W9-BDD-142

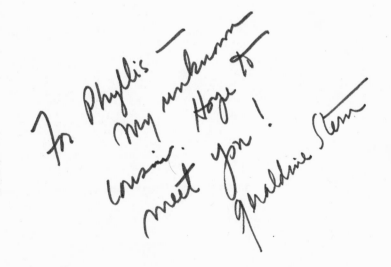

For Phyllis —
My unknown
cousin. Hope to
meet you!
Geraldine Stern

ISRAELI WOMEN SPEAK OUT

Books by Geraldine Stern

Daughters from Afar: Profiles of Israeli Women
Israeli Women Speak Out

ISRAELI WOMEN SPEAK OUT

by Geraldine Stern

J. B. LIPPINCOTT COMPANY
Philadelphia and New York

Passages on pages 74–75 and 77–78 are taken from *Prison Diaries* by Edward Kuznetsov. Copyright © 1975 English Language Translation by Vallentine, Mitchell & Co., Ltd. Reprinted with permission of Stein and Day Publishers.

Passages on pages 173–75 are taken from Geula Cohen's *Women of Violence* by permission of Georges Borchardt, Inc. Copyright © 1966 by Geula Cohen.

The quotation on pages 203–4 is taken from *I Saw the Battle of Jerusalem* by Harry Levin by permission of Ruth Levin. Copyright © 1950 by Harry Levin. Published by Schocken Books, 1950, New York.

U.S. Library of Congress Cataloging in Publication Data

Stern, Geraldine.
     Israeli women speak out.

     1. Women—Israel—Biography.   2. Feminism—Israel.
I. Title.
HQ1728.5.S73   301.41′2′095694   79–1256
ISBN–0–397–01352–3

For Nan and Elmer,
who turned me once more
to the East.

CONTENTS

Foreword

"WHY ONLY THE ISRAELI *women?*" a man asked in Jerusalem when I began these conversations. "Are they so different from the men?"

"Yes," I said, "in certain obvious respects, and some more subtle. I write about the women because, as a woman and a Jew, I identify strongly with them."

On my first visit to Israel, in 1949, the extraordinary events in the lives of the women I met struck me so forcibly that I wrote a book about them a few years later. How did they cope? How did they overcome? They answered the questions for me. And much more. By comparison, my life and the lives of most American women, no matter how difficult, emotionally or materially, seemed then, as now, relatively benign.

The nation was a year old. Israel had survived its first war, started on November 29, 1947, when five Arab countries responded with violence to the United Nations resolution on partition, which had been accepted by Israel. The War of Independence ended with the armistice agreements of 1949.

Immigration, brutally thwarted during the British Mandate, became a swelling tide of Holocaust survivors, Jews ejected from Arab countries, and others who came by choice. The Law of Return welcomed all Jews as instant citizens. It was this period that largely influenced my choice of the women I interviewed then, as well as my interest in the early *aliyah* (immigration) and the kibbutzim.

As this book goes into production, the one woman known throughout the world as *the* woman of Israel has died. I had the privilege of interviewing Golda Meir for my first book, while she was foreign minister. Unfortunately, her illness prevented her from speaking out for this one.

Israel has since suffered three more wars. The new Russian immigration has been significant. The Holocaust trauma continues to affect the lives of the survivors and their progeny. And as with women throughout the world, there is a growing awareness of the Israeli woman's need for a change of status. All of these factors recur as leitmotifs in the lives of the twenty-six women I interviewed recently. I regret deeply that only ten of these interviews could be included in this volume.

Among those who had to be omitted, I would like to mention Naomi Chazan, thirty-one, a Ph.D. lecturer in African politics at Hebrew University. She is a sabra, the word used for the native-born. The sabra is the indigenous cactus plant, tough and prickly on the outside, sweet and tender inside.

Naomi was awaiting her first child during the Yom Kippur War of October 1973, and her husband, who was at the front, was given leave for the birth.

"Almost two weeks overdue," Naomi said, "I was determined not to have my baby until the war was over. As soon as the lights went on in Jerusalem, ending the blackout, I took myself to Hadassah Hospital. They called my gynecologist out of surgery, where he was helping with the terrible overflow of casualties from the front. He took one look at me, was horrified that I was still in the state I was in and gave me intravenous injections to induce labor, went in and out of surgery to check on me, and eventually, but not easily, my seven-pound son was born.

"The husbands of ninety-five percent of the women who had babies when I did were in the Sinai or up north. Most of the fathers found out if they had a boy or a girl by an announcement over the army radio, like this: 'David Cohen, congratulations on the birth of your son.' The maternity section was the happiest place in the hospital. Children were being born! But there were a number of women who had just lost their husbands. . . . Because the war had ended, we named our son Shai Shalom, 'Gift of Peace.' Hopefully, he will be."

Another woman whose interview does not appear in the book is the Government Press Office's Bella Diamant, a university graduate, educated in France and Israel. Single, polylingual, she serves as liaison with foreign correspondents and Israeli journalists. Without her constant assistance I could not have accomplished what I did. We spoke almost daily from Tel Aviv and Jerusalem, sorting out the dizzying possibilities of women to interview. She then followed up with the arduous task, over static-ridden phone connections, of making appointments for me.

"I was born in France the day Israel became a State," she told me. "May 14, 1948. My parents, who were born in Poland, brought me here a year later. My mother had been in Auschwitz. My father hid from the Nazis for three years after escaping from the Warsaw ghetto. I think no one can ever understand it without living it, but it is part of our brain."

About her job: "Officially I am called a secretary. This keeps the pay down. You won't find men who are secretaries. That is not fair. I have been on my job for seven years. If a man had this job, they wouldn't dare pay him what they pay me. They wouldn't dare!" For her giving far beyond her job description, I am most grateful.

I am keenly aware of what a tremendous request I make of a woman when we meet, usually as total strangers, and I say, "Please tell me about yourself, your origins, your family, what you do, what you think about the condition of women in Israel, or anything else you may want to talk about."

With my first interview, I realize that I am actually asking a woman to reach deep within herself. It is an emotional experience for her, as well as for me. Sometimes there are tears. Often we kiss each other good-bye. On one occasion, a woman followed up my visit with a note: "It seems to me that I talked too much about matters irrelevant to your book. I trust that all references that don't belong were for your ears only. It's odd how one can talk to a comparative stranger so much more easily than to a friend. Maybe that's what psychiatrists are for."

Her assessment proved to be accurate when I sat down with an old friend who has a patchwork background and is doing important work in Israel. She said, "I can't do it, Geri. We know each other too well and too long."

To the women who shared their lives with me, I am forever indebted. My thanks also to my live-in editor, husband Milton

Wayne, and to Beatrice Rosenfeld, my empathetic editor at Lippincott, who made the preliminaries to publication a pleasure.

Jerusalem, March 1977–
Harvard, Illinois, February 1979

ISRAELI WOMEN SPEAK OUT

1 Rebel with a Cause

"IN THIS COUNTRY, if you ask objective people, they will tell you that the one woman who did things in this country for women, and is known for this, is myself. And it's because I never do it on the basis of sex, but of human rights."

Shulamit Aloni, who locked horns with Golda Meir in the Knesset (Israel's parliament) and then started her own political party, was, bluntly and with no false modesty, laying out for me some of her achievements in her many fights against the establishment. Having followed her career for some time, as hers was the first voice I had heard raised politically in Israel for the rights of women, I arrived with considerable expectation at her home in the Tel Aviv suburb Kfar Shmryahu. I was not disappointed.

A coral tree in full bloom and brilliant yellow Scotch broom welcomed early spring in the front garden of the unpretentious house as Shulamit Aloni and a large dog welcomed me at the door. Blond, curly-haired, wearing patch blue denims and jacket, this medium-tall, nice-figured woman did not immediately suggest the fighting crusader, although the set of her full lips could mean stubbornness.

"Good morning. Come in. We'll sit in here," she said in an extremely tired voice as she went to the record player to turn off a Mozart quartet.

"Lovely," I said.

"Yes. It's almost at the end. We'll get started. Would you like coffee?" It was Saturday, the Sabbath, and she was giving up part of her one free day for our talk. Sunday begins a six-day week for Israelis.

/15

She went across the front hall to the kitchen. The living room reflected cultivated tastes. The comfortable but simply furnished room had interesting art objects on shelves, paintings on the walls, attractive area rugs, and well-filled bookshelves. She returned with a pottery coffeepot and cups.

"So, all right," she said as she sat down on the couch and the dog settled near us. "I'll start at the beginning. I was born in Israel. Sex: woman." She laughed as she said this, and her tiredness seemed to leave her. "I am married and I have three children. I grew up in this country. I was born in Tel Aviv November 22, 1929, which means I'll be coming forty-seven.

"By profession I am a teacher, a radio commentator, a journalist, and a lawyer. I published four books, thousands of articles."

"Remarkable! What have your books been about?"

"The last book which I published is *Women As Human Beings.* I took this title because in Israel women are not accepted as equal human beings.

"I tell in there the story of Eleanor Roosevelt, who was the head of the Commission on Human Rights in the United Nations. The first draft of their proclamation said all men are born equal. When they stated 'men,' people in Oriental countries said if you write 'men,' people in our countries will say this exists only for men and not for women. So they changed it to 'human beings.' In Hebrew it's *adam,* because *adam* is the common word for both man and woman."

"Isn't it true that in Hebrew there's only one word for a woman, *geveret,* which doesn't designate her marital situation? This has always impressed me, long before 'Ms.' was invented."

"*Isha* is also woman. But you are right. *Geveret* is like Ms.— or Ms. is like *geveret.* But they are always looking at your identity card, not what you say about yourself. I don't know any other government in the world, including the Russian, which is so curious to know all the details about everyone as in Israel. If you go to the police telling them you've had a robber, someone was stealing from you, the first questions will be 'Where are you from? Where is your father from? Your age?' Et cetera, et cetera."

"Were your parents born here, too?"

"My parents came from Poland. During the Second World War both of my parents went into the British army. I went to school, as everyone did. I lived in a boarding village for children."

"One of the Youth Aliyah villages?"

"No, but there were Youth Aliyah children there as well, because children were already coming from Germany and Czechoslovakia. This was the beginning of the '40s. We had very good teachers. I wanted to go to a kibbutz and work in agriculture in '45, but my father wrote to me from Italy that there are so many refugees, I should become a teacher.

"So I left Ben Shemen Children's Village, a beautiful place on the way between Ramle and Lod, and went to Jerusalem. Now Ben Shemen is under different auspices, but then it was a private enterprise of the idealistic Dr. Lehman, who came from Germany and brought children with him. It was very much influenced by Jewish-German intellectuals and Zionists. At that time it was something which can't be compared to any other place. Today it's Aliyat Hanoar, for poor children, children who have been brought to the country without their parents, or children who come from broken families.

"I finished high school in Jerusalem and, later on, the seminary training. It was the time of the rebellion before the end of the British Mandate."

"Did you pick up English during the Mandate? You speak so well."

"Yes, then and at school. I was still in school, at the age of fourteen, when I was already drafted to the Haganah, our Jewish defense forces, even before the war started. November twenty-ninth, '47, was the declaration of the UN for partition of Palestine. In December the riots started and I went with the Haganah to defend the Old City of Jerusalem."

"Were you carrying arms?"

"Oh, yes, of course. All of us did. I was already eighteen. Since it was still the British government, we went to the Old City pretending we were teachers for the children."

"You had been trained underground?"

"Yeah. First in the Haganah and then later in the Palmach, the Jewish strike forces. Girls and boys fought together. I was in an active unit."

"Which the women aren't in today?"

"No. Only very few of them, and only in very separated and

special groups. But then we were together. After the war I started working with the newcomers, the immigrants, and I met my head-master of the seminary, Professor Ben Zion Dinur, who then was the minister of education. It was after the State was established, and he told me that now it was time to teach the Jews how to live in their own government and how to keep the rule of the law, and he told me to teach them civics.

"And I told him, 'Dear Mr. Dinur, it's a good idea, but you didn't prepare me for those things in the seminary.' He said, 'Well, it's still not too late to learn.' " Shulamit laughed at recalling this. "So then I started to study law, not to become a rich lawyer but to teach civics and basic rights and the connection and the relation between the State and the citizen. So I studied law, and I started to teach in the high schools, in the very highest classes, basic civil rights."

"Where was this?"

"Oh, in Tel Aviv. It was a very difficult time. It was '52. I was studying; I got married and later got pregnant. I had two children. I was working all the time."

"Two children just like that?"

"No. During the four years I was studying law. But during these four years I was teaching in high school, I was a housewife, studying, and enjoying life. I was very much involved in the bohe-mian life in Tel Aviv. I don't know. . . . Take a busy person and he can do everything." She laughed. "So I managed."

"Right. The busier you are, the more you can do. Was this planned parenthood?"

"Yeah, more or less."

"When did you marry?"

"On the second of April, next week, it will be twenty-five years already that we are married."

"*Mazeltov!*"

"It's a long time. He was a member of a kibbutz. He left it and became a civil servant. He came from Alonim, and that's why the name is Aloni. *Alon* is an oak tree. My parents are Adler."

"What was the political orientation of his kibbutz?"

"Achdut Avodah, which is left-wing. And, really when I was a child, I was in the youth movement of Hashomer Hatzair, also left-wing. Then, much later, the two of us joined Mapai because we wanted to join all parties together. Some of our political activities started here in this house. It's a prefabricated home, Swedish. We didn't have the money to buy or to build a home. So we ordered it, and part by part we enlarged it, with the children. This is an additional part," she said, pointing to the other end of the room that had a lower ceiling, "and some other places which are not prefabricated."

"And you've been here how long?"

"Twenty-five years. The three children were born here, grew up here. They went to the same kindergarten and the same school."

"You were very advanced to come out here twenty-five years ago, weren't you? It must have been wilderness."

"Oh, yes, we were the first. There was no water and no electricity. But we wanted a little piece of air around us. I have three boys. The oldest is married already, and he has a daughter already, so I am a grandmother already!" Shulamit laughed at this change of status.

"*Mazeltov* again! How old is the baby?"

"Seven months."

"It's exciting, isn't it?"

"Well, being honest with you, no."

"When they get a little older, I've found there's a very special relationship, without the stresses and strains of bringing up your own."

"Yeah. When they start to talk. But not at this age. I hate not to make a kind of a show-off, because they expect it of you, but later on I believe it will be different.

"Now, so, the idea of my studies as a lawyer was to bring to the public basic knowledge of democracy. And Jewish people don't know what democracy is. The majority of them came from Eastern Europe and the Middle East, which means they don't know. Even today, people believe that democracy is the rule of the majority or the despotism of the majority. And it's a terrible thing. We don't have checks and balances. We don't have a written constitution. We don't have a Bill of Rights."

"You don't have a constitution?"

"No. I'll give you an article about it." I was interrupting her train of thought. "Then I decided that instead of teaching school I should use the media, and I started with programs on the radio:

'You and the Law,' 'Basic Law.' At the same time I prepared a book, which was the first book I wrote. The name of it: *The Citizen and the State*. It is a book which is studied in high schools."

"At that period your orientation was not especially towards women?"

"No. It never was especially women, never was. Now, through this radio program, I became the unofficial ombudsman in a society which didn't respect basic human rights. And there was always talk of the society, to sacrifice for the State, to sacrifice for the society, which means that the person, the individual, is less important, and the mission of the people is more important. And that's why basic rights, which you take for granted in America, we didn't know. And people were patronized."

"This was the chauvinism at the beginning?"

"We still have it. It's become even more so."

"You think so?"

"I know so. I know so. We pay more lip service, but in many cases we are worse. It's unbelievable! Now," she said, collecting her thought again, "people started to write to me where their rights were abused and every program became a kind of a scandal. And because there was a scandal, and I was fighting for those things publicly, it became the most popular program in the country."

"Were they people from all levels who wrote to you? Not just the Arabs, immigrants, et cetera?"

"All levels, because newcomers didn't know the law and they didn't understand what we want from them; their rights were abused. Ninety-five percent of the people who answered polls— you know they have those kinds of Gallup researches—said that for this program they stayed home to listen to it. So I became popular. The government wanted to shut me down, but they couldn't because the public wanted me."

"You were a sort of governmental consumer advocate."

"Probably. It was free legal aid, really. Not yet consumerism. Consumerism came later. So in '65, when there was a split in the Labor Party, the Rafi Party sprang up and Levi Eshkol invited me to come on his list. I brought three conditions: one of them was to have an ombudsman, an official ombudsman; second, to declare that we are going to have a written constitution; third, that we are starting to work on civil rights.

"Now they adopted it formally. We don't have yet the three of them. We have the ombudsman already, but we don't have the other two. And the ombudsman is not very official because they don't give names. There is no responsibility."

"You don't know who he is?"

"We know who is the ombudsman, but when he says that somebody abused rights, or behaved not properly, we don't know the name. In the meantime, I published a second book, which is *The Rights of the Child,* social and educational rights of the child, all legislation and other rights, including education, including the relations between parents and the child, and other things like this.

"Now I was a bencher fighting. It was '65 to '69. And then we had the Six-Day War and Golda Meir became the prime minister. She couldn't stand me because I didn't accept her authority. I thought she's mistaken. I thought she's a Bolshevik . . . an ignorant woman with self-righteousness, and I fought some of the things. And she couldn't stand me because of my knowledge, because of . . ."

"Your chutzpah?"

"And my chutzpah. Well, it was about the Arabs, I suppose, and about many other things."

"When you describe her as a Bolshevik, do you mean authoritarian?"

"No. Not only authoritarian. Authoritarian, it's O.K. But her mentality, her system, is a Bolshevik system, which means she is patronizing people. They have to listen to her. There is a self-righteousness. 'Only we are right!' And then, added to this, she has the mentality of the ghetto, which you can see very, very easily through her meeting with the pope, when he asked her why aren't we more human to the refugees. She could say, from her point of view, that it's a political problem and not a humanitarian one. Or it's not ours, but the Arab countries' problem. She could have said that from her point of view, although I don't agree with it. But what she said was striking. She said, 'How dare you ask us refugees, who suffered from pogroms, to be nice to refugees!'

"And I had the same thing with her in the Knesset. She was talking about liberating the West Bank. And I said, 'How can you speak about liberating the land when here you have a million people who don't see the Israelis as liberators but as conquerors!'

And she stood up in the middle of my speech, *furious* with rage. 'How dare you say of the Jewish people that they are conquerors? Jewish people are not conquerors! They are victims and not winners!' "

Shulamit was warming up to her subject in oratorical tones and emphases. It was the most undiluted criticism of Golda I had encountered, and Golda, I understand, felt the same way about Shulamit.

"But they *are* winners!" Shulamit continued. "And if there is a war, it's better to be a winner than to be a loser. And then Golda came up with 'There are no Palestinians.' Because she was a Palestinian and she is not one anymore!

"So, O.K. I was a Palestinian, too, and I'm not a Palestinian because we got our self-determination. Now what are the other people? They didn't get their self-determination, and they still exist. What *are* they? Call them *Kugellager*—"

"What is that?"

"*Kugellager* is something which you put into a car, which means nonsense."

"Junk, you mean?" (The German-English dictionary defines *Kugellager* as ball bearings, without giving an idiomatic or slang definition, for which I accept Shulamit's "nonsense.")

"Call them whatever you want, but they exist. You can't just ignore them because you don't like them.

"Now, what I wanted to point out is something else. During the time that I had this program on the radio, which was almost nine years, which is a long time—two programs a week, and for a time I had some special programs as well—I found out, working on the problems of human rights, how deeply and how terribly women are discriminated against in this country. Women and minority groups, but especially women, and how superstitious we are against women.

"And I started to study Jewish law, which is enforced here as far as marriage and divorce are concerned. I studied it not only at the university, but I went to very well-known rabbis and I studied with them. And then I started the whole business of women and women fighting for equal rights."

"What year was that?"

"In the '60s—even before, I would say—women's rights and

equal rights and equal opportunities. But my point of view is not women as a group, because I don't accept human beings divided into groups. I hate these groupings—blacks, women, whites, Sephardic [Jews from Spain, Portugal, and Arab lands], and so on. My point of view is that people were born free, but they are not equal. It would be boring if all of us would be equal.

"We are different, and we have the right to be different. But although we are different, we are entitled to equal rights and equal opportunities. And not to generalize groups. Because if ninety percent of a certain group want one thing and ten percent don't want it, you can't make majoritization from this ninety percent if the ten percent don't want to do what they want. You can't tell the others to conform. Because women as a group are not a group—are not a group! Every woman, every man, every child, is a one-hundred-percent individual, with his own rights. So how can you say, by vote of the majority, that all women should stay at home and make cookies?

"But in Israel a married woman is her husband's property. I mean in her body and in her soul. She cannot divorce him. If he ignores her, if he leaves her, if she's neglected, she can't remarry even though nobody knows where he is for ten or twenty years!"

"She can divorce him, can't she, if she goes along with the religious laws—spit on a shoe and all that business?"

"No. This is something else. This is a problem of *halitza*. This is only when she's a widow and she has no children. Then she becomes the property of her late husband's family. And then she needs to go through all those things. . . ."

"Oh, yes. Not to marry his brother?"

"Not to marry his brother."

"No possibility of divorce?"

"A man can divorce a woman if he wants and when he wants. But a court cannot nullify a marriage. They cannot decide, 'Well, those people cannot live together, we decide there is a divorce.' Because she is his property and because, according to the law, it's not only property, but a taboo. She's not only his, but not somebody else's. And you know, in the Bible it's written that you can't take the property of somebody else—you will see in the Ten Commandments—not his wife, not his house, not his cattle, and so on. Divorce is the same thing. And it's so today. If, after ten years being completely neglected, she lives with somebody and has a child, the child is excommunicated."

"The child is a bastard, isn't it?"

"A bastard, but not in your meaning of bastard. It's a *momzer*. Because a bastard is a child which is born out of wedlock. Now if she's not married or was never married, the child is not a bastard. A child that is born out of wedlock to a free woman, not to one who was married, has all his rights. A child who was born to a free woman is completely living in equality. And the father has all the duties towards him. It's only a child that was born what they call 'out of adultery,' which means out of a woman's adultery, that is a bastard."

"What about this case where the woman had a child by her lover and she wanted to marry her lover but wasn't allowed to?"

"Because she was married, and because she knew her lover before she got a proper divorce. I'll tell you a story which I'm dealing with now. The woman came from South America twenty years ago. Her husband stayed there and didn't want to give her a *get,* a divorce. She asked for it once or twice, and she was waiting for a few years, and because he didn't want to give her a divorce, she started to build her life with somebody else in this country.

"They had four children. After having these four children, the husband finally sent the divorce. Now, well, the two of them went to the rabbinical court and made a terrible mistake. They said, 'Well, now that I have the divorce, we want to marry.' The court said, 'No, you cannot because you are a whore and your children are the children of a whore. They are bastards, and you can't marry.' "

"She had no children from the first marriage?"

"No. None at all. And then this couple kept it as a secret that they weren't really married. Time passed by, and the first daughter wanted to marry, and she went to the rabbinical court for registration. They said, 'We'll send you. We'll tell you.' And for months they were waiting. In the meantime they were living together, the two, and she became pregnant. They told her, 'One day you'll get the certificate.'

"But the certificate didn't come. So they went to the rabbinical court again, and she was told, 'You can't marry. You are a bastard, and your child will be a bastard, excommunicated.' And they told her boyfriend, the father of the child she was carrying, 'Leave her. You shouldn't live with such a woman. And this child, ignore him!'

"And she came back to her family. The family is completely, all of them, collapsed. Because the other children didn't know the whole thing, they had breakdowns and need a psychiatrist, so on and so forth. And this girl now lives by herself."

"He actually left her?"

"He left her! She tried to commit suicide. Now she's in the sixth month. And she left her family, as well. She couldn't stay with her parents and brothers. Just by chance, some woman working in the neighborhood found her. They brought her to me, and I'm trying to solve the problem. Now, this is the status of a woman in Israel, in a nutshell. The tragedies are unimaginable."

"Incredible. In 1977!"

"Yeah. According to laws which I'm not sure that they were up-to-date three thousand years ago. But none of those rabbis lives today the way those people used to live three thousand years ago. We have the telephone. We have the radio, television. We've reached the moon, up in space. But here the status of a woman is still a second-rate citizen. It's unbelievable!

"Always, when I am talking about it, they say I am a traitor. If to tell what Israeli law is means to be a traitor, just look what kinds of laws you have!

"Even more: the hypocrisy, the double standards and double morals in this country, as far as human rights are concerned. . . . They tell the children that in Russia and Syria there is racism. Why? Because they register the Jews, being Jewish, as a minority group. And they tell it to the children in the schools. And they develop hatred.

"But in Israel, registration is even worse. They don't write you down as being an Israeli citizen. We are divided into twelve ethnic religious groups, by birth. And if you have a mixed marriage, if the woman is a Gentile, then the children are Gentiles and they can't marry in this country. They point out every minority group on an identity card, which you have to show everyone because of the security problem. You have to show it when you go to a bank, when you go anywhere."

"There are only twelve groupings, with people having come from so many countries?"

"Twelve ethnic religious groups. It's not Jews, Moslems, different Christians, Druze, and so on. Because the Jews which are accepted by the Orthodox Jewry are accepted, all of them, the same. It doesn't matter if he came from Morocco or Russia. It's according to the religion."

"If you're an Orthodox Jew . . . ?"

"No. They decided that I'm an Orthodox Jew, although I'm not religious at all. But I am pure because my parents are pure. For instance, an individual cannot get a certificate that he's single, that he's not married, unless he goes through a routine. They look into blacklists which they have, if he's a pure Jew and a proper one. Many families are brought down here because they came to this country from Russia or from the United States or other places where they have mixed marriage. And here the wife and the children are discriminated against in a most dreadful way."

"Wasn't there a case where a child could not be buried in a Jewish cemetery?"

"Because the mother was not Jewish."

"Horrible!"

"And we had a case where a soldier was killed in the army and they didn't let him be buried with the others."

"So what do they do with the bodies?"

"They bury them outside the cemetery. They call these a donkey burial, *kvurat chamor*. You see, Israel is a country of contradictions, not only controversial. On one hand, you'll see things which you wouldn't believe even in the darkest Middle Ages. On the other hand, you'll see—and probably those are the people you meet —very broad-minded people, Western people, who will never tell you about what I'm telling you because they are ashamed. And they are brainwashed not to talk about it. Now, 'If you don't talk about it, let the Gentiles not know.' The Gentiles don't know, and the people don't know. And then they go from one tragedy to another. And there are thousands of them. It's not just a single case.

"And the corruption around those things. Some cases you can buy with money. Some cases, if you are very important and they are afraid it will cause a scandal, then they are finding the individual way to settle it."

"The big mystery to me has always been how they could set up a democracy and have no civil rights," I commented.

"There is no democracy. O.K. We don't have civil rights, and what we have is no democracy, but the formalities of democracy. We worship, and this is the only thing which people worship here, is the rule of the majority, which is the despotism of the majority. And they use the majority to overrule decisions of the Supreme Court. You go to court and you win against the government. And then, if the government doesn't like it, the next day they overrule it by legislation."

"How can you have a democracy and please everybody? Don't you have to observe the will of the majority in some sense?"

"When there are things which you have to decide for the future, what to do and how to do it, you have a majority and minority and you work according to the majority. But the majority should be restrained. There are certain things which they cannot overrule. And the idea is that a human being is free, was born free, and has certain rights that you cannot overrule."

"Inalienable rights."

"That's right. That you can't overrule it by majority. For instance, if you take away freedom of speech and of the press and academic freedom, what do you do? Then the democracy really is cutting her basic rights."

"Is your model American democracy? British democracy? Our Bill of Rights, our Constitution?"

"I'll tell you. Usually you have to adapt it to the country, how big it is. But the main thing is, you have the Bill of Rights of the UN. And what I want is these basic human rights, to teach them to the children, to make them part of the legislation, to make them above the game of the majority and the needs of the coalition."

"Do you think the United Nations has been effective?"

"No. But I think that they prepared a very good declaration. The declaration is the minimum a country should adopt. You adopted more. In your Constitution today, with the help of the Supreme Court, you really safeguard more rights than the UN prepared. The UN prepared something which can be the common denominator, and we don't have even that.

"So the main thing I'm fighting for in this country are those minimum rights. The religious people in this country are really a minority group. But the Labor Party makes them so powerful because they never have a majority and need them." (The same is true of the new government formed by Menachem Begin since my conversation with Shulamit Aloni.) "Not having a constitution, you can bargain everything. So each election they give them more and more power, more and more money, more and more authority. And the individual loses more of his rights. Once you have a constitution, you can't bargain away those things."

"Have you been in America?"

"Yeah. A few times, only for short visits."

"What is your impression of democracy working in America?"

"Now, I'll tell you. First of all, I'm glad that every child in every school is taught civics and knows his constitutional rights. Which means that every individual has the tools to fight against despotism. You never expect people who are in power to restrain themselves. It's a game. It's a game!" she said with great emotion. "The most important thing is to educate people, individuals, to know his rights and to stand for his rights. This is what America has done. And this is very important. Sure, there are abuses. Sure, there is the game of power and so on."

."And wealth in America."

"And wealth and everything. But the moment the individual knows, and the teacher knows that he should give it to the child from the very beginning, that he has some rights and those are his rights and they are constitutional rights and no one has the right to abuse them—and if they are abused, he has a way to fight it through —then you have democracy."

"It doesn't exist here?"

"It sure doesn't. This is what I'm fighting for. And I'm a loner, unfortunately, because people in this country—maybe I'm assuming this—they don't feel secure in themselves. They don't have self-confidence."

"Did you start a civil rights party?"

"Yeah."

"How many members does it have? Has it grown?"

"Well, we went only once for election. Nobody believed that I'll get even one seat, and we got three. Three seats in the Knesset out of one hundred and twenty, in '73. I don't know what will happen this May because people don't like what I'm doing. I'm making them think about things, and they don't want to. For instance, I was once the baby of the media. Now it's closed to me."

(In the May 1977 elections, the Citizens Rights Party received 20,621 votes, enough for only one Knesset seat, filled by Shulamit Aloni.)

"You're too controversial?"

"You'll have twenty or thirty programs a month by rabbis, brainwashing people, telling them only to believe in the mission of the Jewish people, what sustains us and so on. Superficial things. They won't give me two minutes to say that it is nonsense and against basic rights."

"Has your party grown since '73?"

"Well, I don't know. We are going through so many changes. It's a party which has no membership. In this country nobody gives donations to a party because they have their money from the government. The establishment has it arranged that the big should stay big and the small should stay small."

"And you have no list of members?"

"We have. But people are afraid, because of the system, to say that they belong to a small party which criticizes the government. We have about a thousand people who come and do some work. But for one seat we need eighteen thousand. But then we didn't have anyone and we got thirty-five thousand."

"So you are persona non grata on the radio, in the media?"

"I wouldn't put it so badly because I am enough well-known and I can always make a scandal. It's difficult to say to me 'No.' They have to have an excuse to say this."

"What kind of a scandal have you made lately?"

"Well, many of them. For instance, we had one for the environment. They wanted to put an atomic station for electricity in the middle of an overpopulated area."

"Is that the Negev?"

"Not far from the Negev. The chairman of the Knesset wouldn't let us do things to protest it. The government tried to shut us up. So we said we are going to the Supreme Court. We are going to rebel, provoke the people, and so on. And we won, and they decided to postpone it."

"You went to the Supreme Court?"

"No. We didn't have to go that far because they knew I would if necessary."

"And now you have a woman justice on the Supreme Court."

"One of them. She's a good person. Another scandal we had was over abortion. The fight is still not finished. They called me murderer. It was unbelievable!"

As Shulamit raised her voice, the dog, lying well-behaved beside us, decided to join in, resulting in large yelps into the tape recorder. She let him out of the house and resumed.

"A rabbi told me, 'Today when the Syrians are coming to our borders, you want to murder the children!' So I said, 'Well, take the yeshiva *bochers* [young male students at Orthodox religious schools], take them to the army. I don't want my children to be killed for you.' Can you imagine? They called me murderer, and they wanted physically to harm me."

"Of course, yeshiva *bochers* are exempt from army service."

"Yes. They pray for us."

"That's very helpful. What's the present status of the abortion situation?"

"It's legalized now, but it's not effective because a woman has to go through a committee of three: two doctors and a social worker. It's a country which thinks in terms not of the needs of the individual and the right to decide for herself, but the needs of the people. Now we have some very totalitarian symbols here. We've had some very strong signs.

"A woman's body is her own. It is not there to service the State, the army, or the nation. To make children is very easy. To bear them is harder, and to bring them up, harder still. Every woman has the right to decide for herself whether she will do so or not. Family planning is at a terrible level. They keep it a secret because they want many children for the people. You will find brainwashing: 'We need children for the army.' "

"And the Arabs are multiplying fast."

"Yeah. This is another excuse. So I have to fight women, and I have to tell them, 'How can you carry a child for the army? You carry him because you want him, because you want him to be happy.' They say, 'No, I bring ten children for the army. That's why the country should support them.' And things like this. You won't believe it. It's very difficult."

Shulamit's voice was sounding tired again, but she continued.

"On the other hand, the people who you meet are nice. You are of the opinion, how democratic they are. But there is no one who is more deaf than the one who doesn't want to listen. And they decided not to listen to those things. If you bring a human case, they feel very touched. But for the unity of the country, they say we have to sacrifice those people. But you can't stop, like this, the problem."

"How is the abortion law working?"

"It's not working yet. But there is the law and it will start working during the next year if the minister of health will prepare what is necessary to begin it."

"Isn't it quite remarkable that they passed such a law?"

"The decision was accepted when I was a member of the cabinet. When I joined the cabinet I was the minister of nothing. I was a minister for five months, without portfolio, but I worked to cut red tape and bureaucracy and I pushed for a better abortion law."

"This was under Rabin?"

"Well, I made Rabin, unfortunately, prime minister because I wanted Golda and Moshe Dayan and the others to resign after the Yom Kippur War."

"How did you make him prime minister?"

"Because he needed our three votes. He didn't have a majority."

"And that did it?"

"And that did it. That did it. We kept the religious party outside. I was in. Golda and Dayan went out. So during these five months, unfortunately, they wanted Mafdal religious party so badly that we only passed two decisions, one of them about abortion. We were able to get the abortion law because the religious parties were out during those five months that I was minister in the cabinet.

"The other law we passed was cutting censorship of theater plays and some other things. And then the party wanted the religious party to join the government. I mean Rabin wanted it because then they could do everything the way it was before Golda left. He's still the baby of Golda and runs to her every week. And that's why, for idealistic reasons and on matters of principle, we left the government."

"We, meaning the Citizens Rights Party?"

"Yes. That's right. My party. We managed, in one day or so before the party registration deadline in '73, to recruit a list of people to run for election, sign up seven hundred and fifty supporters, put down the necessary deposit, and start life as an independent party."

"What a push that must have been! That must have set some kind of a record."

"It sure was. And it sure did. Now, to get back to Golda. She is strong. She is very strong. She knows how to deal with things she's in charge of. She's very emotional. She has self-righteousness. She never listens to other people."

"She's a great speaker."

"No. She's an emotional speaker. She influences people. But if you read later on what she said, you'll find she said nothing but emotions. But the moment people listen to her, she is hypnotizing them. The woman is ignorant. She plays unbelievably with her five hundred words in Hebrew."

"She has a limited Hebrew vocabulary?" I asked incredulously.

"Very limited Hebrew. But all that I've said up to now shows that she is a great woman. But greatness sometimes gives power to destroy things. And I think that this woman destroyed the Labor Party because she's emotional. She hates people and she destroys people, very good people, who had to leave the party because of her. And because everything was done according to what she wants and people were afraid to discuss things with her."

"That didn't stop you, did it?"

Shulamit laughed and said, "It did not. I remember the time in the Knesset when I said something which she didn't like. You could hear a fly in a room with a hundred people. Everyone was holding his word to see what would happen. I think we should accuse her for what brought us to the Yom Kippur War."

"And not Dayan?"

"The two of them. They were together. But she was the prime minister. That's why she is responsible. Her policy was to ignore the Arabs. We were big. We were strong. We had had a great victory in the Six-Day War. And if we would be more flexible and more generous, I think we could achieve many things from a strong starting point."

"Did you feel that earlier, when Nasser was beginning to lean in the direction of peace?"

"Yeah. But she acted, with her mentality, as if the whole world is against us. And we Jews should have a safeguard, not to give in on anything. I think the woman never went through the metamorphosis from her ghetto trauma to the fact that here we are the majority. We are the government. We are the legislature. It's our language. It's our people. It's our policies. It's our army. And we have minorities. She can't get it!

"And she said openly, on television, 'Why should I put myself in somebody else's shoes? We are right.' This self-righteousness is something unbelievable. She doesn't have to explain it. And she never explains it in words. It's the kind of power which ignorant people with self-righteousness usually have. Because intellectual people always see two sides to the coin. She, never. The second side of the coin doesn't exist."

She sighed heavily and asked, "O.K., what else would you like to know?"

"I'd like to know about Marcia Freedman."

"Marcia Freedman went on my list, and she gained her seat in the Knesset on my list and my name and because of me. She was not known. Even I didn't know her. If I would know her, she wouldn't have been third on the list. She's thinking in a completely American way, which doesn't suit this society and makes the people irritated." (When I met Marcia later, she denied this, saying, "Women's struggle for equality in this country has a long and honorable history. But my ideas are often attributed to my American background.")

"Then her attitude to the Arab problem—although you understand that I myself am a dove—I don't think we should have a kind of guilty complex towards the Arabs," Shulamit continued. "Marcia seems to be on the side of the Communist Party. Now, this movement of the women, starting a Women's Party, here you have a joke. We split because of her ideas of, not women, but of political cases. This thing is a good joke. They took my money. She took it, Marcia. She gave it to this group."

"She gave it to them to start a new party?" (I learned later from Marcia that every outgoing Knesset member gets money from the government, a sort of pension.)

"She gave it to them to start a new party. The joke about this is that they sent me a formal mission to ask me to go with them. I told them it's nonsense."

"You mean *Kugellager?*"

"Yeah. *Kugellager* is right." She laughed. "I told them, 'You should come and join me.' Now this group is a feministic group with an American style, which won't work in this country. They know it, and that's why they came over to me, just last week, asking me to go with them. I said, 'Don't be silly. You know me. Come and join.' "

"Have others besides Marcia been in your party?"

"Part of them were. Marcia became all that she is because I took her to my party and I brought her to the Knesset. But today it's kind of a selfish thing, which happens in your country with the blacks. At the beginning, you people were fighting for the rights, then for equality and equal opportunity, and then you have groups for separation.

"Now I told them I am against one-sex community, whatsoever, because it gives all the tools to the men to say that women are different."

"It's another kind of racism."

"That's right. They said they'd have another discussion. I said, 'You're welcome to join us. You know me, and you know the work I'm doing and my past achievements. I'm the only one in this country who is for civil rights for everybody. And every individual is a one-hundred-percent human being.' "

"But isn't it true that women, as a minority, have been denied some of the rights of equal pay, et cetera?"

"Yeah. But in Israel all the discrimination comes from a very basic thing, the religious basis, the religious status. And it infects both sides."

"You mean, 'I thank you for not making me a woman'?"

"Yeah. I have to stand before a court where all the rabbis pray each morning, 'Thank you, God, that you didn't create me a woman,' who decide that, in their rabbinical court, I cannot be a witness, I cannot be a judge.

"Some of those things influence both sexes. For instance, this girl I told you about. If she cannot marry, then the man cannot marry her. If a divorcée cannot marry somebody, then her man cannot marry her. If a woman is a second-rate citizen and her duty is to stay at home, and the head of the family is exclusively the father, it means that, since I work, my husband won't get any of my pension. And all the money that is kept for me will stay with my employer and not be given to my family.

"A widow can be as rich as a millionaire, and she'll always get her husband's pension. A widower can be poor, and his late wife had some benefits because of her work, but they won't give him the money. It's because of discrimination against women. But the one who suffers is the man. You can't divide the whole complex.

"Everything that will be done only by women, except for charity, will arouse the Israeli people against them. Charity done by women is acceptable because it's in the Jewish tradition. Social work, volunteer work, et cetera. But not political work. Every kind of political work that the feminist groups in the United States are doing will raise public opinion against them in Israel.

"I always say, 'Only a woman and a man make life fruitful. One sex is fruitless.' So why should women build a separate party? It is another kind of ghetto which will boomerang. I won't accept it, and I will never, in my life."

2 Thunder on Mount Carmel

I HAD COME TO SEE Marcia Freedman with certain misgivings. I had heard everything about her since I arrived in Israel: "She's a kook!" "She's a maniac!" "She goes off the deep end!" "Starting a separate women's political party is ridiculous!" "She's so aggressive. Women shouldn't be like men!" "Her ideas might work for America, but Israel, who needs it?"

No one was dispassionate about her, even those who said, "You must see her. She began the whole thing here." "I don't go along with her a hundred percent, but a lot of what she says is true." "She's brilliant!" "I'm all for her!" "My consciousness-raising group has been very important to me."

Strangely enough, in my rather extensive reading about the women's movement in Israel, which had blossomed since I was last there in 1971, I hadn't come across the name of Marcia Freedman, or if I had, it hadn't registered. On my return home, after meeting her, I found four publications in my mail with something about her.

I came to her apartment, halfway up Mount Carmel, dotted with spring's wild flowers and blossoming trees, with the magnificent coastline of the Mediterranean and the Haifa port below, prepared to find a wild-eyed Amazon. When this four-foot-ten, under-100-pounds woman in jeans and sweat shirt opened the door, I said disbelievingly, "Marcia Freedman?"

"Yes," she said. "Geraldine? Please come in."

So there I was, confronted not by the monster I had been warned about but by a soft-spoken, pleasant-mannered thirty-nine-year-old woman with cropped gray hair and large, rather sad, dark eyes, sharply focused on the lot of women. We sat down in the living room to talk.

I told her of my continuing interest in Israeli women since my first visit in 1949—that their lives contrasted so sharply with the usual American woman's life story. And I mentioned a conversation I had had the day before with the wife of an American dentist who had moved to Israel with his family a few years ago.

She said, "Why are you writing about the women here? Are they different from women in America?"

I was stunned by the question. It was inconceivable to me that this woman couldn't see the difference. "They've come here from all over the world, most often forced to leave the country of their birth. Many have had the most traumatic experiences and have had to start their lives again in a new country with a new language, and usually without money and with few possessions. Did many of your American friends have to do that?"

"No," the dentist's wife agreed, "I suppose not. I hadn't thought of it that way."

"Some people are in their tight little corners and don't look outside of themselves to see what goes on there," Marcia commented, "but more and more women are becoming sensitive to other women. It took me a while to get to that point."

"I understand that you're the one who started it all in Israel. Please tell me about it."

"I found myself, in the late 1960s, early 1970s, in a situation that women all over the world of my background and generation are finding themselves in, and that is that you are highly educated, skilled, have built up a certain amount of expectations in terms of a career, in personal development, personal identity, and at the same time the expectations and obligations to be a traditionally good mother, housewife, wife, daughter, neighbor, hostess, and so on were all there upon you. I was then in my early thirties, feeling that all this was about to drive me absolutely mad, not quite understanding what was wrong basically. I was already in Israel by this time. We came here in 1969."

She was born in Newark, New Jersey, and stayed there until she went to college at the age of nineteen.

"The Newark I grew up in is the Newark Philip Roth describes in his novels. It's exactly that neighborhood, and sociologically his descriptions are so valid. Growing up in a very cut-off Jewish community, cut off in the sense that having grown up in the city of Newark, I did not know anything other than the neighborhood that I was born and raised in—the Weequahic section, which was the section where all of the Jews lived."

"What section?"

"Weequahic."

"How do you spell that?"

She laughed. "I'll give you the high school cheer: W—double-E—Q—U—A—H—I—C!"

It was an understated cheer, but it answered my question.

"To this day I have no sense of the geography of Newark, in which I grew up," she continued, "which shows you the closed-in community, ninety percent Jewish, as was the high school I went to.

"Then I went to Bennington College and did a B.A. and M.A. in literature. For me that was a sort of coming out into the world, getting a bit of sophistication and a very, very fine education. I got married in '61 to William Freedman, who also grew up in Newark. Now he is a professor of English literature at Haifa University, and he's also a poet. We are no longer married," she added casually. "I had a daughter along the way, whose name is Jennifer. She is now almost twelve. And I did not do very much else. I picked up an M.A. in philosophy and I taught at Brooklyn College, but it was part-time."

"You came to Israel with your husband?"

"Yes. I came with my husband and daughter. It's very difficult for me to explain why we came. The first time we came was in '67 when we came for one year. The idea then was to come just for one year. It was a sabbatical year. We were just visiting. Bill was then a visiting lecturer at the university, and I didn't work. We wanted to get out of America. We wanted to see what it was like to live someplace else.

"I had been in Israel in 1959 for the summer. I had had the one strong fit of Zionism in my life, Zionism in the sense of not knowing what Israel was all about, et cetera—it's out there in the Middle East and is a Jewish State."

"Was your family involved in Zionism?"

"My father was an active Zionist towards the end of his life. He was always a very strongly identified Jew in a kind of mystical, ethical sense that I have inherited from him. My relationship to the Jewish community was the kind of relationship of gefilte fish and Yiddish, and not too much of either."

We took a small nostalgic pause. I asked if Yiddish was spoken in her home. She explained that her mother's father and mother, who had come from Russia as teenagers, lived in the same building as her family. "So I was very close to them. My parents spoke Yiddish when they didn't want us to understand. . . . The usual story of second, third generations of American Jews. Very, very typical.

"My father was active in the labor movement in the '30s and '40s. He was one of the original organizers of the CIO, so there was a strong political atmosphere, a very strong idealistic, ethical atmosphere in the home. And for me, that was what Judaism was all about. It was all mixed up into one thing. It still is to this very day.

"As a teenager, I did my own bit of research as to what the Jewish people were all about because I felt very strongly identified as a Jew. But looking around my neighborhood, I couldn't figure out what I was identifying with. This was something I wanted to get away from. I found my own roots, my own sense of identity in the history of the Jewish people, which I studied for several years, on my own, privately, just by reading, partly haphazardly, and not very scholarly. But for me the question was very strong: Who am I and what am I?

"In 1959 I was a junior in college. Those were the Eisenhower years. I had looked for many, many years for barricades. There were just none to be found."

"Barricades? Meaning what?"

"A cause. A cause to which I could feel myself dedicated. The civil rights movement hadn't even started yet. Because for me then, and I think now, the meaning of my existence was defined in terms of the kinds of changes that I want to participate in bringing about in society. By putting all of this together for you in terms of time-space, on tape, I think you can understand that as far as I'm concerned, my existential makeup, my political commitment, my ethical commitment, and the idealistic and Jewish commitments are all one thing. Don't ask me to define it. It's just there, and that's what it is. I think it's very much a part of my early childhood background."

I said, "You're explaining yourself deeply. I appreciate the effort involved in pulling all this up."

"I don't often take the time to look back. So in '59," she continued, "I met some young Israeli sabras who were in America for a short time. One of them was my cousin, it turned out, my first cousin, in fact. I got very excited about Israel and decided I wanted to come, so I entered an essay contest that the American Jewish Congress ran. If you wrote two thousand words on why you wanted to go to Israel, you could win this contest, and I was determined in advance that I was going to win this contest because I really wanted to go. So that obviously came through in the essay, and I won it and spent the summer in Israel. I was very impressed."

"You won! *Mazeltov!*"

She laughed. "Thank you. Israel in '59 was still very anti-American in the sense of being anti-materialist in values, anti-capitalist in very strong terms. I'm still very much identified with the Socialist world, Socialist values and ideals—very, very simple in terms of living standards."

Her apartment is true to her words. It is not large, and the furnishings are minimal, the upholstery a little worn. It is located on a rather heavily trafficked road coming down from the top of Carmel, which is the posh area. Occasionally we had to pause so the noise of a motorcycle wouldn't drown out her soft-spoken words.

"I came with three dresses," she continued, "and I put two of them away because the prints were too bold. I ran around with my little black pinafore and sandals. I came home quite impressed and wanted to come back to live here. But at that time it was not possible. I wanted to do my M.A. at the Hebrew University, but there was then no financial help for American students to study in Israel. I was a talented student and had fellowship offers from various universities," she added matter-of-factly. "The problem here was—and I spent six months working on it—all the answers I received said the Americans have to help themselves. We have to help the Israelis. There wasn't a developed consciousness, at that time, of the importance of promoting *aliyah* by getting young people who were in their student days, as is now the case.

"Then my life just went on. I started to do my M.A. I got married. My contest trip was my one exposure to Israel and Zionism, and my life went on in ways that had nothing to do with anything very much, I must say."

"There was nothing you could do to take your M.A. at Hebrew University?" I asked.

"No. I did not come back then. I wasn't able to. I didn't get a fellowship. I didn't get financial aid, and I didn't have the money to do it. So I continued at Bennington with a fellowship."

From the moment I came in, I had been wondering about the stenciling on her sweat shirt, SAN FERNANDO STATE COLLEGE, which so far hadn't been mentioned. "That sweat shirt, did you go there to college, too?"

She laughed. "No, this sweat shirt—so you know something quite typical of Israel—was left at my house accidentally by an Israeli-born woman who spent many years of her life in France and who is today in Venezuela. God knows where she got the sweat shirt from San Fernando State College. I had no idea. But that's what Israel is all about."

The incongruities in Israel are endless. One that struck me and my husband every time we saw it was the sight of a young Orthodox Jew, bearded, with long curling sidelocks, wearing his black silk Sabbath coat, knickers, white stockings, and wide-brimmed fur hat, out for a Sabbath stroll, wheeling a baby stroller with one hand and often guiding a couple of older children with the other. Marcia would say, "It's about time he took his head out of the prayer book and helped with the kids."

Marcia went on, "We came to Israel in 1967 because my husband and I were very much involved in both the civil rights movement and the antiwar movement in America at that time. If there was a demonstration, we would be there. If money was needed, we would give it. But we weren't active leaders. We were both very involved in our very small nuclear family, in our little jobs, and so on.

"But I, for a long time, I think for almost all my life, felt very alienated in America, and Bill began to feel the same way, and we began to think about leaving. The period of emigration from America was just beginning. There was a whole wave of emigration from America to all parts of the world at that time amongst people of my generation. From about the mid-'60s to '72, '73, many of the Jews came here."

"This was after the Six-Day War?" I asked.

"We had got here just one month after the Six-Day War, but the plan to come had been made before. So it was not a result of the war, as far as we were concerned. For us, it was accidental. We would have gone anyplace in the world to live for a year, and, very coincidentally, a job as a visiting lecturer was offered to Bill here. Then I began to remember my experiences here, which had really faded from my consciousness. So, based on both of those facts, we came. We both liked it and decided to stay. We went back to America to get our stuff together and came back again in 1969 permanently, and we've been here ever since."

"You had the baby you were taking back and forth?"

"Right. When we came here finally to settle, she was four years old. It took her about a year to learn the language, to acclimate herself. Now she's totally bilingual—I think, in many ways, bicultural, in ways that I like very much."

"How soon after did you get the idea of starting the women's movement in Israel?"

"I founded the women's movement in 1970–71 without, I think, any strong intention of doing so. Certainly without having been a feminist when I came, and certainly not an activist. Just as I said, just very much involved in my own daily life. I think I began to wake up after a long period of slumber in 1970–71. I think I began having to deal with and to confront the dilemma of what my life was about. And I think in a way that was very standard for the supposedly quote/unquote 'emancipated' woman of the '50s and '60s.

"I will never forget, a friend of mine in New York—where we lived before we moved here—had her Phi Beta Kappa key hanging over the kitchen sink! To me that was very symbolic of what we were all into at that point, where you felt the oppression even though you were not supposed to be oppressed anymore . . . the tremendous mystification that went around, that Betty Friedan described in 1961 but that didn't catch on until later.

"Some friends of mine in America were beginning to get involved in the women's movement at that time. They sent me some literature, and I began to read with enormous interest, I think with more interest than anything I had read in years. I spent three to four months almost in religious conversion, gobbling up all the feminist literature that I could find because it explained my life to me in very much the same way, but even much more directly than as a teenager starting to read about Jewish history to find out who I was as a Jew. And finally I was finding out who I was as a woman. And finding out—as a consequence of that—that as a person, as an individual, Marcia Freedman, I'm really not yet, I have not even begun. To quote a poster in the women's movement: 'Today I feel like I've given birth to myself.' That process started around '70–'71. As a consequence of that—the energies that generated in me —the women's movement got started here. First as a study group at Haifa University, and then it spread rather rapidly."

"And it met with the same scorn and ridicule that it did at first in America, I gather, from some of the opinions I've heard here?"

"The communications media, smelling something new to make fun of—obviously, they smelled a new sensational subject— they were mostly men and exploited it in the worst possible way.

"And the first women reporters who wrote about the women's movement would come and sit with me or somebody else for five, six, seven hours. They couldn't stop the interview because they were getting their own consciousness raised."

"I promise not to do that."

"No, you're, anyway, I'm sure, not at those first stages. But you must understand that in those first stages nobody here knew at all what feminists were saying. Nothing. So at first a few of us who were talking about these things and spreading the ideas were doing the original consciousness-raising with every individual we talked to."

"Most of what is written today in the American press about the women's movement in Israel," I told her, "says that it's almost nonexistent."

"It's not true. We are a force that has been in existence in this country since 1971. At the start we were only eight women. Today we are about a thousand in the women's movement. It's called the Feminist Movement of Israel. There are branches in Haifa, Beersheba, Tel Aviv, and Jerusalem. We have been active in all of those years—six, seven by now."

I thought, What an amazing force the words of this low-keyed woman have. I can believe that she's influenced many of the thousand in the movement. I found her genial, very bright, and not the aggressive personality I'd heard about. "Would you describe the kind of woman the movement has attracted here?"

"Very similar to what's happened in America and in Europe, maybe with some slight changes," she said. "Most of the women are middle-class, anywhere from the ages of sixteen through seventy-five. What we have is a total and very representative cross section of middle-class Jewish women in Israel. There are some Arab women in the movement, some women from Eastern-oriented Jewish background, but for the most part, this is it. Probably the same number of divorced women and married women, mothers and nonmothers, students and nonstudents, educated and noneducated, housewives and women who work outside their homes that you have anywhere else. We have been responsible, I think, for having the abortion reform passed, which happened last year."

I didn't question Marcia about the abortion law since I had heard the provisions of the law from others. Later, I read the following: "Those who had been advocating legalization of abortion wanted it stated that women could have it on demand during the first three months of pregnancy. One of those advocates, Marcia Freedman, called the new law 'a victory first and foremost for the gynecologists, who retain their control over women's wombs.' " It seems in retrospect that she and other proponents of the law feel it's a beginning and a decided victory. There was a bit of Talmudic irony connected with its passage. Some members of the Orthodox bloc, who vigorously opposed the measure, missed the vote because they were outside the Knesset demonstrating against it when the vote came up.

The law permits termination of a pregnancy after approval by a three-member committee consisting of two doctors—one a gynecologist—and a social worker. Some of the reasons for which a legal abortion can be obtained are as follows: if a mother is under sixteen or over forty; if the pregnancy resulted from incest or rape or occurred out of wedlock; if it can be determined the child would be born physically or mentally handicapped; or if the birth would injure the physical or emotional health of the mother.

In effect, the law ratified a common practice in Israel. A recent study has shown that 46.7 percent of all Israeli women have had at least one abortion by the time they reach forty. The estimates of the number of abortions in Israel, which has a population of 3,500,000, range from 40,000 a year, a figure stated by the government, to 70,000, a figure used by the Feminist Movement. Contrary to the American experience, the abortions are done under relatively good conditions in a gynecologist's home clinic. Since 1952 there have been no prosecutions of doctors who performed illegal abortions.

The fees, of course, are excessive. Under the new law, the cost is covered by existing national health insurance.

"But I think the most important thing about the women's movement is that it works here, probably more than in America, as an underground force. The movement here means to any woman who's exposed to it, and lets herself hear what's being said, that her life cannot go on in exactly the same way as it went on before. It also is a political force, so that there is amongst women in Israel today, because the women's movement exists, a new consciousness about the rights of women, about the status of women in the country. All the old myths that this is an egalitarian country, that it ever was an egalitarian country, have been broken down. I don't think there are many people who will say that anymore."

"In what sense is the movement underground? You have announced yourself as a party. You have open meetings."

"Its effect seems to me to be quite an underground effect. That is to say, there are changes in the lives of women—in growing numbers of women—and those changes in the lives of women mean changes in the lives of men with whom they're living, changes in the lives of children whom they bear, changes in the lives also of the people with whom they work."

"You mean it has created an undercurrent in women who haven't necessarily been affiliated with the movement?"

"Absolutely. I think there's really been a very significant change in Israel in the past four or five years for sure. I don't know if you could feel it now when you come here. I don't know the last time you were here, but I know there is the beginning now, only the beginning, of the sense of women, that it's good to be a woman, that it's exciting to be a woman. That there is potential and possibility for us."

"This is the longest I've been away from Israel since my first trip in '49. At the end of '71 I didn't hear a murmur of a women's movement. From the moment I arrived I've been getting lots of messages and reactions—negative and positive. It's clear that you've stirred up something."

"I think we've succeeded in at least raising the consciousness on a minimal level. Up until the time the women's movement got started, there was a very strong myth in the country that this was the best place in the world for women. The kibbutz, if it wasn't

absolute equality, was something very close to it. That it was good
to be a woman. The fact is that it was not, and never was, correct.
Women have now begun to do some research on what it was like
thirty, forty, fifty years ago. We're beginning to understand what
was, in fact, going on then." (The sociologist Judith Buber Agassi,
who has recently done a study on the role of women in the kibbutz,
was to tell me more about this later.)

"As a result of my own activities—let's go back to my own
story—I became somewhat well-known in the country, not quite
intentionally and not in the most positive light, because I was the
one who took all of the first angry and aggravated and threatened
reactions to the beginning force of the women's movement and
became the only name actually that was identified with it publicly.
As a result of that, in 1973, when Shulamit Aloni, who was not
associated with the women's movement but who had associated
herself politically with women's rights issues, decided to leave the
Labor Party and run on her own ticket, she turned to the women's
movement and offered us third place in exchange for support. It
was quite late. It was two or three days before the filing deadline,
and she needed organized support quickly. We made a very quick
decision that we would do this because there was a woman at the
head of the list, and we would have third place with another feminist on the list, and I was that woman. Nobody, including ourselves
or Shulamit Aloni, expected that I would be elected. But that's
exactly what happened. So in January 1974, having been in the
country for a total of four years, I became a member of the Knesset.
It was an enormous shock, I think, to everyone, especially to me."

"I gather from Shulamit Aloni that it's been a shock to her that
you've left her party now and formed the Women's Party."

"It's something I had to do. When I first began in the Knesset,
my Hebrew was not terribly good. I was making speeches to audi-
ences, reading and translating simultaneously from a text written in
English, in Hebrew words which I had just learned the day before,
written in with the dots."

"You didn't go to an ulpan?" (An ulpan is an intensive Hebrew language course for immigrants with higher education.)

"Sure, I studied Hebrew intensively my first year in the
country, and I had begun lecturing in philosophy in Hebrew the
following year. Nevertheless, I certainly wasn't able to give

extemporaneous speeches in Hebrew at that time. And even now I find myself limited, although my friends say it's not the case. But I feel the difference when I speak in English and when I speak in Hebrew.

"When I was elected to the Knesset, I was in somewhat better shape, but not all that good. I still found it very difficult to express myself forcefully in Hebrew and to make my point persuasively. And there were many areas in which I couldn't discourse at all because I didn't have the vocabulary. In a way, the Knesset was a very fine ulpan for me because there's certainly nothing for me today that I can't talk about in Hebrew."

"Is there anything that you won't talk about?"

"For sure. I saw my task in the Knesset basically as one of trying to put the whole subject of the status of women into the political sphere, to make it into a political question, that it would be one of those things that politicians address themselves to, that it would be one of those things that the Knesset addressed itself to.

"I can't say that there were very many significant legislative achievements during the four years that I served in the Knesset. But it seems to be clear today that certainly every political party that is going to run in these elections is going to have a very nice and clear section on women in their platform. There's no doubt that that's the case." (This was about seven weeks before the May 1977 elections.)

"I decided that I did not want a second term in the Knesset. I was in for one term—four years. It is now just ending. I did not want it because there are other things that I want to do, and also because I believe very, very much in the principle of rotation, particularly for women today. It's terribly important, now that I've become all this famous. Let me get out of the limelight, and let other women come and fill it."

"Are there others ready to come in? And what are the other things you want to do?"

"Absolutely. Of course there are. We are still in the position where there's not very much room for many of us, and so one has to stand aside and make room for other women. First, I'm going to take a little rest. Then I'd like to set up a women's counseling center in Haifa. If I do any future teaching, it will be teaching specifically for women." (Since then, Marcia has established this center in Haifa. Other crisis centers and shelters for rape or for battered women operate successfully in the major cities.)

"Will your women be elected in May?"

"We will have to see about that. We have organized the Women's Party for the elections to the Ninth Knesset. It is not something new in Israel. It was called the Union of Women for Equal Rights in Israel and ran in conjunction with WIZO, the Women's International Zionist Organization. They elected one member—this was to the First Knesset [1948]—and her name was Rachel Kagan.

"My history in the Knesset is in many interesting ways quite parallel to hers. We were both considered to be slightly absurd because we were both totally preoccupied with the question of women. Which means that we were totally preoccupied with the question of fifty percent of the population of the country. Which was, nevertheless, considered slightly funny, not very serious, and certainly not a political issue.

"If that precedent means anything to us today in 1977, we will elect at least one person. My own feeling is that the potential is there for at least one seat. And one seat for us is very, very significant. It would be something above and beyond another small splinter party in the Knesset. It would be, I think, a very clear signal to the whole political structure that women are beginning to organize themselves on the basis of what has been called sex solidarity, and to identify with women as women, and to organize around their own clear personal interests.

"Part of the reason that that's possible is because the subject has been raised politically in the past four years. The other part of the reason is that, as an outgoing member of the Knesset, I can provide state financing for a Women's Party, so that for the first time here there is a group of women which has a bit of money to work with. Not a great deal, but at least some. We've never had any before."

"Did you say 'state financing?' "

"All political parties are state financed in Israel, from the government. But that's only if you're a successful political party. New parties have to go on their own. But since I'm an outgoing member, I am eligible for it."

"Has the Women's Party considered aligning itself with Aloni's Citizens Rights Party, which got you into the Knesset?"

"No. The Women's Party will not align itself with Aloni's civil rights movement. If you look at the platform, it deals only in part, and not very deeply, with the whole question of the status of women. Shulamit Aloni has been a very, very forceful and outspoken advocate of separation of church and state and against religious coercion. She basically sees the problem of women as a subheading under the whole question of church and state, which is an analysis that we don't agree with."

"You don't agree that it's a civil rights problem?"

"It's partially a civil rights problem. But it's different to say that the women's issue is partially a civil rights problem than to say that the problem of civil rights is partially a women's issue. In other words, what we see is that the question of the status of women is a question of a systematic and ongoing exploitation of the labors, the bodies, and the emotions of women. You say, 'By whom?' Then obviously it's by the men through institutions that have been set up to make it possible for it to happen without anybody being consciously aware of what they're doing. This is something that has to. be fought, attacked, and explained at all levels.

"And to say that it's just a question of the influence of religious parties through coalition agreements, and that this is what's responsible for the question of women, I think, is worse than saying nothing at all. Not broad enough. It's very, very misleading. This, I think, has been very much the attitude in the country for a long time. That if, somehow or other, the National Religious Party wasn't in the coalition, there would be full equality for women. Everybody has hidden behind the religious party, in a way, not to face up to what is clearly around them.

"The Women's Party has a platform of seventeen different sections on the question of women: talking about housewives; talking about employed women; talking about soldiers in the army; talking about prostitution, rape, battered wives; talking about children's rights; talking about the image of women in the media; talking about values and ideals in the whole cultural sphere."

"There was a letter in the *Jerusalem Post* from a battered husband! I hadn't heard of one before. Did you see it?"

"Yes, I did. The difference between a battered wife and a battered husband is that the battered husband can leave the house, for one thing. He has the money. Secondly, battered husbands are usually battered by wives who are severely mentally disturbed.

Actually, this was the case. Battered wives are battered by men who are rabbis, who are policemen, who are generals in the army, who are doctors, lawyers, and who are perfectly sane but who are violent, and whose violence is not permitted in any other sphere in the society, under penalty of law and punishment. But it is permitted in the home because of the very old attitude that a wife is the property of her husband, and his home is his castle in which he may do as he likes. And it's nobody's business what he does. By the way, that's one of the issues I raised in the Knesset, and I believe most successfully, at least to bring it out from under the carpet. Today I would say that there are at least fifty thousand such abused women. We've uncovered a great deal of violence towards women in this country. There are a minimum of three thousand rape victims a year in a country of three and a half million."

"Are the men brought to justice?"

"Very rarely, because, as in Western countries, there is a requirement that the woman prove that she tried to resist. Where you know you can be killed, she has to bring what is called corroborating evidence! That is, an eyewitness. It's just ridiculous.

"Secondly, there's a lot of male identification between the police and the rapist himself. There's always the suspicion that the woman is lying, that she seduced him. 'What were you doing out on the street alone at night?' And so on. So that when the case gets to court, which is rare, and when there are convictions, even though the law provides a fourteen- to twenty-year penalty, the usual penalty for the most brutal cases of rape is five to six years. Only ten percent of the three thousand cases are reported to the police, and an even smaller number gets to court."

"I think that's quite comparable to the United States record."

"Yes. One of the interesting things we've discovered about the women's movement in general, because we are such a mixture of women from different parts of the world, is that the situation of women in one or another part of the world is basically the same. The dentist's wife's remark has a deep level of truth to it. A very deep level of truth."

"The question: Are Israeli women different? You think, essentially, there are the same problems here, although Israeli lives, backgrounds, and traumas have been very different. But as women their problems are the same. I agree."

"O.K. The kinds of oppression and exploitation that women have suffered everywhere they also suffered here. I had meetings with Druze women, for instance. When we talked quietly, without men around, about our lives as mothers, as daughters, as wives, the similarities between our experiences are much more impressive than what seems to be the enormous difference between a Western woman with two degrees who teaches philosophy talking to Druze women who are still in purdah, wearing veils and sitting on the floor barefoot.

"That, to me, has been very impressive and instructive. That also goes back to answer the question of why the Women's Party would not join with the civil rights movement. The Women's Party has invited Shulamit Aloni to join the Women's Party. She has refused. We have also invited Violet Khoury to join the Women's Party, and she has still to let us know. I'm still very hopeful that she will join us and take a high place on our list." (I had an appointment to see Violet Khoury the next day in the Arab village of Kfar Yassif, north of Haifa. She was the first and only woman mayor of an Arab village.)

"You said you started the women's movement, not realizing that you started it. In what sense did you not realize it?"

"It was not a product of direct intent to start a women's movement, although one can talk about intentions that aren't direct, that aren't fully conscious, and they are probably correct."

"Have you been analyzed? Have you had analytic therapy?"

"I had six weeks of therapy in 1973, after the war. But I spent many, many hours in consciousness-raising groups and also by myself. My mind is very analytic."

"I would agree with you. What you have plowed through to arrive where you are is really amazing. Are there many consciousness-raising groups here?"

"Oh, yes. I think that's the most important thing in the women's movement in Israel, where we are still at the beginning stages. Unless women can understand and analyze the woman's problems from their own personal experience, it's never very meaningful."

"And to compare with other women . . ."

"Yes, to compare with other women, and also to build the bonds of sisterhood, which for us is the major political tactic. Our major advantage is that we are half the population. What we really do need is to stay together."

"Supportive understanding . . ."

"And more. If I could choose between support from a woman or from a man, it must be a woman. It's a political obligation. There can be no question about that. If that point were firmly fixed in the mind of every woman, we could end discrimination in ten years."

"Has lesbianism become an issue here, in the women's movement, as it has in the States?"

"No, it has not become an issue. There are lesbians in the women's movement. We have been aware of what has happened, both in Europe and in America, on the fight between lesbian women and straight women. But I think we've also been able to benefit from the experience of women outside the country. We're about five to six years behind those movements, so we can see both behind and ahead at the same time.

"When tensions began to develop, we began to talk about it openly between ourselves, and what came out of it was that a lot of the tensions developed because women who were not lesbians found themselves very much attracted by the idea of a possible alternative or an option which, up until then, had been so taboo. They had never even thought about the possibility."

"Or they didn't allow themselves to, consciously."

"Yes. So when those kinds of feelings began to come out and be expressed, much of the tension eased. Today, in Israel, very recently, there has been formed an Association for the Protection of Individual Rights—something which is again a liberation group —and most of the lesbian women in the country are active in that, and not active in the women's movement. Among the feminists, there is a minority who are lesbians, and for us it has not become a divisive factor. There is just now beginning to be talk in the women's movement about the whole question of women's sexuality and the effects of oppression on women's sexuality, which has been an open subject in America and Europe for many years. This is a very puritan country, in which you do not talk about all sorts of things."

"According to the article in the *Jerusalem Post* yesterday, you are now talking about some very taboo subjects. What reactions have there been to your sexuality statement?"

"Some of my colleagues in the women's movement were terribly upset. I'm not upset. I think some very important and vital information got out, at least to English-reading women. One of the effects of the women's movement has been to break down many of those taboos, so one section of the platform of the Women's Party is on sexuality, very clearly. You saw what the *Post* did with that." (The headline on the *Post*'s article was WOMEN'S PARTY PLEDGES TO PROMOTE SEXUAL SATISFACTION. Then it reported: "Marcia Freedman's new Women's Party yesterday pledged to develop studies and open institutions to help women achieve greater sexual satisfaction. . . . Their platform says, 'With whatever regards sexuality, the male's real or conditioned needs are preferred, so a behavioral pattern emerged which prevents sexual health for both male and female.' ")

Marcia explained, "The behavioral pattern is based on the model of the conquering male and the submissive woman. As a result there are many women who engage in sexual intercourse unwillingly, even when married. This model prompts the male to initiate sexual intercourse and determine its style, while we, the women, are conditioned to passivity, feelings of guilt and shame, which accompany us during sexual intercourse.

"The platform, therefore, pledged to develop studies and public debates on sexuality, give equal sexual education to boys and girls from an early age, open clinics for sexual education, and abolish the law prohibiting 'unnatural sex.' The platform also proposed abolishing the law which defines prostitution as an offense. It pledges 'essential services' to prostitutes, including medical treatment and supervision and police protection. Women who want to quit prostitution should be able to enter special quarters where they would be given shelter, moral support, and taught a new profession.

"The platform recommended giving women self-defense courses to protect themselves against rape, and said the requirement that women prove in court that they fought a rapist should be abolished."

"I also saw the ad," I told her, "of the Women's Party that asked: 'When your daughter grows up, will they still be saying that she "doesn't do anything," that she is just a housewife?' It's certainly been a perjorative term for years. I know I always felt it demeaning, before I worked professionally, when a form of some kind was filled out with 'Occupation: Housewife.' "

"That's the problem. First of all, it's important to realize that seventy percent of all adult Israeli women are housewives, that our analysis of what it is to be a housewife is to be a worker within the society who is working twice as many hours as any other worker in the society, providing absolutely essential services, and not having her labor recognized in any way whatsoever, not officially, not nonofficially, not culturally, and certainly not in terms of money— no protection, no pension rights, nothing."

I didn't think of it at the moment, but now, writing this, I recall some personal propaganda that I disseminated in 1952 when I first moved to New York from Los Angeles and started reading *The New York Times*. A now-defunct woman's magazine ran a full-page ad with a photo of a young couple. She was holding a baby. The headline said, in bold type: DO YOU KNOW THAT IN THE NEXT TEN YEARS SHE WILL SPEND $40,000 OF HIS MONEY? (Today they would probably have to say $100,000.) The ad was appealing for advertisers. It ran three times. The first time I saw it, I winced. The second time I saw it, I winced again. (Coincidentally, I was working on my first book about Israeli women at the time.) The third time, I interrupted my work and wrote a letter to the publisher to the effect: "How can you pretend to represent the interests of women in your magazine? Don't you realize that while he's at the office putting in an eight-hour day, she's working about sixteen hours taking care of the kids, doing the cooking, the cleaning, the laundry, the marketing, chauffeuring, entertaining his boss, et cetera, et cetera? She is not spending *his* money. She is spending *their* money!" I promptly received a lengthy and thoughtful letter from the shocked publisher. These facts had never occurred to him before he gave his advertising agency the go-ahead on this and a series of ads on the same theme to follow. He was grateful to me for bringing this to his attention, and he canceled the series. I should have carried my message much further. The status of the housewives of the world has changed little since 1952.

To get back to my conversation with Marcia: "This seventy percent doesn't work out of the home? Are these recent statistics?"

"Absolutely. The point of our ad was to attack the idea that women who are housewives don't do anything, that they don't work. One of the things we're calling for is official recognition of the home as a place of work, and being a housewife as an occupation, with everything that it implies. What we've done in our platform is to call for the establishment of a national committee of economists who would find a solution to the question of providing a just remuneration for the work of housewives."

"And benefits?"

"And, of course, benefits. We're calling for pension rights for housewives, accident insurance for housewives, and fringe benefits which are allowed to all workers. In addition to which, we want all those years of experience in housework to be counted as experience in order to get a job outside of the home. All the years that she has put in early childhood education, in management, in budgeting, in consumerism, and all the rest of that should be counted as work experience, which it really is, enormous work experience. Most of the housewives I know could run corporations quite easily. They prove that when, at the age of forty or earlier, they go into volunteer work and they're running enormous organizations. Again there's no money."

"Are there adequate child-care centers when the woman wants to go out of the home and has young children?"

"No, there are not. One of the other things we're working for is exactly that. In addition to organizing baby-sitting services, we're also calling for the establishment of community centers in which much of the work in running a home would be communalized— done on a communal basis—just as in the kibbutz. There is no reason why in this neighborhood there is no communal laundry. Not one where I can bring my laundry and run the machine with a few other women and talk at the same time. I mean where the family can drop its laundry off at the beginning of the week and pick it up at the end of the week at a very low price because these would be state-financed services.

"There's no reason why there could not be a communal dining room in every neighborhood where those working families who don't want to, or cannot, prepare their own meals every single day can eat well and cheaply. There's no reason why there can't be a communal baby-sitting service, right in the neighborhood, in addition to day-care centers.

"What we're trying to do is to provide a vision of the way a society might look, could operate, in a practical sort of way, where there's real equality between the sexes. We have called for the return of parenthood to fathers, and this means that both fathers and mothers get childbirth leave. Both fathers and mothers get paid sick days for their children's sicknesses. We want there to be flexible workdays for the parents of young children, with full pay."

"It shouldn't be just the mother's responsibility."

"Absolutely!"

"Are any marriage contracts as such being written in Israel?"

"This is one of our special problems. As you know, marriage and divorce are under the jurisdiction of the religious courts, whether one is Jewish, Moslem, or Christian." (This was a recurring theme, in one way or another, in many of my conversations.) Marcia went on. "I'm not an expert on Christian or Moslem religious law having to do with marriage and divorce, but I've become an expert on Jewish law in matters having to do with marriage and divorce.

"It is very clearly and openly, without any fudging of the issue, based on the fact that the woman is the property of the man. She is married according to a contract, a *ketuba,* which is signed between her father and her husband, that she promises all of her personal services, plus sexual services, plus bearing his children. These are the terms in which the contract is put for life, in return for room and board."

Of course, when I asked about marriage contracts, I was referring to some of the personal contracts that have been written between couples in the United States, defining what each partner is committed to in specific terms, and what he or she is not. But it's clear that in Israel the term "marriage contract" has only one meaning, and more often than not those are fighting words. One woman in high public office told me, off the record, "The religious laws for marriage and divorce are a disaster!" "Disaster" is a favorite word with Israelis for all manner of political and social unpleasantness.

"Our claim," Marcia continued, "is that, for the most part, women are subjected to a feudal hangover in what is supposed to be an exemplary democracy in the Middle East. The Jewish marriage contract makes it absolutely clear. And Halakah, Jewish religious law, is what determines the conditions under which men and women can marry, what their married life is supposed to be, and the conditions under which they can divorce."

"A friend told me the other day of a man she knows who wants to divorce his wife because she is frigid. She said, 'It's so outrageous! Would a woman go to court and claim a divorce because her man was impotent?' How would the law rule on that?"

"The fact is that the Halakah demands not that the woman give the man sexual satisfaction, or that she experiences sexual satisfaction, but that they bear children, and that the husband has regular intercourse with his wife at stated periods. The woman can sue for divorce here on the grounds that the man is impotent. Her function in this world is to bear children, and if he cannot give her children, then she cannot perform her rightful function. Therefore, she's not going to be a good Jewish woman. This is not for a woman's protection.

"It's also possible, according to Jewish religious law, to have children out of wedlock without any legal stigma. The illegitimate child here is the child of a woman who is already married, where the father of that child is not her legal husband. That is an illegitimate child. But to have a child without being married, that child is not then called illegitimate. That's something that not too many women are aware of because of the social stigma."

I recalled, "I heard about a Beersheba rabbinical court that wrote a clause into a woman's divorce decree forbidding her to marry her lover. A group of women, protesting outside the court, carried signs that read, 'When a man commits adultery, the children are kosher. When a woman does, they're bastards.' So if you don't have a husband you are responsible to and you give birth to a child," I asked, "it's all right?"

"In terms of the legal status of the child, it's quite all right. In other terms, it's not all right. It's very difficult for the women to support themselves without being married, because the average wage for women, which is forty-three percent less than the average wage for men in the country, is below subsistence level."

"Is that true in the higher echelons, of doctors and lawyers too?"

"In the higher echelons—that is, in the free professions—what you find is, first of all, fringe benefits are not equal, although the salary on the books is equal. The benefits are unequal because men are the heads of families, and this has an effect on the tax structure and all kinds of fringe benefits which have to do with getting loans for housing, cars, and so on.

"And what you find is that most of the women who are lawyers
—and only seven percent of the lawyers in the country are women
—most of them are working for the State's Attorney's Office, which
is a kind of legal-clerical work, for the most part. Very few are in
private practice, and then their clientele has mostly to do with
women, marriage, and divorce.

"Twenty-five percent of the doctors are women. There seems
to be a quota system operating in the medical schools, because only
twenty-five percent of the students can be women. Of course, there
are always exceptions. We're living in the 1970s. Women have had
higher education now for fifty years. What you find in most cases
is that the woman is a hell of a lot more talented than the average
male with whom she's competing."

"She has to be to get there."

"Absolutely!" Her use of the word leaves absolutely no doubt
of where she stands. "Also, in a high percentage of cases, she has
never been married, or married without children, or divorced or
widowed at a young age. That is to say, having a decent ordinary
family life and being a woman with a serious career seldom go
together. And that is the kind of choice that women still have to
make, which men obviously don't have to make.

"Most of the women doctors work in clinics of Kupat Cholim
[the national health service]. You find very few as heads of medical
departments. You don't find them in the higher echelons of the
medical schools or of the hospitals. There are about four hundred
women in this country who have high positions, but not more. It's
a country of three and a half million people, and approximately
fifty-one percent of them are women. Which means four hundred
out of one and three quarters of a million women. Not a very
interesting ratio.

"One of the problems we have to face is that there are all of
these token successful women who deserve all credit and all sympathy. But because they've become successful under conditions that
prevent their becoming successful at every turn, they feel themselves to be superwomen and, in fact, they probably are. But because ninety-nine percent of their colleagues are men, they identify
with men and not with women. In addition to which, one could
always say, 'You had a prime minister who was a woman, and you
have a woman who's a Supreme Court judge.' A woman here, a

woman there, a woman everywhere. Everything's all right. It's not. And every good sociologist knows it's not."

I was interested in knowing Marcia's views on the situation of women in the Israeli Army. I had been told they weren't being treated seriously.

"Women fare worse there than anyplace else. They are theoretically drafted together with men when they are eighteen, for compulsory service. But only sixty percent are actually drafted. They're exempt if they're married, or on grounds of religious conscience. Or they are refused because of substandard education if they are dropouts before finishing eighth grade. Men with substandard education are offered remedial training in the army; women are not. It is absolutely necessary for us to demand equal obligation for women in the military. Not just in law but in fact. The army is emphasizing the economic and political gap between men and women.

"Of those drafted, seventy percent of the women are trained to be clerk-typists. Most of the rest are loaned out to other ministries to cover womanpower shortages. Or they fold parachutes, work in the base kitchens, or are a part of entertainment troupes. Some become junior officers, training other women to work in the kitchen or pound a typewriter. Very, very few hold anything like responsible positions with any direct military importance.

"The Women's Party is calling for service for women to be changed from eighteen months to two years, as is the men's; that the image of women as morale boosters for male soldiers be changed; and courses in cosmetics and home economics be canceled.

"Perhaps the army's attitude towards women is best illustrated by the recent call to reservists to join the standing army for a year. It is called 'volunteering.' But there is a salary and fringe benefits. Women are also being asked to volunteer, but with them, volunteer means volunteer—twenty to forty hours a week of unpaid labor!" (Since our talk, the religious bloc, traditionally against women serving in the army, has succeeded in passing a new bill that so relaxes the requirement for exemption that now a girl, on reaching eighteen, can simply declare before a judge that she observes *kashruth* [Jewish dietary laws] and the Sabbath. Opposing groups, outraged by the new law, claim that the old law was so permissive that in one case a girl who convinced the former board of examiners that she could not uphold her high standard of modesty in the army later competed in a Miss Israel contest wearing a bikini.)

"Tell me about your projections for the future. What do you anticipate may happen to your movement? What do you hope will happen, and what will some of your problems be?"

"It's very hard at the moment to answer that. If the Women's Party wins at least one seat in the Knesset, we'll have a jumping-off base which is very significant—extraordinarily significant. The point is not only having one representative in the Knesset, but it means having eighteen thousand women or more who have united around their own interests. You need that number to get one seat in the Knesset. In addition to which, the very fact of having a Women's Party means the beginning of a mass movement and an organizational structure that is effective and efficient.

"Even if we don't win, the women who are involved are getting the first real opportunity they've had, without directions from men and without a man looking over their shoulders, judging and approving or not approving, to discover what their own abilities and talents are. We're finding we are really a very able group. We're doing everything ourselves, from the very highest policy planning—advertising and so forth, using no professionals, because the professionals are all men—down to stuffing the envelopes." (The Women's Party received 5,674 votes, indicating the embryonic condition of feminism in Israel and/or the preference of some women to fight for their rights under the established parties.)

"Did your activism in the Women's Party and feminist movement have anything to do with your divorce, or did your divorce have anything to do with your activism?"

"I don't think it had to do with activism as much as it had to do with developing consciousness both in myself and in my ex-husband—things like self-growth, self-actualization, living existentially, and so on. A feminist awakening in women really means being reborn in a very significant sense.

"Anyway, what we both began to feel was that the family structure was confining and, having lived together for thirteen years, we had sort of used up whatever there was that had been holding this thing together for all of those years."

As Marcia was saying this, the doorbell rang. She answered,

and introduced me to Bill, her ex-husband, who joined us momen-
tarily. He's a nice-looking young man of slight build, with sandy-
colored hair and mustache.

Marcia continued, "I started out by saying that I don't think
the activism itself had anything to do with the separation, but on
the other hand—"

"Not ideologically, but on a practical basis," Bill added, and
said he'd go into the kitchen to have something to eat. This seemed
to be one of the rare divorces where a friendship maintained.

"Bill is somebody who likes a quiet life very much—a life
within the home. And I don't. I simply don't. What happened was
I was beginning to develop, in my own way, after such a long time
of not developing at all, and I began to see that I really do like to
live in a way very different from the way I'd been living.

"There was a basic reexamination of values, of life-style, of
how I want to see myself ten, fifteen, twenty years from now, that
I had not thought about since I was a teenager. I think the same sort
of thing began to happen with Bill and, at that point, both of us
started to go our separate ways. I think it was good."

"Do you anticipate a future marriage, or do you think a
woman gets along better without one?"

"No, I do not believe that women ought to marry at all unless
they can marry in a very clear way, on an egalitarian basis. I also
do not believe, and this is my personal view, that those kinds of
marriages can be genuinely egalitarian. Because if it is, then both
people will be developing in their own individual ways. And there
is no reason for assuming that a relationship that existed at point
x is going to exist at point y. Both people will be developing and
changing all the time.

"I think that women today should not marry. It's both unneces-
sary and harmful." With statements like this, it wasn't hard to see
why the name Marcia Freedman brought out such violent reactions
in people. "If one takes a look at the history of the marital institution, it's very obvious that it has been designed to guarantee the
continued existence of the patriarchy. Because that's what it's all
about. It's designed to make sure that men can be fathers, and from
that you move to godfather and everything in between. Women
have to fight that institution. On the other hand, I do see a possibility of permanent relationships between men and women."

"With children?"

"With children."

"What about illegality? If children aren't legitimate, it creates a problem for them. Or do the laws have to be changed?"

"The problem isn't law. The problem is attitude within the society. Attitudes change as people change their attitudes about themselves. The more women who bring children into the world, at the same time refusing to marry the fathers of their children because they cannot marry them on an egalitarian basis, the quicker we will bring about equality between the sexes. It means a change in the whole structure of the economy, in the whole policy. Basic, basic, deep, deep changes in conceptions of what your relationships are all about."

"You say it's just a problem of the woman, of being able to support a family. But it also creates a problem for the child. He may not even know who his father is if there isn't a continuing relationship."

"The human race, up to 6000 to 7000 B.C., had absolutely no notion of biological fatherhood at all. That is to say that the function of the male in the reproduction of the species was not understood. The patriarchal family has existed probably only three to four thousand years. You know that Freud himself was patriarchal in his attitude. So the idea of a mother image and a father image means you have to have feminine and masculine. I reject those concepts. They're not biological concepts.

"I don't think that a child who is raised in a typical nuclear family today is being raised in a very healthy way. I think the boys are being raised to take their part as equals in the patriarchy, and the girls are being raised to be servants. That kind of constriction creates a typing in the family that results in very strong dependencies on a small number of people and is damaging to both adults and children. So I'm open to all kinds of possible alternative life-styles, including alternative ways of raising children."

"Do you think it's important for a child to have an identification with a father, with a father figure, with a male, in his life?"

"Not necessarily. Why?"

"It just gives him both sides of the coin."

"There are plenty of males in this world."

"It doesn't have to be the one who conceived him."

"Of course not. There are males all over the world. There are males ruling it. The problem for feminists is exactly to try to break down this kind of identification that 'I'm a member of the privileged class.' "

"You mean that I have a mother and a father and that I can point to them?"

"No, I think it's important for us to break down the identification between boys and men, and between girls and women. What we're trying to do is to break down all those kinds of stereotypical distinctions. Freedom begins at home."

"Including relating to a mother and father."

"On a sex basis. If you want to change the society, then you don't want your child to be adjusted to the society as it exists."

"Do you think there are many women in Israel who espouse that sentiment?"

"I think there are a growing number of women who are deciding to have children, and not marry on grounds of principle. It's still small, but growing. And the fact is that because Israel is so interested in increasing the birthrate, there's a certain amount of encouragement for this."

"Internal immigration?"

"Yes. That's an interesting way of putting it. I hadn't heard that term before. Is it yours?"

"No. As far as I know, it was coined by the late Miriam Baratz, in 1911, when she gave birth to the first of her seven children in Degania, the first kibbutz in the country. She told me 'internal immigration' was her answer to the immigration restrictions of the Mandate government."

Marcia took up the phrase. " 'Internal immigration' without marriage now is another form of protest against the age-old mandate of men over women."

―――――

In other days, Deborah, prophet and judge, sat under her palm tree in the hill country of Ephraim and sent for Barak. She told him, "The Lord commands you to take ten thousand men and go towards Mount Tabor, to the river Kishon, where I will draw out Sisera, the captain of Jabin's army, with his chariots and with his multitude, and I will deliver him into thy hand."

Barak, brave warrior, answered, "If thou wilt go with me, then I will go. But if thou wilt not go with me, I will not go."

And that's what happened. Deborah went up with him.

Barak's troops slew the multitude, except for Sisera, who alighted from his chariot and fled to the tent of Jael, the wife of Heber the Kenite. She told him to fear not, opened a skin of milk to quench his thirst, bade him rest himself, and covered him with a rug.

When he made the fatal mistake of falling asleep, "Jael took a tent peg and hammer, went softly to him and drove the peg into his temple." Barak, in pursuit of Sisera, was greeted by Jael at the flap of her tent, with a fait accompli. It came to pass that Deborah knew what she was talking about. A woman, not a man, had delivered Israel from tyranny.

Will Marcia, on Mount Carmel, though not sitting under a palm tree, be Israel's contemporary woman prophet? Will she deliver the women of Israel from the tyranny she describes? Will enough women want her to?

 # "Crime" and Punishment

"IF SOMEBODY WOULD EVER TELL ME that when I would finally get my permission, after years of trying, to leave for Israel, I wouldn't want to leave, I would never believe it. I left Russia with a very heavy heart because I left my husband and two brothers in prison, and my father and other brother, and I didn't know when I would ever see them again."

These were the words of thirty-year-old Sylva Zalmonson when she started to tell me of the ordeal she, her family, and companions lived through in Russian prison camps as a result of their efforts to emigrate to Israel. I had followed her turbulent story since the first press reports appeared in 1970 and particularly wanted to meet her to learn firsthand of Russia's oppressive policies. It is one thing to read about inhuman happenings. It is another to hear about them from a person who lived through them.

Since we were meeting after her work as a mechanical engineer, it was already dark when I came to a large complex of new apartments on the outskirts of Tel Aviv, near Ben-Gurion airport. As with buildings in Europe and Israel, you grope in the dark to find a button that lights up for a few seconds, then again plunges you into darkness. I eventually located her building and walked up two flights to number nineteen.

A nice-looking young woman welcomed me. She was slim, of medium height, well dressed in a plaid skirt, pullover sleeveless sweater, and blouse, her dark hair cut in short Sassoon fashion. Brown eyes reflected the sadness that is always with her.

I entered a surprisingly comfortable apartment, furnished with simple Danish pieces. Books lined the walls, and bowls of nuts and fruit were on the coffee table. I remarked on her good fortune, as most single people have difficulty in finding apartments, since they are built for couples or families.

"You see," she said in her limited English, "I hope soon my husband will be with me, and the apartment is for both of us." She showed me the bedroom, bath, and kitchen. Though small, the rooms were well designed. It was obvious that she gave them loving care.

I looked around expectantly for the person who would translate for us. "I am sorry," Sylva said in a quiet voice, "my friend who would translate has unexpected guests and can't come." She quickly allayed my fears of our not being able to communicate when she added, "We will go there."

As we walked past several buildings, playgrounds, and lawn areas on the way to her friend's apartment in the same complex, she said, "I am sorry not to have my car. I would have called for you, but I loaned it to a friend for a few days."

"You have a car?" I was surprised, since so few people in Israel can afford cars, especially new immigrants.

"Yes. Not a very good one, an old car I bought with royalties from my husband's book, *Prison Diaries.* It was smuggled out and printed in America. But the royalties have stopped, and my lawyer gets no results. It was printed in Italy, England, France, and other countries, also."

Having arrived at her friend's apartment, we walked up three flights and were greeted by a pleasant young woman named Rita Harrow, who works as a technical librarian in the city library, all of the literature being in English. She and her husband emigrated from Russia in 1969 with the first group allowed to leave for Israel. Her husband, an economist, has also found work in his field in Israel. Both learned Hebrew in an ulpan and are happy to be in "our own beautiful but difficult country." I was introduced to her husband and their guests, who had recently come from Russia. Sylva, Rita, and I went into one of two bedrooms, which was furnished as a study, with books piled high on every available surface. They sat together on a daybed, and I sat next to them on a chair.

"Where did you learn your beautiful English?" I asked our translator before starting.

"My English is not of Russian origin," she explained. "It is of Chinese origin. I was born in China, in Harbin. Then I lived in Tsinan and Shanghai. When I was fourteen my father took me to Russia, and when I was seventeen my father was imprisoned. He was sentenced to twenty-five years in prison."

"For what?"

"For being Jewish. He was a musician, pianist, and cantor. He was arrested because he was singing in the synagogue in Odessa. Because he came from China. He was suspect for that and because he worked with Jewish youth in China. My husband served six years in prison—also for nothing." Every encounter in Israel brings another extraordinary life to explore. Time being limited, we turned to Sylva.

"I came to Israel in September 1974, after being freed from prison," she said. "My husband and two brothers and a group of our friends, after trying for many years to leave Russia legally with permission, and after failing to get permission, decided to leave illegally.

"In February 1970, Hillel Butman came to see us in Riga, from Leningrad, and told us there was a plan to use a plane to leave Russia illegally. I can't say that at that time I thought that this plan would be carried out, but I was in such an extreme mood, I felt I was at a standstill, that we weren't moving, that we weren't able to get out. My friends and I wanted so much to dedicate our lives to Israel. We had the feeling that without Israel we just couldn't survive. So I agreed to this plan.

"There were two plans, actually. The first plan, which the group from Leningrad disagreed about, was that our group was supposed to buy tickets to Murmansk, as though we were going to a wedding. While in Murmansk we would enter a plane at the airport without causing any bodily harm to the pilot and copilot and crew. We wanted to push the crew out and take over the plane. We thought we could do it without bloodletting, that we could just take the positions. We had no arms. Our objective was to get out to Sweden, and then to Israel. We had a pilot among us, Mark Dymshitz. Since '65 he wasn't allowed to fly, because he was a Jew."

"Did he apply to go to Israel?"

"He didn't apply. Because he was a pilot, it was absolutely clear that he wouldn't be allowed to go even if he applied. He agreed to take over the plane. He was the only pilot among us. This plan was dropped. But what I wanted to say was our mood at that time. We understood that this plan had hardly any chance of succeeding. When we invited people to our group, we told them there was a fifty-fifty chance of staying out of prison or going to prison.

"We felt we wouldn't get to Israel this way, but we wanted somehow to move from this standstill. We were in a sort of quagmire. We couldn't get out of it. So we thought we'd do something. It was a desperate act to do, to move, to cut this line.

"Then we thought and hoped that maybe the West would back us, that we would get publicity and the people in the West would back us, give us a push to this whole thing. We wanted to say, with our actions, to the Soviet government that it's not in their power to decide the destiny of any people, especially the Jews. On the other hand, the people in the West will understand what we wanted because, as they say, actions speak louder than words. People would hear, think about it, and maybe understand."

Sylva's muffled but rapid words, intensely concentrated on what she was saying, showed how difficult it was for her to relive her experiences, which she did in an almost numbed manner, focused on the insurmountable problems that must leave her with little hope. At this point, Rita's dog scratched on the door and barked. She let him in and he joined us, providing temporary relief from the tension that Sylva was undergoing.

"Had you tried to contact the outside world in any way?" I asked.

"Yes, we had. I saw what was happening to the people around me, that some had to apply for ten years, without success. I felt that it was really hopeless to try and wait for legal permission. After trying the local authorities, I wrote to the higher authorities in Moscow and even went there from Riga, where I lived. We risked sending letters outside of Russia to international organizations. We asked the United Nations to help us leave Russia. We wrote to U Thant. The authorities don't want people to write independently, to go outside the country. Actually, sometimes it's considered a crime.

"There was no reaction from abroad and we felt abandoned, especially after Kosygin declared that there's no problem, anyone who wants to leave has just to buy his ticket and leave. We felt abandoned and that a noose was getting tighter around our necks."

"Yes," I recalled, "that was back in 1966 in Paris when Kosygin announced that the Soviet Union would make it easy for Jews who wanted to leave. His word was no better than Russia's pledge at the Helsinki Human Rights Agreement in 1975. It becomes clearer and clearer that Russian anti-Semitism is an unchangeable historical fact. My father came to the United States from Kremnitz in the Ukraine, in the late 1890s, to escape from pogroms."

"You were very lucky," Sylva said with a faint smile. "They lie when they make agreements. They mean nothing. All Jews will have to leave to be free human beings. Of three million in Russia, only one hundred thousand have gotten out. I had the feeling that there was no future for the Jewish nation in Russia, that there was a policy of discrimination and a future of spiritual assimilation. The future was assimilation with the majority, with the Russian people. Besides spiritual assimilation, sometimes there was physical discrimination, as in '48, when Jews were destroyed as individuals and as a people, and in '53. I didn't see that in the future there wouldn't be such another wave of anti-Jewish feeling.

"An example of physical destruction is Mikhoels, who was run down by a car. People were arrested only because they had some Jewish feelings or talked about them. They were taken in groups and destroyed in camps and prisons. Mikhoels is one of the examples that the world knows about."

"I've read a great deal about Stalin's purges and his purge of Jewish doctors," I said, "but I'm not familiar with this name. Who was he?"

"Mikhoels was an artist and head of the list of people prominent in Jewish culture, like Peretz Markish, the poet. And they were destroyed for that, for being the leaders. People whose names are not known were also destroyed because they were Jews. Babel, a writer, was killed a year later, in '49. Many non-Jews were killed and imprisoned, but what happened to the Jews happened because they were Jews, because of their Jewish nationality."

"I joined the first French tourist group allowed after Stalin's death, a cruise from Le Havre to Leningrad. When we were in Moscow, the ambassador from Israel, General Yosef Avidar, told me that the anti-Semitism was alarming. After one of our group, a Jewish French schoolteacher, returned from visiting Moscow relatives, I asked her about their situation. Her answer was 'Je ne sais rien,' claiming to know nothing, for fear of reprisals against her family. That was 1956. What year were you born?"

"In '44. My background was Jewish. Both my parents graduated from Jewish schools in Latvia, and although the atmosphere at home wasn't religious, it was traditional. Just the same, I was a member of the Komsomol youth. Like everybody else in my school, all my girl friends—it was just the thing. You couldn't stay out of it. Nobody stayed out of it. It didn't have any meaning for me.

"I was born in Siberia where my parents were evacuated during the Second World War. I have three brothers. My mother stayed at home to take care of the four of us. But she was very sickly and she died young. My father was an accountant. In '45 we left Siberia for Riga.

"At school it so happened that I was the only Jewish girl in class, and I always felt the anti-Semitism. I always had fights with girls about that. My teachers never interfered. I always had the feeling that my marks were lower—maybe it's true, maybe not—because I was Jewish. I always felt abused. And I was abused.

"The atmosphere among the Jews in the country at that time was that people tried not to speak Yiddish. I never heard a lot of Yiddish spoken around me. Later, at the Polytechnical Institute, where I majored in mechanical engineering, somehow I felt the anti-Semitism less. Maybe because I was more grown-up and didn't react. But it really didn't matter because if somebody else among my Jewish friends suffered anti-Semitic attacks, it was all the same for me, as though it was I."

"When did you start to think seriously about going to Israel? I met young people in Russia who told me their grandparents, or great-grandparents, were Jewish. They were very vague about it, although they had a typical Jewish name. They said they weren't Jewish, just Russian. I'm sure, to identify yourself positively as a Jew, even in '56, presented problems."

"Before the Six-Day War, in '67. I was always searching for my identity. I was always probing and trying to understand. It was difficult at my age to withstand the massive propaganda that was directed against the Jews and Israel. I was twenty-three then. Before that, even, it was very difficult to hear such massive propaganda against Israel.

"You have to have something inside you and around you to withstand it. Even before that, I had the feeling, although I heard a lot of bad things about Israel from the Russians, that it was my duty to go there and do something, and give my life for Israel.

"But after the Six-Day War I felt a surge of pride, of identification. I felt that this is what happened to my people, which was very important to me. I was elated with their victory, as were many of my friends. I became close to a group of young girls and boys who collected literature about Jewish history, about Israel. We tried to learn Hebrew. We had Zionist literature among us, and we circulated it."

At this point, Sylva's energy seemed to run down. She said her back was bothering her, and she stood up for a few minutes. "If you aren't too tired," I said when she sat down again, "will you tell me more about your group and how you tried to escape?"

"Yes, I feel all right now. My father is there still, and my brothers and my husband. My husband is in prison, and two of my brothers, Izrail and Wulf. The third, Samuel, is going to have his trial now. I write five letters every week. Sometimes I think of things I want to tell them and then I forget when I write." She looked at my tape recorder. "I'd like to learn to use a tape recorder to refer back to." I agreed it would be helpful to her. (Since our meeting, I read that her youngest brother, Samuel Zalmonson, was sentenced to ten years in prison on a trumped-up charge of taking bribes. The report stated that the actual reason was the same zeal for going to Israel that motivated his sister, brothers, and brother-in-law; that he was imprisoned to muzzle his protests, his one-man demonstrations, and his activity on behalf of his brothers.)

"In '70 I married Edward Kuznetsov in Riga," Sylva continued, having gotten a second wind. She kept her maiden name, as is customary in Russia. "We met in Moscow in '68 soon after he had come out of prison camp where he served a seven-year sentence for printing and distributing *samizdat* literature and for reading dissident poetry in public."

"What is the exact definition of *samizdat?*" I asked.

"It comes from the word Gosizdat, which is the state publishing house. Anything published personally is *samizdat,* meaning 'own' publishing house. My husband was a philosophy student at Moscow University and is a fine writer. He had published dissident literary publications and was editor of the magazine *Phoenix*, an anthology of poetry, which was published abroad. He is only half-Jewish, but proclaims himself as a Jew.

"In the '60s he and a friend, Ilya Bokhstein, drew large crowds reading the poetry of Vladimir Mayakovsky in Mayakovsky Square in Moscow on Sundays. The KGB watched, but reading from a classic Russian poet was not illegal. When they started reading dissident, unpublished poets who challenged Soviet ideology, they were seized and given the maximum sentence in a 'strict-regime' labor camp, where he is again now."

"He must have been very young then. How old is he?"

"He is thirty-eight years old. Sometimes I have to stop and think and calculate, because when we parted seven years ago, time stood still for me and I just have to remember back. For me he is still thirty years old. He was in his twenties the first time."

"What was the final plan that your group decided on?"

"Yes," Sylva said, suddenly realizing that she had gone back in time. "A group of our friends in Leningrad disagreed with our first plan because they were sure it was going to fail. So we began our search for another plan. It was something like four to five months that we were searching for some other way out, and we separated from the Leningrad group, leaving only sixteen of our original thirty, who had been planning for two and a half years.

"We were in a constant mood of feeling that we had to do something, we had to get out. We were hoping for a miracle, another Jewish miracle, that would carry us out of there. We talked it over all the time. We constantly talked out all the details and planned it all.

"Our plan was to seize a twelve-passenger plane at Priozersk airport on June 15, 1970. Twelve people, including my husband and Dymshitz, the pilot, were to fly there as normal passengers from Smolny airport in Leningrad on a plane bound for Murmansk. When the plane stopped at Priozersk, they were to tie up the first and second pilots, without harming them, put them in a tent in sleeping bags, and then take aboard four of us, who would take the train and be waiting at Priozersk. Dymshitz would then fly us to Sweden.

"The four of us, two men and two women, were in the forest at night outside of Priozersk, before going to the airport at the appointed time in the morning, when we lost our way. Having enough time, we decided to wait till morning, when we could find the right direction, as it wasn't far. We lit a fire and ate the little sausage we had, and each of us kept watch for an hour. When I was finishing my watch at three A.M., a KGB man suddenly appeared and asked me for a match to light his cigarette. I was paralyzed with fear, but I gave it to him. He lighted his cigarette and without a word disappeared in the darkness.

"Before any of us knew what was happening he came back, shooting a revolver over my head and shouting, 'Hands up!' Then more men with barking dogs rushed at us, shooting in the air and squirting gas in our eyes. They tied us up back to back, and took us in a truck to police headquarters in Leningrad. My husband and the others were seized as they started to board the plane in the Leningrad Smolny airport at eight thirty in the morning."

"Had you had any idea that the KGB knew about your plan?" I asked.

"We found out later, when we were interrogated, that they knew everything. They heard it, maybe, when we talked on the telephone to each other, but they never stopped us. They let this fruit, so to say, ripen so that they could do something with us, destroy our group and make us out as criminals, as bandits, although we didn't want to hurt anybody. We just wanted to leave Russia. It just would mean that we would vanish from Russia and that's it, that our presence wouldn't be felt there. But they let this thing go on. They knew all about it. It was their purpose to try us and make us out as bandits and criminals.

"The day before our arrest we noticed that we were being followed. The first to notice was my husband because he had experience before and after his other prison sentence. He was the first to notice it, but as I said, we wanted publicity, we wanted the world to hear what was going on. It didn't stop us, although we were afraid, of course. We had to break through this wall of silence.

"The next day, people were arrested in Leningrad and Moscow, Kishinev and Riga, which proves that the KGB people knew all along, because they did it simultaneously. They knew all the people. They knew who was where."

"How many people were arrested?"

"Something like thirty people—everyone who had been in-

volved in the planning since the beginning. When we were tried
by the Soviets, in a secret trial, and when they handed down the
verdict, they thought they finished in one beautiful sweep with the
Jewish problem—people would be frightened in Russia, and that
everything would simmer down.

"They didn't expect the reaction in the West. There were
waves and waves of protests all over the West, as a result of which
the death sentence of my husband and Dymshitz was commuted to
fifteen years' imprisonment, the maximum. I had ten years. Because
I was the only woman in the group imprisoned, the whole problem
focused on me and I was in the limelight. The other woman who
was arrested with me was released because she was several months
pregnant. I wasn't so lucky. I was at the beginning of a pregnancy
and had a miscarriage shortly after I was imprisoned."

Although the trial was closed to the public, family members
attended, as well as reporters from the world press. The immediate
families of nine of the accused were offered exit visas to Israel two
weeks before the trial opened, in an attempt of the government to
counteract the support of the West. All refused. F. Lee Bailey, the
prominent American criminal lawyer, offered to defend the accused
without charge. His request was denied, as well as the request of
four well-known Washington lawyers to interview the accused and
to attend the trials. After the prosecutor's summation speech, in
which he said there is no anti-Semitism or any Jewish question in
Russia, but spoke of the "conspiracy of international Zionism,"
demanding the maximum punishment for all, Sylva made this he-
roic speech, recorded in her husband's book:

> I cannot gather my wits together. I am stunned by the sentences the
> prosecutor demands for us. He has suggested that heads be cut off
> for something that has not been done. If the court agrees, then such
> remarkable people as Dymshitz and Kuznetsov will die. I think that
> Soviet law should not regard as treason someone's intention to live
> in another country and I am convinced that according to law it is
> those who unlawfully violate our right to live where we like who
> should have been brought to trial.
>
> Let the court at least take into consideration the fact that had we
> been permitted to leave, there would not have been the "criminal
> plot" that has caused us so much pain and even more pain to our
> families.

Israel is a country to which we Jews are tied spiritually and historically. I hope that the government of the USSR will soon solve this question in a positive manner. The dream of uniting with our ancient fatherland will never leave us. Some of us had not even believed in the success of this plan, or believed very little in it. We noticed we were being followed, but we could no longer return to the past, to the waiting, to the life of sitting on suitcases. Our dream about life in Israel was incomparable with the fear of the pain that might be done to us. We would have harmed no one by our departure. I wanted to live there as a family, to work.

I would not have engaged in politics. My entire interest in politics is exhausted by the simple desire to go away. And even now, I don't doubt for a minute that someday I shall go and live in Israel. This dream, sanctified by the two thousand years of hope, will never leave me. "Next year in Jerusalem! If I forget thee, O Jerusalem, may my right hand lose its cunning." [She repeated these words in Hebrew and was stopped.]

Her words were prophetic. "As a result of the many protests, demonstrations, and petitions around the world," she said, "I was freed after four years in prison, and actually I was given a present. Six years of my life were presented to me by the world."

"Four years in prison must have been a terrible time for you. Where did they send you?"

"The first year I was in the KGB prison in Leningrad. And then I was sent to a prison camp, where I was for three years. I worked in the prison camp, as did everybody else. Everybody had to work and had to fulfill the norms. If one didn't fulfill the norm, one was punished. One punishment prevented us from buying soap and cigarettes in a little place there, for our own money. There were other punishments—for instance, we were allowed two parcels per year from our relatives. We were refused these parcels or a meeting with our relatives.

"Or we were sent to a confinement cell alone, without any food or without warm clothing in the cold. There was a whole set of things with which we Jews were punished. So I worked like everybody else did." She spoke with no sign of self-pity and always in rapid, hushed words.

"What kind of work?"

"We sewed work gloves. The work itself was not really very

hard, but the norm was very high, and we had to make many of them. It was difficult to fill the norm. The work maybe is not hard for a person who lives well and eats normally, but for people who eat substandard food and who are without vitamins, for them it's not that easy.

"Physically, I wouldn't say that we were abused. They didn't beat us. But everybody knew that there was a chance of being put into a psychiatric ward, as happened with Vladimir Bukofsky and others. We were afraid of that. For a person with a healthy mind, to be drugged by the psychiatrists, with insane people, can be worse than death.

"In prison I was in a cell to which I was confined. In the prison camp it's a limited, small territory, but you can go out from the barracks where we lived and slept and worked and ate. We could go out except for working and night hours.

"There were so many rats that very often they jumped on people. And often we would find a mouse in our soup. We were led to get washed together with women who were sick with venereal disease. Absolutely unhygienic conditions. Also, I had to be in the constant company of Nazi collaborators. I mean murderesses who helped the Nazis. I had to be with them constantly."

Looking at this refined young woman, it was difficult to imagine her in the situation she described. How she came out of it as whole as she seems to be is even more remarkable.

"Medical help was minimum," she continued. "To get some help from a doctor, once we had to go on a hunger strike because one woman had to be operated on urgently and they wouldn't take her. We went on a hunger strike so the prison authorities would do something about it because we felt she might die. Even the simplest thing, a dentist, one could go around with a puffed-out cheek for ages and never get to a doctor.

"Speaking of medical services, my husband, now in prison, has ulcers. It would probably be easy to heal here outside in the free world. But there he is not treated, and it is getting worse. He had to go on a hunger strike before they took him to the hospital. When he was very insistent on getting a medicine, they gave him pills so he won't have children's diarrhea!"

Reading Edward Kuznetsov's *Prison Diaries* is a terrifying experience. How he got it outside of prison camp is not known, but the authorities have accused and sentenced several dissidents in connection with it. He was determined to tell the world what thousands of desperate young men and women, in no sense criminals, are subjected to in a totalitarian state. He played a constant game of hiding his writings from the guards but often did not succeed. At one point he says, "I write only to stay human," and at another, "They just came and searched me; just managed to get the papers out of the way in time. I've lost the track. I feel more like howling like an animal than writing!"

He is a powerful writer and a spunky, fearless man. When his jailer learned that one of those accused with him was going to wear a yarmulke (skullcap) during the trials and said, "I have never met believing Jews; the only thing they believe in is money," Kuznetsov told him, "The Jews, stretched out on sheepskins, looked up at the sky and thought about God while people like you were hanging from the branches of trees and swinging by their tails."

Excoriating the so-called Soviet social democracy, he says:

What of those who may have shown the slightest lack of confidence in Big Brother's divinity and refuse to betray themselves or their friends under the spreading chestnut tree? For in the camps, treatment of the recalcitrant convict falls basically into two categories: loss of rations or the punishment cell, both of which abandon him to the whim of as many levels of persecution as you could possibly imagine: registration, apartment, work, family, neighbors, friends. There's a metaphorical, though not very appetizing, saying that illustrates one of the most popular methods of re-educating the dissidents that they have, "They beat you till you shit yourself, and then they beat you for shitting yourself!"

He describes one of many beatings:

One of the guards discovered my hiding place and relieved me of a whole pile of my papers. I made a dive for him, grabbed the bundle out of his hands, then I jumped onto the water closet, tore the papers into little pieces and flushed them down the Neva, or Fontanka, or Moika, or wherever the pipes lead to down there. A couple of guards thereupon gave me a good beating and even now, nearly a week later, my face is still covered in bruises, my neck and arms are black and blue and my left shoulder feels as if it has been dislocated.

The impossible work norms mentioned by Sylva are reported in *Prison Diaries:*

I started working on the presses today, the hardest work you can do here. The presses are antediluvian, the norms incredible. I'm not surprised a good dozen convicts have lost their hands over the last two years.

The most terrifying part of the book deals with self-mutilation in the prison camps:

I have many times witnessed some of the most fantastic incidences of self-mutilation. I have seen convicts swallow huge numbers of nails and quantities of barbed wire; I have seen them swallow mercury thermometers, pewter tureens (after first breaking them up into "edible" proportions), chess pieces, dominoes, needles, ground glass, spoons, knives and many other similar objects.

I have seen convicts sew up their mouths and eyes with thread or wire; sew rows of buttons to their bodies; or nail their testicles to a bed, swallow a nail bent like a hook, and then attach this hook to the door by way of a thread so that the door cannot be opened without pulling the fish inside out. I have seen convicts cut open the skin on their arms and legs and peel it off as if it were a stocking.

Or cut out lumps of flesh (from their stomach or their legs), roast them and eat them; or let the blood drip from a slit vein into a tureen, crumble bread crumbs into it, and then gulp it down like a bowl of soup; or cover themselves with paper and set fire to themselves; or cut off their fingers, or their nose, or ears, or penis.

Having tried all other forms of protest against the lawlessness and caprice of the prison and all other authorities, they have finally resorted to self-mutilation, have been reduced to the ultimate despair.

Undoubtedly Sylva has to push her knowledge of these horrors back in order to maintain a measure of hope and to carry on her daily life. She told me of her complete surprise when she was released from prison. "When I was freed, it was very sudden for me. I mean I didn't know what was going on. Then, as soon as I was out of prison, they wanted to push me out of the country. Although they were really blackmailing me and frightening me and not allowing me to move altogether, I insisted on staying and seeing my husband, whom I hadn't seen in such a long time. If I would leave, it meant that I wouldn't see him for eleven years more. So after my insisting on seeing him, they brought him to Moscow for our meeting, and to the Fortiva prison, where we met.

"About my leaving, I wasn't sure I had to leave, but my husband insisted on my going, feeling, first of all, that I would be out of the danger zone, and secondly, here in the free world in Israel, I would be able to help more effectively than if I were there. Opinion was divided among Jewish circles and my friends.

"When I was freed, my father and one brother were in Riga. Two of my brothers were in prison. They are there still. They were together with me in our group. They are twins, and today happens to be their birthday." She paused, closed her eyes, and then spoke again. "I went to Riga, where I stayed for nearly a month. I stayed with my father and brother for three days, and then I prepared myself for my journey. Before leaving Riga, I went to the cemetery to say good-bye to my mother. Then my father and brother and I all left for Moscow, where I said good-bye to them and boarded the plane."

"Have they applied for emigration to Israel?"

"Father doesn't want to leave the country while my husband and brothers are in prison. He won't leave until they're free."

"Is he earning a living there? What does he do?"

"He works as an accountant. They haven't bothered him yet." She continued with her voyage. "In Vienna I was taken to the Israeli embassy, and after being there for half a day, I was flown to Tel Aviv, where I was met by friends and acquaintances and many, many people who fought for my freedom. The airport was filled with people. They spilled outside the entrance. It was very touching.

"At the beginning there were many meetings and interviews and many people that I saw. Then I went to Europe and America and Mexico to meet other people and to thank them for all they did for me. I met a lot of people who worked very hard and, as I said, saved me six years of my life."

"What was your impression of America?"

"My main impression was of the American people. I like Americans very much. First of all, they're very kind and sort of open-minded and ready to help. What's really striking about them is their ability to employ all they can to organize this desire to help and to really help.

"The main difference, of course, is that in Russia there is absolutely no individual freedom. The norm, the ideal, is a robot-like party member who just doesn't think, doesn't act independently. In the free world, the person is in the foreground, while in Russia, everything is done around him and it's not the person that's in the foreground."

"What has been your experience as a citizen of Israel?"

"The main thing for me is a feeling of belonging. I don't have to ask myself what is it to be Jewish. I'm Jewish, and I belong, and this is my place. After six months at an ulpan, where I learned the language, I got my apartment. I feel at home, which is very important for me. I work not far from Tel Aviv as a mechanical engineer in the constructors' bureau. I have friends here. I see them sometimes. If one can say life is normal without a family, I lead a normal life." Sylva gave a heavy sigh.

"My husband has nine years in prison. That's a very long time for him and for me. I want to get permission from the Russian authorities to visit him, at least to see him for a short visit, the same as they gave me when I was freed. I don't know what to do about it, but I really do want to go and see him. I can't see those nine years without ever seeing him again." I was told that there had been a recent story in the Israeli press to the effect that Sylva wanted to return to Russia to see her husband and become pregnant. When I asked about this she shook her head, and Rita explained that the subject was too delicate for her to talk about.

Sylva concluded by saying, "The demonstrations and petitions of the people, especially the women of America and England, is what gave me my freedom. It's what they did for me, the power of their protest meetings and declarations, that made the Soviets free me. I'm very grateful to them for that, and I want them to remember that they have power in their hands. They can do the same for others who are now in prison and suffering and not seeing their freedom in the near future. Those women who helped me can help the others."

———

Early in 1978, since I saw Sylva, both she and her husband went on hunger strikes—she briefly at the Western Wall, Edward for several weeks in prison camp—for the purpose of obtaining permission for her to visit him. He stopped when the authorities agreed to grant her a visa, but they did not do so. Kuznetsov's name was mentioned in a possible exchange, with Anatoly Scharansky, for Soviet prisoners in the West, but that, too, failed to materialize. In mid-August 1978, Izrail Zalmonson, one of Sylva's twin brothers, was released from prison after serving eight years. Sylva met him in Vienna, and they went on to Israel.

On January 29, 1979, dozens of protest meetings were held throughout western Europe for the liberation of Edward Kuznetsov, seriously ill with a stomach ulcer and tuberculosis. Among the American and European writers who called for his release were Saul Bellow, Simone de Beauvoir, Jean-Paul Sartre, Heinrich Böll, and Raymond Aron.

4

"I-Thou" Redefined

JUDITH BUBER AGASSI, sociologist and political scientist, arrived at our apartment the afternoon of Passover Seder. She had come up to Jerusalem, with her husband and son, from her home in Herzliya Petuach, a northern suburb of Tel Aviv, to have Seder with her artist sister and family.

She is a tall, slim, handsome woman, fifty-three, with black hair pulled back tightly from a high forehead and falling down her back. Dressed for the festivities in a colorful long printed skirt and blouse, she put down her shoulder bag, a utilitarian knapsack, saying, "I planned to help my sister an hour before Seder, but I'm running a bit late." Her strong clipped English has a hint of German accent.

"We'll start at once," I told her. "Would you like tea or coffee?"

"Tea, please, would be fine." We sat at the table of the small dining alcove of the furnished apartment, where the light was best. I brought tea and we began.

"O.K.," she said with a sigh, having rushed through her usual overcharged day. "First of all, I call myself Judith Buber Agassi, keeping my maiden name as a middle name. I was born in Germany in 1924. I grew up, as a child, up to the age of twenty-plus, in the house of my grandparents. My grandfather was Martin Buber."

A few days before, my husband and I had seen a copy of one of philosopher Martin Buber's books displayed in a case with others burned by Hitler. It is one of many chilling and numbing objects and photographs in Yad Veshem, Israel's stark memorial to the six million, a grim and deeply emotional reminder of the Holocaust, set high in the Judean hills of Jerusalem. We were too affected to remember if the book was Buber's *I and Thou* or another.

"As to my early family history," she went on, "it is simply this: My parents are Rafael Buber, the son of Martin Buber, and Margarete Buber-Neumann, who is a well-known author and political publicist. *Under Two Dictators* and *Mistress to Kafka* are two of her six books that have appeared in English. She is German and spent seven years in concentration camps.

"I have one sister, who is two and a half years my senior. My parents, who got married when very young, separated when I was about two. The divorce court decision transferred my sister and me from my mother to the custody of my paternal grandparents, Martin and Paula Buber. So I grew up in their house, from age four onwards, first in Hoppenheim, in Germany, and then in Jerusalem.

"I came with my grandparents from Germany in '38 to, then, Palestine. I was fourteen. I went to school in Yerushalayim, to high school in Beit Hakerem. And after that I went to Hebrew University and studied history, sociology, and education. Sociology, or, as it then was called, anthropology of culture, was the subject that my grandfather taught."

"Did you study under your grandfather?"

"*Ja, ja.* He taught, as I said, anthropology of culture. There was, then, no sociology course as yet, as a subject. Shmuel Eisenstadt, who is now—it's a bit early to say—the 'grand old man' of sociology, was, I think, his first doctoral student in Israel, and Yenina Talmon Garber was his second doctoral student."

"They are both now at the university?"

"No. Eisenstadt is well-known, worldwide, as the Israeli sociologist. Yenina, unfortunately, died young of cancer, but she did the first work on the development of the family in kibbutzim and moshavim [cooperative agricultural settlements]."

She spoke quickly, her large, dark, penetrating eyes, under ample eyebrows, focused intensely on the matter at hand, with the complete concentration of the student and scientist. "Then came the War of Independence, '47, '48," she continued. "I was in the siege of Jerusalem. I was a youth leader, so I was exempt from military service proper, and my main duty during the war was keeping a soldiers' club. I had to tell parents and wives what had happened to their sons and husbands. To the lucky ones, I just could say they were wounded. And the less lucky, that they were missing, or worse.

"I was shortly in Europe in '47, just before the war, for half a year. I accompanied my grandfather on a lecture tour, so I had a chance to see Europe after the World War and before our War of Independence."

"What year did your grandfather die?"

"In '65. He was eighty-seven years old."

"Do you feel you were greatly influenced by his philosophical tenets?"

It was a difficult question. She drew in her breath before saying, "Oh, I think I must say, first of all, where I am not influenced. I am not a religious person; therefore, the religious aspect of his philosophy, there I really do not see. I very much agree with him as to the moral aspect of his philosophy, that the basis of any morality is not using your fellowman as an instrument for some purpose, but to treat the individual as a human being in his or her own right. This is, I think, in short, the 'I-Thou' relationship. But I don't accept his claim that you cannot really achieve this 'I-Thou' relationship without a divine or personal God. This leaves me simply where I am not with him."

"That leaves you cold?"

"It leaves me cold. Where was I influenced? I was influenced in his social science ideas. His idea was that a change of the society for more, for better, human relationships is only possible by reform of the community from the society and not by some kind of political edict from above. Because of that, he was really, you might say, a religious socialist, anarchist. He had a strong suspicion of the political factor and the state. When offered the Ministry of Education, he did not take it.

"He was constantly in opposition in the Zionist movement, from his young days. He was a Zionist from the age of nineteen. He was a representative in the Third Zionist Congress, as a nineteen-year-old, and active in the Zionist labor movement. But on the topic of the Jewish-Arab relationship, he very early on got into opposition and remained in opposition."

"His position was very pro-Arab?"

"Not pro-Arab. His position was that, if the Zionist movement is based on not recognizing the rights of a second people in this country, then it was doomed. He was in opposition to Herzl very early on. He was in the group of Ahad Ha'am and Weizmann, who saw the establishment of the Jewish homeland as he did. Ahad Ha'am was the theoretician, the philosopher, of the Zionist movement."

"Why did he turn down the education post?"

"That was already when the State was established. Because he did not want to serve in a political office. The point is that for him to establish a Jewish homeland or a Jewish State without aiming at a better society, a society that was something special, then this was not really worthwhile. And certainly, to establish it on constant tension with the second people in this country, and in constant warfare, this would be a very sad prospectus."

"He was quite correct."

"*Ja.* His organization, the Brith Shalom—he was one of the founding members and, under different names, this continued all the time—was treated very much as a nuisance by the officials, by the Zionist establishment. Brith Shalom means 'the peace covenant.' So I accepted from him this idea of the primacy of the social as against the political, of the importance of decentralism. If you want to have an active citizen consciousness, you have to have him determine how he lives from the community, from local government on, and not do everything from above in a centralist way, which was very much the attitude of our first generation of statehood.

"Ben-Gurion was in favor of doing everything from above. He did not like voluntary organizations, and he certainly did not like decentralization. My grandfather was a decentralist, which I accepted. I was certainly influenced also by my grandfather in seeing the importance of the Arab-Jewish relationship as primary, of very great importance for the future of the society that we built here."

"Did you marry someone who agrees with your philosophy?"

"Yes, fortunately." She laughed, turning less serious. "Immediately after the War of Independence I married Joseph Agassi, who is a philosopher, his main field being the philosophy of science."

"Is he an Israeli?"

"He's a sabra. His mother's family is from the old Yishuv,

meaning the pre-Zionist Jewish settlement of the Old City of Jerusalem. His father came at the beginning of the century. Joseph is now professor of philosophy at Hebrew University and at Boston University."

"Where did his father come from to Palestine?"

"His father came from Hungary." She poured herself more tea. "Before we were married, and after, I worked for a time as a teacher in the boarding school for sick and crippled children of Youth Aliyah. And then, after the birth of my daughter in 1950, I worked as teacher and teacher of teachers in Beersheba. That was at the time of mass immigration. Then, in '52, after we'd both got our masters at Hebrew University, we went to England and got, both of us, our doctorates at the London School of Economics."

"Simultaneously?"

"Yes. We went with our baby daughter. We left the country on the basis of a loan, by a cousin, of one thousand dollars."

"That couldn't get you very far."

She laughed heartily. "We managed! We lived on that for ten months, and by then my husband got a small scholarship in London, and we managed somehow. Later on he became assistant professor to Sir Carl Popper, for five, six years. And then he became a lecturer at the London School of Economics.

"But in the meantime, for one year, we were in the United States because Carl Popper went to the Center for Advanced Studies for Behavioral Science in Stanford, California. Carl Popper was invited there and said he couldn't go without his research assistant because he then was in the middle of a book. So we went there, and Joseph became a junior fellow.

"I studied a year at Stanford. Formally, my field was political science. In fact, what I did was political sociology. So we spent a year there. My doctorate is on the role of local government in the actual working or functioning of parliamentary democracy. I did a comparative study of the British, Dutch, and Belgian systems, on two research grants, each of fifty guineas. Remember that a guinea is a pound sterling plus a shilling, about three U.S. dollars. I spent twice a month doing fieldwork in the villages, small towns, and cities of Holland and Belgium."

"You must have been a very good budgeter."

"*Ja, ja.*" Judith chuckled, but again resumed intense concentration on what she was saying. "I then went on the second lap of my fieldwork to Holland and Belgium. I also was expecting my son. He was born eight years after the daughter. In fact, it was the first year that we knew how we would pay the rent!" She recalled the hard times with laughter and added, "British landladies being a terrible experience."

"Different from American or Israeli landladies?"

"Students! Married students with a child! The London area was terrible, like nowhere else. Students were not expected to be married. Students were not expected to have children."

"You had a hard time getting housing?"

"*Ja.* We lived in the most terrible digs, as it's called in England. And also British universities did not expect women students to be married and have a child! They looked at that, from the very beginning, as a very bad bet. All the American universities have married students' quarters since World War Two. In London there were only dorms, and of course dorms were for the males separate and females separate. And marriage or children was not dreamt about. In fact, I was twice offered a scholarship by the university women, and twice this was on the condition that I would live in their dorm in London. I couldn't accept it, so it took me almost seven years to do my doctorate.

"Then we wanted to come back to Israel, but there was no job at that time. So my husband accepted a job in Hong Kong, at the University of Hong Kong. And we were there for three years. He taught philosophy and became the chairman of the philosophy department at the University of Hong Kong.

"I taught in the extramural department at the university, Chinese students and the monks and nuns that abound in Hong Kong. And I also worked and did research for the USIS, the United States Information Service, on the so-called cultural exchange of China abroad, analyzing the material of this cultural exchange of China with Asia and Africa in order to find out what the policies and the goals of China in this area were.

"I did my first research in Hong Kong. I wrote a paper on the social stratification of Hong Kong. This was for the University of Tokyo, where they have a United Nations body for research on the Far East. I did some research on popular housing in Hong Kong.

"The local Chinese language, of course, is Cantonese, and in

Hong Kong I would not be able to be fluent and be able to read properly within three years, even if I would study it every day. I chose, second best, a language that is also a very useful language in the Far East and Southeast Asia, which is Malay—which is, in fact, the basis of the Indonesian official language and is also the basis of the most commonly spoken Philippine language. So I learned Malay and did my first little piece of research on political development in Indonesia."

I was somewhat stunned by Judith's matter-of-fact recital of multiple virtuoso performances and her adaptability to any place that her husband's work brought her. There was more to come.

"From there, Hong Kong, we went to Illinois. My husband got an offer from the University of Illinois at Urbana, and I, immediately on arrival, became assistant professor at the sociology department and taught there for two years, '63 to '65."

"Those were about the years of the beginnings of the women's movement in the United States, following the publication of Betty Friedan's *The Feminine Mystique.* You probably recall hearing about her then," I said.

"*Ja.* I remember, upon arrival, the general topic of talk was Betty Friedan's first appearance on television. Up to then, I must say, I had taken women's rights and equality of women as a thing so absolutely basic that I didn't worry much about it. I had been impressed, however, in England at the relative backwardness in the popular approach to that. Lower-middle-class attitudes in the '50s in England were that a woman's place is in the home, advising girls not to aim too high, but to settle for marriage and children. That was the popular attitude. That was not the attitude so much among the intelligentsia."

"It's marvelous how you managed, from the very beginning, all that you accomplished academically, plus marriage and children. Did you have much help with the care of the home and children?"

"Minimum. If you want to, you manage. And I don't think my children suffered from it."

"Where are your son and daughter now?"

"My son is here with us, about to go into the army, and my daughter is at Berkeley doing graduate work in the social sciences. Now, to come back to the attitudes I encountered about women," she said, steering the conversation back on course. "In the year that

I was in California, I also was somewhat impressed by the conservatism of American attitudes at this time. In Hong Kong, I had been active in the university women's group, and after some research we appealed for equal pay."

"Was there a great discrepancy at that time?"

"*Ja*, certainly. Where isn't there one?" she replied, laughing ironically.

"Did you succeed?"

"*Ja*. We got the government to come out for equal pay in government service. It has to be remembered that in the '50s in Britain—and Hong Kong is a Crown colony—there was officially unequal pay scales for the government service. Women got three quarters of the pay men got. The same was true in the universities.

"When I came to Urbana, I continued being active among university women. What we did there was make a campaign for granting women graduate students the right to continue studying part-time. At the time, the president of the University of Illinois did not see this at all."

"They had to take a full curriculum?"

"Anybody who wanted to study part-time was put at the very end of the line. And many subjects, many courses, were closed. Which means that there was an enormous public of women, university graduates, who could not go on. Partly, these were people who had started studying and then got married. This was a kind of academic island within the flatland of Illinois, a monster university sitting in a big cornfield.

"So these were mainly the wives of students and graduate students. Their studies were usually interrupted upon marriage, and they had to go and work in offices or as grade-school teachers in order to keep their husbands at the university, which struck me rather as an inequity. The net result, usually, in a very large percentage of cases, was that by the time the husband got his doctorate, he got sick and tired of the wife who had kept him all those years and had fallen behind in education."

"And had babies, probably."

"*Ja*. And an enormous number of these marriages of graduate students ended in divorce. Also during these years, there was a federal education act coming through. It must have been '64, '65. I'm not quite sure. It was at the time of the assassination of

Kennedy. The education act mentioned the right of women for continued education. Then we had a legal basis to act on.

"My husband didn't like the philosophy department very much at Illinois. Perhaps they didn't like him either very much. He didn't belong to either of the warring factions in the philosophy department, he being neither a language analyst nor an existentialist. So we went to Boston, and he became then a professor at Boston University, where he is until today. And I taught for two years at Simmons College.

"Then, at long last, we went back to Israel to try if we could fit into any academic cloth, '66 to '67. We were, the two of us, at Tel Aviv University to see how things went. My husband decided he wanted to get a double appointment, so we went back again to Boston.

"There I worked at MIT two years, as research associate, writing research on mass media in Indonesia, for the first time using my Malay. I also taught at the same time, as associate professor at Bentley College in Waltham, Massachusetts. Then I got a fellowship in the Radcliffe Institute, which belongs to Radcliffe and Harvard, and started, at long last, on research of my own that I wanted to do, on a very small scale, on the relative impact of technology and the attitudes or the ideology of managers on the quality of jobs."

"That sounds like something apart from what you had been doing earlier."

"My interests had shifted during those years from social stratification to the problems of the quality of working life. I did this research mainly in southern Massachusetts and Rhode Island, in electronics and needle trades. I came across the reality of women's jobs in industry and decided that if ever anybody would fund a larger research—if I would ever have the chance—I would do research on women's jobs.

"After that, in January 1970, we finally went back for good to Israel, my husband having this arrangement of double appointments at Tel Aviv and Boston—one semester here, one semester there. I taught at Haifa University and also at Hebrew University, part-time, and tried very much to get a similar arrangement. This was promised to me by Tel Aviv University. But while I was in Boston, the then rector of Tel Aviv University fired me behind my back, claiming that there was something in the statutes of the university which did not permit a double appointment. My husband had a signed contract to that effect, so they couldn't change that, but I was only staffing."

"Did you think it was discrimination?"

"No. I think they wanted to force my husband to give up his Boston appointment. Anyway, since then I have had no proper appointment. I taught for one year at the Ruppin Institute, which is the management school of the kibbutz movement, and I was a guest lecturer at Hebrew University at the Rehovot campus, the agricultural faculty."

"With all your credentials, the world of academe is still a man's world, like most other fields, with the woman moving from place to place, according to his appointments, and picking up what you could when you got there."

"Unfortunately, *ja*. It will *have* to change. In the meantime, I have managed to publish a variety of papers, such as 'The Worker and the Media,' 'Man Incorporate,' 'Technology and Culture,' 'The Mixed Blessings of Technology,' 'Women Who Work in Factories,' 'The Quality of Women's Working Life,' and others. I have recently completed a study on 'Kibbutz and Sex Roles,' in which I take issue with the book by Lionel Tiger and Joseph Sepher, *Women in the Kibbutz.*"

"Yes. I read it and didn't agree with it either."

"The book attempts to answer why in the kibbutz, where women were declared to be on an equal basis with men, sharing all the same work, they are today, for the most part, doing traditional women's work: teaching, care of the children, kitchen, and so forth. In short, the authors hold the position that where, as in the kibbutz, women are liberated from ideological, social, and economic pressures, they have freely chosen to return to traditional feminine social sex roles. And that this freedom from constraints has permitted them to follow their natural inclination for motherhood and all it entails.

"I say not so. As far back as the '50s, research done among kibbutz girls showed a considerable majority did not want to work either in the kitchen or in child care. They considered their mothers prematurely old, limited, ignorant, and unambitious as a result of work in the services only. And many of them openly broke the taboo and suggested that boys also should work in infant care, saying, 'Why not? Are they going to kill the kids?' And the same in sewing: 'Can't a boy sew on a button or iron?'

"The most positive thing I can say about the book is, despite its severe flaws and its wrongheaded bias, it may serve as a catalyst for kibbutz women to get their just deserts. There is a massive exodus of second-generation women, out of discontent with their role. If the kibbutz would resolutely allocate production and service duties on an egalitarian basis, including child-care activities, then the outcome may be entirely different as to women's aspirations, occupational achievement, and political participation. And this still remains to be seen."

"Have you lived in a kibbutz at any time? For the short time I spent in Ein Hashofet in '49, doing token work in the tree nursery, it seemed, contrary to the kibbutz principle, that most women were in service activities or teaching. I'm sure it was not always out of choice."

"As a youngster, I was a Marxist. I was in Hashomer Hatzair —as you know, Ein Hashofet is of that group—but I never went to kibbutz. I got through that period, and got through it as one should get through children's diseases, by really going through it all the way, not patching it up and making compromises, but seeing where the real weaknesses in Marxism lie. And seeing also the contribution that Marx made to social science and keeping the important points in socialism.

"But now I wouldn't call myself a Socialist because I think that the new socialism is such a wishy-washy thing. And if, under the same name, you include the regime in the Soviet Union and of Sweden, then I don't see that this is useful for me. If you declare that you want to have a society in which nobody goes hungry or without medical care, and that you want to grant the maximum of equality of opportunity to all the citizens of that society, men *and* women, that's very important for me."

"And children . . ."

"And children. *Ja,* rights for children. Opportunity, of course, is anyway aimed mainly at the young people, and without any regard to the national origin or religion or no religion. If you call that socialism, fine. Then I'm a Socialist. But otherwise, if it means that a trade union is always right and the employer is always wrong, then I'm not a Socialist.

"I do not think that if property is owned by the State that this is more just or moral than if property is owned by groups of private people or by cooperatives or by collectives. I think it's a good thing if, in one same society, you have an economy which is pluralist and where you can have the freedom to be active economically, as individuals or in cooperatives or collectives.

"This is particularly important in our days where it is essential that the State has some influence on the development of the economy. But I don't think that State companies have proved themselves anywhere as either being efficient or as granting the people working in them better conditions or a better quality of living."

"Do you think the kibbutzim have been successful as Socialist communities?"

"I don't know if this is Socialist. I think it's a very important experiment in an alternative way of ownership and social and economic organization. Certainly I would not want to make a sacred cow out of private property. I don't make a sacred cow either out of State or private property. But I think that we have to look for what we want of it. Do we want to put out a good-quality product for the people in the society and, necessarily, for export in order that we can import things which we need? And do we want that the people who work in making these things have the maximum quality of life while they work there? This, for me, is the goal. And in the meantime, there is no 'ism' that fits my goal."

"How do you place yourself politically?"

"I'm a liberal, I might say. I'm a radical liberal. For me, the rights of the individual, the well-being of the individual, the freedom of self-expression, of thought, of movement of the individual are the prime goals. And I think you can have no decent society in which you do not fight for these rights. Because only the individual who has those rights will be one who will be ready to contribute to society.

"Now, coming back to my political activity—after a long gap of activity since my Marxist days, activity which I and my young friends stuck to until we realized that the Soviet Union is not only not Socialist but was an absolute false prophecy and created, in fact, much less freedom and much less well-being of the individual than Western society. And it also established a new anti-Semitism.

"For years I did not find, in the Israeli political setup, groups that I could work for and with. I certainly did not like the political system that developed here, that evolved from the pre-State political Yishuv into the State. It is a system of narrow party cliques whose main aim was to continue ruling or to share in ruling, who became more and more conservative and even reactionary as to the status of women."

"How is that manifested?"

"We have no constitution. We have no basic laws of the equality of rights of women. We have no separation of State and religion. We have, in fact, in part of our laws, the laws of the Halakah, the religious laws, where the woman is unfit to be a witness, unfit to be a judge, unfit to rule. And it is according to those laws that we have to lead our family life.

"The political system that evolved here repels me from political activity. And I think it is just in the last months, perhaps since just before the Yom Kippur War, that this old system is now more and more coming under fire and lying in shambles. The system was one of a coalition government in which the Labor Party gave up its principles in order to continue to rule.

"It could never achieve a majority. Therefore it decided to continue to rule, not by fighting for the votes of the majority, but by establishing its rule on a coalition with the religious bloc, thereby giving up the fundamental principles of democracy and of a liberal democratic society.

"The coalition with the religious bloc was bought by, first of all, giving up the promise in our Declaration of Independence, that we would have a constitution. Israel has no constitution. To the public, what is it? I voted, as a very young woman, for the constituent assembly. We had a constituent assembly, but we never had a constitution."

"When the promise was made, when was this supposed to be realized?"

"Immediately. The constituent assembly was supposed to form it, instead of which the assembly was declared the First Knesset. So we have only basic laws, and the basic laws are not really laws that are constitutional laws. For instance, we have a basic law for the rights of women. But this law does not invalidate laws that are based on inequality, that have different treatment of women and men."

"So how do they reconcile the equal rights law with the other ones that do not give basic equality?"

"It says there, in a paragraph, 'not changing any already existing laws.' Now, with the existing laws, the most important thing here is that marriage and divorce are in the hands of the rabbinical courts. We should remember that this is not just a typical representative religious organization of all the Jewish religious organizations we have in Israel.

"The only Jewish religious stream in Israel that has any power, in whose hands are the rabbinate and rabbinical courts, are Orthodox. This Orthodox stream does not permit Reform or Conservative Jewry any, even an inch, of influence in this country. They had to fight for years in order to establish their synagogues here, but they have no right to perform marriages or divorce. Nothing! Each municipality has a religious council, *mo'atza ha'datit.* Conservative and Reform Jewry have not one share in those councils. They are exclusively Orthodox and completely patriarchal in their attitude.

"Now, I see two reasons for the retrogression in the status of women in Israel. The one is this which I just now mentioned. And the other is that in order to somehow gloss over this unholy coalition—to my mind, unholy coalition—the elements in the secular Zionist Israeli ideology were emphasized, which we, more or less, have in common with the Orthodoxy. And that is an emphasis on the family. 'Familism,' I would call it, the all-importance of the family and the emphasis on having large families.

"Ben-Gurion gave a prize for the mother of ten children. It was a disaster! It has only made the social and educational gap between our Oriental-Afro-Asian community, now fifty-one percent of our population, and those from Western origins much larger because it has perpetuated the backwardness and the low standard of living. They are those with the large families, with the low incomes. They are those with the lower education.

"The emphasis on familism means there is no normal existence for any human being but being married. And you have to get married young. There's housing only for married couples. You have to buy your housing, which means clipping the wings of young people—of young men, too, but of young women even more."

"Yes, they strap them financially from the beginning."

"*Ja,* from the beginning. And this familism has encouraged the view that the proper place of women is first and foremost in the home as wives and mothers. Sure, we have a rising participation of women in the labor market. It has risen to thirty-one or thirty-four percent if you take the whole population, not only the Jewish population. But this is still low, compared to Western Europe and the United States, where it is forty-plus.

"So we certainly have an increasing entry, especially of Israeli-born women, into the labor market. But we have extreme occupational segregation of women's occupations and men's occupations, and women being only in a very small part of the occupational—what would you call it?"

"Spectrum?"

"*Ja.* And women being backward in all the technological occupations. We have a good representation of women in medicine. But we have a very weak representation of women in the technological occupations. We have a considerable income gap."

"For the same work?"

"For the same work. But it is very difficult to find the same work because we have segregation not only in occupations, but we have segregation in the same enterprise. And we have a very, very high concentration in all the lower levels, in all occupations. Even in women's occupations the women are in the lower levels. Even in education, which is a woman's occupation, nearly all grade-school teachers are now women. A smaller proportion of the secondary-school teachers are women. The men are the supervisors, and the men are the principals. And the men write the curricula in the Ministry of Education. This situation adds to that which we have in the physically segregated oriental communities in the villages and development towns near the borders, where the quality of education is considerably lower than in the center of the country. There it even goes so far that we have girls growing up receiving a very much inferior education because, in these large poor families, patriarchal conditions continue. The mothers keep the girls at home to look after the smaller children. They do not attend school regularly. They barely go above grade school, perhaps a year or year and a half more."

"Even though it's compulsory for them?"

"*Ja.* It is compulsory, but if you are somewhere in the sticks, then the law is not properly enforced. We have not only a considerable group of the older women, who came in the mass *aliyah,* who are analphabetic, illiterate, but we have a new generation of their daughters who grew up with barely being able to read and write. This—to my mind—this is a scandal!"

About a year after my meeting with Judith Buber Agassi, a report on the status of women in Israel, prepared by a ninety-two-member commission headed by Knesset member Ora Namir, was presented to Prime Minister Menachem Begin on January 23, 1978. It is a 140-page report, listing 241 recommendations to improve the status of women at work, at home, in education, in political, economic, and social life. Notably omitted, no doubt because of the influence of the religious bloc, is the problem of discrimination in marriage and divorce, which is the sacred province of religious law, administered by all-male rabbinical courts. Corroborating Judith's statement, the commission found that half the women in Israel have had education for only eight years or less, and that half of that half have had less than three or four years of schooling; that there is a strong connection between education and status; that women must be educated to seek equality. "What won't be done by women," said Ora Namir, "won't be done!" As for kibbutz women, one of them, a commission member, stated that the basic problem is a change of male attitudes towards women in the kibbutz: that the male, in sharp contrast to past attitudes, now sees his ideal woman as a homemaker to provide him with love, warmth, and aesthetic satisfaction. Women who do not fit this stereotype are regarded as deviants.

"How about the army being the great equalizer?" I asked.

"What is said about the army as an equalizer is not so. An enormous percentage of oriental girls never get to the army. They declare they are religious, which exempts them. And also, although I have no statistics, an enormous number of the girls get married before they are eighteen, which exempts them. So they never get to the army.

"So I think we need a real push to do something about raising the status of women in this country. Since the Yom Kippur War, there has been a raising of consciousness of concern in this area. I am active in the political group which I not only think is truly democratic, but which has done a lot in order to break away from this paternalistic pattern and party clique method that was the vogue here for too many years. This is the Citizens Rights Party, whose leading personality—I think, typically—is a woman, Shulamit Aloni."

"Yes, I've met with her. In fact, she suggested I meet you. Tell me, how did the Yom Kippur War stimulate activity towards change?"

"People suddenly saw that the leadership they had believed in, which had constantly told them that everything was fine, that you never had it so good—they found that leadership couldn't be trusted. At least, the first few days of the Yom Kippur War were disastrous. Things were far from fine and dandy.

"But as for women, suddenly when all the men were in the army, it turned out that the economy was at a standstill because of this segregation. In no technical position was there a woman. All plants, where nearly all the production workers are women, couldn't work because there were no mechanics. Only men were mechanics and setup men, and the women couldn't work!"

Judith's voice rose in exasperated outrage. "Women staying home had no gas for cooking because there were no women drivers to deliver it to the tanks that we use here. There were no women bus drivers. Traffic was at a standstill because Egged [the national Histadrut—General Federation of Labor—bus system] didn't accept women as bus drivers.

"This was our first war since the War of Independence [from November 29, 1947, when Arabs responded with violence to the United Nations resolution on Palestine, to the signing of the armistice agreements during 1949] that lasted more than a very short time. [The Yom Kippur War started October 6, 1973, and ended October 24.] So the anomaly of the position of women became clear. Women jumped out of their skins! They wanted to help. They knew that things were terrible. And they were told to bake cakes and knit caps."

"And entertain the soldiers?"

"And entertain the soldiers. Keep the home fires burning!" She spoke in a solemn, lowered voice. *"Ja,* keep the home fires burning, I repeat!"

"You're hopeful that the Citizens Rights Party will correct some of these problems?"

"In spite of being such a small group of only three members in the Knesset, it has to its credit many bills and many reforms of existing laws, constant activity in the Knesset committees, and a constant serving as a channel for the complaints of thousands and thousands of citizens—Jewish, Arab, and many, many women among them!" The last was accompanied by ironic laughter.

"Its civil rights position has strong appeal for me. They have asked me to be on the ticket for the coming elections, and I have accepted to run for the Knesset. However, the party is not in a terribly good position because we're having the formation of quite a number of new groups. So the picture is very unclear, and the unsophisticated voter is now confused. I can only hope there are enough people who remember what has happened in the past and who are sophisticated enough to see what is what, not only to continue, by returning our present members to the Knesset, but to augment our representation." (Judith's fears were justified. In the May 1977 elections her party received only enough votes, 20,621, to return one member to the Knesset: Shulamit Aloni.)

"What are your plans if you don't go to the Knesset?" I asked her.

"I will continue with my teaching, of course. I am also chief researcher on a study of 'Women's Jobs and Job Attitudes.' Being done on a grant from the German Research Foundation, it is a comparative, multinational project concerning the characteristics of typical women's jobs and their correlations to women's attitudes to their work. As you know, it is a subject that interests me very, very much."

5 Kibbutz: Whither Equality?

THE KIBBUTZ HAS ALWAYS BEEN an elite group of Israeli society. Although less than three and a half percent of the population lives on kibbutzim, the representation of kibbutzniks in the Knesset, in army volunteer units and top army posts, in intellectual, artistic, and industrial life, in agriculture, and in political activity is about ten times greater than the actual kibbutz segment of the population.

Communal goals remain the same, but with age and prosperity there have been changes. The emphasis has shifted from pioneering to a more middle-class type of achievement, and much has been written and said about a retrogression in the status of women in the kibbutz. The dream was to have equal sharing of all work, regardless of sex.

In the early years, women did almost every job the men did, building, running tractors, managerial jobs. Today they do, almost exclusively, "women's work." The question is why. Is it because they prefer child care, teaching, kitchen work? Have they been put back into those jobs because the men covet the prestigious positions? Or has this happened for other reasons?

When I met the late Miriam Baratz in 1952, she told me that when she had the first of her seven babies in Kibbutz Degania (the first kibbutz in what was then Palestine, founded in 1911 by Miriam, another young woman, and ten young men), she had to fight to keep her job in the milk shed. She had a passion for milking cows and had no intention of stopping. She was sixty-two when we met and was still going strong at the job. She came from Russia in 1906, when she was sixteen.

"I used to take the babies with me to the shed when I milked the cows," she told me, "and they sat or slept in the trough. Nobody approved! Sometimes the cows licked the baby. Everyone said, 'Miriam, it's unhealthy! Manure!' I told them the cows are cleaner than the people. Don't bother me. You are worried about the child? If the diaper has to be changed, change it!" Her stand resulted in the first cooperative care of children in the kibbutz, which continues today.

Twenty-five years later, on a visit to Israel in 1977, I heard of Senta Josephthal, distinguished for being one of the diminishing number of kibbutz women who are in high managerial or executive positions. I went to meet her in Kibbutz Galed on the Sabbath, when she was at home from her work as head of the Agricultural Center, an umbrella organization serving all the settlement movements.

The kibbutz is beautifully situated in the hills of Menasheh, southeast of Haifa in northern Israel. All was green and fresh in early spring, with blossoming trees poking up through the green. On arriving at Galed, I found my way to the community dining room, where a slim, ascetic-looking man was stacking orange plastic dishes after lunch. He offered to escort me to her room.

Having seen nothing as chic as these dishes when I was a kibbutz guest some time ago, I asked about them. My guide, who was born in the Netherlands, managed enough English to tell me that they were produced by their own kibbutz, as partner in a factory at nearby Kibbutz Mishmar Haemek.

On the way, he pointed out a large poured-concrete building, nearing completion, which would be a new dining room and kitchen facility. We also passed the new cultural house, an impressive-looking building which is the pride of every kibbutz that can afford one. It contains a library, lounge, and meeting room, as well as a stage for theatrical and musical programs that come to the kibbutz.

"Hello, I've been expecting you." I was greeted pleasantly by a sturdily built sixty-five-year-old woman of medium height. She wore a comfortable knit suit and heavy glasses, and her straight white hair was cut in a short bob. In a group of one-story row houses, the room that I came into was familiar to me from other kibbutzim. A small entrance area led to a short hall and bathroom, on the right, and to the room itself, straight ahead. A daybed, desk, bookshelves, a few small tables and chairs furnished the simple but comfortable room, which I admired, as I have since my first exposure, years back, to the minimal, uncluttered life-style of the kibbutznik.

"Oh, yes, it's fine for me. I am a single person since my husband died, and therefore I have only one room. Most of the single people today have more than one room. I am not interested." It was clear that this was a no-nonsense woman, and we got to the business at hand immediately after she brought coffee from a hot plate in the hall.

I sat on a chair and she on the daybed. "It's a beautiful kibbutz," I said. "When was it started?"

"My husband, Giora, and I came in the first group of eight from Germany in '38, when we were both twenty-six. He had finished law. I began law studies in Nuremberg, but I was thrown out of the university when Hitler came to power. I had my earlier schooling in Fürth, where I was born. It may interest you," she added, "that Henry Kissinger's father was my teacher.

"We saw there was no future for us in Germany. From the end of '34, until we left, we worked in the central organization of the Habonim Zionist youth movement in Berlin, preparing ourselves and other young people to go to Palestine. My husband was responsible for Youth Aliyah, for bringing children from fifteen to seventeen to Palestine.

"We set up agricultural training farms in Holland, in the Scandinavian countries, in France, England, Yugoslavia, and Czechoslovakia. There the young people prepared for kibbutz life and also learned a bit of Hebrew while they waited for certificates to come to Palestine. I think this work saved the lives of a lot, a lot of young people."

When I asked how the Jewish youth movement was able to operate in Germany at that time, she explained, "The Zionist movement had a silent agreement with the Nazi regime, that we are allowed to take Jews out, as many as we are able to take out, because they thought it's the best solution if they don't have to expel them or to kill them. So they let us work.

"When we arrived here, we went to an existing kibbutz to see how it's done. We had a big group left behind in Germany. We were very lucky that the parents of my husband and my parents got out and came here just before the war. A very small part of our comrades succeeded in coming before the outbreak of war, but most of them didn't survive. This is the reason why our kibbutz till this day is a small kibbutz.

"We have now a hundred and seventy members, more than half of them already second-generation who were born and grew up here. I think we were fifty or sixty when we started, nearly all from Germany. But some of our friends who made their training year in Holland, like the man who showed you to my room, brought with them their friends from the Netherlands, so we have that additional small group.

"We started our own kibbutz in '39 as a working group in Raanana, which is today a small town close to Tel Aviv. Then it was more a village, based on citrus plantations, which were not cultivated at all during the war because there was no export of the fruit. The sea was closed for such things. We came at a time of full unemployment. So we looked for work all over the country.

"For instance," she said, shifting her position and clasping her hands over her knees, "I learned the building profession, and I went for work to the British camps. The British army set up a lot of camps for the soldiers fighting in the Middle East, and there was a lot of work in the building trade. I went for three months here, three months to another place."

"Did you do different things in building, or were you trained for something in particular?"

"I laid bricks. I have a certificate that I am a trained building worker!"

"Terrific!" We both laughed at this prideful report on her past.

"All the time we were waiting for land to settle on. We trained our people in agriculture, as much as we were able to do, in other kibbutzim. In my agriculture profession I am a cow maid, a milkmaid, a very good one!" This brought more laughter, and I asked if she had known Miriam Baratz. Of course, she said, although they were a generation apart.

"I worked in a neighboring village, Ramat Hashavim, with an old German settler who had six cows. I learned to milk, and I brought the milk to the houses in the village, and I made milk products. This was very useful for us later because this old settler, when he felt the work was too hard for him, sold his cows to the kibbutz, and this was the foundation of our dairy herd. And today it's a very good dairy herd, two hundred and fifty milking cows.

"In '45 we got the land here from the Settlement Department of the Jewish Agency. It's hilly country, as you saw on your way here, but it's only two hundred meters high. It makes the impression that it's in the mountains because you go up and down, up and down. Now it's the nicest time of the year because everything is green and blossoming."

"I noticed the wild cyclamen outside your door. May I pick a few before I leave?"

"Oh, yes. Not too many because it's forbidden." Laughter again from this woman who laughed very easily. "All the land we got was sown with stones. In summer we picked the stones, and in winter we planted trees. All the brush, shrubs, forests, and trees that you see around us, we have planted them. Because when we came, there was not one tree.

"After the war, we absorbed into the kibbutz some of our groups that survived. And one group came at the beginning of the war in '40, with the *Patria*. I don't know if you know the story of the *Patria*."

"I remember the incident but not the details."

"Illegal immigrants had come to Haifa port on two small ships. The British wouldn't let them come in and transferred them to their warship, the *Patria*, to be expelled to Mauritius. The Haganah, the Jewish defense force, and the people on the ship decided that they won't leave Palestine, whatever may happen, and explosives were smuggled onto the ship. They themselves ignited it and the ship went down in Haifa port.

"They took care that most of the people should be on deck. Then they gave the order to jump into the sea, that you are being awaited on shore, where people will help you. Therefore most of them were saved, but the British took them to the detention camp of Atlit, and they were held there for one year. It was to tell those who would make the same attempt that it was not worthwhile doing. But it was worthwhile because those people survived."

"How did they get out of Germany at that time?"

"They succeeded in leaving before the war and waited in Rumania, Yugoslavia, Bulgaria. Then they came through the Danube in very small ships. My husband went to the detention camp in Atlit and lived with them for a year as an instructor, as a teacher, assistant, to help them. After the war, a group of them joined us, so we were almost a hundred members when we started the new settlement here."

"When did your husband die?"

"In '62, of a heart attack." Her firm, low-pitched voice saddened. "He was minister of Housing and Development before he died. He had been head of the Absorption Department for a long time and held many posts in the government. We had known each other from the age of fifteen, from the youth movement we were in together. We were just the two of us, no children."

"It seems you have both done important work since the beginning. What did you do besides bricklaying and milking that brought you to your big job today?"

"I think there is no work I didn't do. I worked in the British police station in Kfar Saba, laundering their uniforms. I had to speak English there, and I had some English in school in Germany. Also, I picked fruit. I worked in the vegetable garden. It was quite clear in those days that every work you may find you have to take, because otherwise there's nothing to live on. I think it was a very good thing to learn so many different kinds of work. It came in very good when we set up our new kibbutz here.

"In '47 I got the job of treasurer of the kibbutz. It was a treasury without money, and it was a terrible job because we had a very small income. We tried to develop the place, and therefore money always had to be found in some way. What did we do? We called it traveler's checks—not like the ones you know. I think it was illegal. Not only I but treasurers from other kibbutzim did the same.

"We wrote out a check from a Haifa bank, on ourselves, to a Tel Aviv bank. We went by bus to Tel Aviv, and in Tel Aviv we wrote out a check on a bank in Zichron Ya'akov, a small town nearby. Then I went by bus to Zichron Ya'akov and I wrote out a check to the Haifa bank, and therefore the round was closed. And there was no money at all behind it."

"Didn't they catch up with you?"

"They knew it, and I think many of the banks closed their two eyes. First of all, they took the interest on it, high interest. And they knew that, after all, we're not doing it for our own sakes. We're doing it for the national sake."

"You were getting loans if they took interest?"

"No. You also pay interest on your current account."

"You had an account with this 'found money'?"

"Oh, yes, we had accounts, I think, with a dozen of banks."

"I'm not used to this high finance," I told her. "I don't quite understand it."

We both had a good laugh at the kibbutz version of traveler's checks, and Senta added, "You see, the late treasurer of the State, Levi Eshkol, who later on was prime minister, always said, 'I need some of the kibbutz treasurers to manage with the finances of the State.'" Still laughing: "I had a lot of experience in finances, and therefore I went to work in the kibbutz movement as director of the bank of the kibbutz movement.

"For two years I was the director of the bank of this movement, which today is the largest federation of kibbutzim, representing about thirty-six thousand members. Then there were less. [This kibbutz belongs to the Ichud Hakvutzot v'Hakibbutzim, Union of Kevutzot and Kibbutzim. The *kvutza* was a smaller form of the kibbutz. Today, all are kibbutzim.] Unexpectedly, in '55, I was elected to the Third Knesset on the Mapai Party list, now the Labor Party. But I resigned after one year because I was invited to the executive of the Histadrut, the General Federation of Labor, where I founded the Department for Absorption of Immigrants and Development.

"When I was in the Knesset, I felt that I don't do anything. There were only words and words and debates." The deliberations of State must have exhausted the patience of this woman of action, and she said this in a long-drawn-out voice. "I had the feeling that I waste all my time. And I was very happy to join the executive of the Histadrut because there I had the feeling I do something real.

"It was the period of the big immigration from Poland and from Hungary. The four years that I worked there were the years of building the development towns all over the country, from Kiryat Shmonah in the north to Dimona in the south. I took an active part in this. It was a wonderful job, and I thought it was *much, much* better than the Knesset.

"When Mr. Lavon, the then general secretary of Histadrut, built his new executive after the elections in '60, he didn't include me because of political reasons. We didn't see eye to eye on a lot of issues. Maybe you know the Lavon affair. It was the beginning of it, and I was on the other side of the fence."

The Lavon affair was one of Israel's major espionage and sabotage setbacks, involving sabotage efforts by Egyptian Jews. Lavon fell from power because of his part in its planning. Recently, the bodies of two spies who were hanged in Cairo in 1955 were brought to Israel, with the bodies of nine Israeli soldiers who died in the 1973 Yom Kippur War, in exchange for fifty-eight Egyptian prisoners.

"Then I worked again in the kibbutz movement," she went on. "I was responsible for all the economic activities. After two years, I became general secretary of the movement."

"Were there many women in these top jobs in those years, or were you an exception?"

"At no time were many women in top jobs. Not here, as in no other country in the world. I think until now I was the only woman to be the general secretary of one of the big settlement movements. It was a time when many new kibbutzim were founded, and it was a very wonderful job. I was there until '65. Then Galed, my kibbutz, demanded, 'Come home and do something for your own home. It's very nice that you do for all Israel. Do something for us!' I came home to be farm manager for two years. And so it went, with one job and another until my present one."

I asked what her job as head of the Agricultural Center involved.

"I am responsible for all the economic activities in all the kibbutzim and moshavim, the agricultural villages. That means five hundred and thirty settlements in all, representing about two hundred thousand grown-ups, who are the members. The center does all the negotiations with the Ministry of Agriculture about prices, about production quotas, about allotment of water and land to new settlements, about training institutions for all the movements together. We take part in security problems of the border settlements."

"How does agriculture apply to security?" I asked, not understanding the connection. "Don't the army and the settlements themselves guard the borders?"

"If you sit on the border, you have a lot of security problems. We don't defend the borders. We have a special department in the Agricultural Center to make the connection with the army and with the special police force. We try to find the right conditions in those

settlements that it shouldn't interfere too much with the development of the settlement. There has to be enough security for the
people living there, like fortifications and things like this."

We came back to talk about the changes in the kibbutz since
Galed was founded. "As I told you, we came here to nothing. The
one thing we thought we had was enough water. We came here in
spring, and in the wadis the water was running. But in summer, not
a drop of water is in those wadis, and we had only a very small well
for drinking water. It took years of drilling to give us the water we
needed.

"We lived in tents. We lived in huts made of straw mats in the
summer. When winter came, in the few buildings we had built, we
lived two and three families in one room. Therefore, in the first
years we had a lot of difficulties. But surely you've heard it from
other people. These were the happiest times of the country because
everybody had the feeling he's building his own home with his ten
fingers. And he's putting in all his strength and all his energy and
all his willpower to overcome all the difficulties." Senta made a fist,
to emphasize the effort they had exerted.

"Today we are a well-to-do community, quite middle-class
standard of living. There is no question of expenses for daily life.
We are able to afford new and better housing for the young couples. And we can afford, every year, to send three or four families
for a trip abroad. When people don't have so many difficulties to
overcome, they think too much about the small things of life and
they are less happy than we were in the harder times."

"Where does your main income come from now?" I asked.
"The man in the dining room told me the kibbutz is producing the
attractive plastic dishes I saw."

"Yes, I'll tell you about it. Income comes from agriculture,
dairy cattle, beef cattle, fruit orchards—apples and pears, very good
ones. And we have a share in a big citrus plantation in the valley,
where we also grow cotton and wheat."

"I remember in '49, on my first trip here, during your worst
austerity period, I brought apples and salamis from Rome. Both
were treated like diamonds by the people I gave them to."

"Oh, yes. We didn't grow our own apples yet. As to the plastic
factory, five years ago we went into partnership with our neighboring kibbutz, Mishmar Haemek. It's a big factory, and the partner-

ship is based on the number of workers we are able to give. It's not the money we can invest because for that there are banks in the country."

"Are you saying you don't have to pyramid nonexisting money from bank to bank, as you did originally?" I asked her.

"Oh, no! Now we are living on money we earn, and we are very happy that the factory runs without hired workers. Our principle is to do every work ourselves. Besides the dishes, the plastic factory makes strings for balls of hay and straw, parts for machines, and helmets for the army, instead of steel ones. They are much lighter and just as strong. And we export them. Many armies in the world think that what's good for the Israeli army must be very good.

"Many of the presses in the factory are automatic, and it makes for easy work, which is very good for the women of fifty-five and sixty who have worked in the children's houses for many years. And that's quite hard work. They are glad to have a new productive job and feel they are contributing to the income of the kibbutz."

"That brings us to the role of women in the kibbutz. How about the younger women? Are they essentially doing women's work, too?"

"Yes. This is one of the problems of women in kibbutzim today. The younger women are nearly all occupied in the children's houses."

"That wasn't the case in the early years when you were a bricklayer."

"No. You see, the kibbutz gives all the opportunities to women. There is really equality of start, equality of rights. But the young women are not interested at all to take those jobs. They are happy to go back to the traditional women's work."

"How do you account for that?"

"Maybe it's a reaction to the first years. In the older kibbutzim I sometimes heard, 'Look at my mother, how she looks at the age of sixty. I won't look like her at that age. I'll take care of myself and I won't work out in the fields and I won't do such hard work.'

"The other thing is that, with the rise of the standard of living, there is much more work in the house. You have a bigger apartment. Today we build three-room apartments for the young couples. You have nicer things to take care of. And you have to have some strength left after your official workday for your own home. For instance, baking a cake. Who dreamt about it in those times? There was no facility for making a cake in your room. And there were no products. But today you go to the kitchen and you get the eggs and the meal and the butter and everything you need. And you have your own oven to bake in. Only last year they decided to have the children sleep at home, and that means a lot of work also. Some kibbutzim are doing that today."

"Why did they make that decision?"

"Oh"—a big sigh—"don't ask me. I think it is such a mistake. It's part of the same trend of going back to the traditional form of life."

"How about the new kibbutzim that are being established? Don't they have to go through some of the same problems that you did?"

"They have a much better starting point. They are given good buildings to start with, big budgets from the Jewish Agency, and in a few years they have all the production, all the means to make. a good life. We got such a small budget we had to build very primitive buildings at first and build them ourselves."

"With community toilets and showers you had to walk to in all kinds of weather," I recalled. "When I stayed in Mishmar Haemek and Ein Hashofet years ago, I made the trek. And today everyone has his own bathroom."

"Sure, sure, sure!"

"Are there two bathrooms in any of the houses, or haven't they got to that yet?"

"No. It's one. But you couldn't imagine it today to build an apartment without a private shower and a private toilet. Couldn't imagine it at all! The children who grew up here can't remember it. They haven't known anything but this luxury. But even when we had nothing, we did everything for the children, so they grew up in proportional good conditions."

"They were the privileged characters. Do many of the children remain in the kibbutz?"

"Yes, in all the movements, about three out of four are staying on. Our statistics show as many leaving as are coming in. Because somebody is marrying out and somebody is marrying in. All the Israelis are marrying early. They finish the army and they get married."

"That means in their early twenties? Do many of them go to the university from the kibbutz?"

"We decide every year how many we are ready to send to the university. We have a committee for higher education. Anyone interested will apply, and the committee will make a decision according to three standards. One, what does the kibbutz need? For instance, we need a teacher for mathematics, or we need a teacher for history. We send our children to a district school, but we have to give teachers to the school. Or, for instance, we need agriculturally trained people for the farm, so we have to send them to the agricultural faculty. Or we need somebody for the factory in Mishmar Haemek, so we send them to the Technion in Haifa.

"The second point is what the applicant may want, even if the kibbutz is not in need of it—perhaps music or philosophy. Then he will be told, 'All right, we are ready to send you to study what you want. But you have to know when you come back you have to be ready to do the work we need you for. And you can't demand that you will work in your profession. You have to decide now if you are ready to take such a decision.'

"The third thing—and this, I think, is special for the kibbutz —we sometimes propose to older people, in their early fifties, to go and learn a new job. 'You worked in the fields till now. You're getting older. Think about your second profession. What are you able to do until a hundred and twenty? Go out and learn something new, perhaps to be an accountant or an economic-trained person.' The children already are on their own, and women are free to go out, too, to learn a new job. People more and more are thinking about this in the last years."

"And it's extremely important," I agreed. "But in your second category, if a young person goes to study music or art or philosophy, how will he or she be able to use the training later if it's required to come back and do the usual jobs in the kibbutz?"

"He may have it as a hobby for his own. He loves music for its own enrichment. He may organize a choir in the kibbutz, an orchestra in the kibbutz, or maybe he will teach music as a part-time profession. There are always people who say they can't agree to these conditions. Then, if the pull is strong enough, they may have to leave the kibbutz to follow a chosen profession. It doesn't happen often."

We returned to early marriages in the kibbutz, attitudes towards premarital sex, and the question of family planning. "Most of them are living, before the marriage, some months together," Senta told me. "Every girl and every boy coming home from the army gets his own room. No problem. Maybe there are single cases earlier. Some couples make arrangements amongst themselves at an earlier age. The kibbutz doesn't interfere.

"We think it's not bad that they are living together. And it is better to do it before marriage than to find out a few months after marriage that they are not very good in making their life together." This liberal philosophy is possibly an extension of the early days in the kibbutzim when couples often waited to formalize the relationship until the birth of a child.

"The young families today have many more children than the old-timers," Senta continued. "The old-timers couldn't afford it because they always calculated how much it cost to bring up more children. Today the couples are encouraged to have bigger families, and three, four is the ordinary case. But also, to have three or four you have to plan the family, and they plan it very well, not too close together, two-and-a-half-year intervals. They get advice in the local clinic by the doctor and the nurse, and the girls get the pill."

"When the babies come, do the fathers take any part in the care of the children? I remember, in the earlier years, some of the kibbutzim were training a few young men to be in the children's houses, as well as the mothers."

"No, we don't train them, but on Shabbat they take their turn also in the children's houses. When they take their turn—let's say in the kindergarten—they take the children on a trip around the kibbutz in a big tender or something like this. The children like it very much when one of the young fathers has his turn. But there is no regular work of the men there."

"Do the children's houses still exist in the same sense if the parents are having the children at home now?"

"They exist. First of all, sleeping at home will only begin two months from now. But they will continue because the child will be brought at seven o'clock in the morning to the children's house, for the mother has to go to her work also. The child will stay there till four in the afternoon."

"I don't know how familiar you are with the women's movement in America," I said, "but one by-product of it is that many fathers are sharing considerably in the care of the children, freeing the mother for work other than 'woman's work.' "

"I don't say that I am very familiar with it, although I've been in the States a few times, having to do with agriculture and education and, last year, with explaining Israel to all levels of groups—black groups, labor groups. It was extremely interesting for me and, I think, for them.

"In Israel, I'm sure the problem is that women don't take the rights, not that they aren't given them. They don't use all the opportunities given, and I don't think they would have to fight very hard to have real equal standing. But they don't fight at all.

"In the kibbutz there is no doubt about it that every woman could get any job she wants. But most of them don't want those jobs that are not the usual women's jobs. Even in the committees, in the economic committee, you have sometimes one and sometimes none. But in the education committee, in the cultural committee, in the social committee, there the women are the majority. That is in the kibbutz.

"Outside the kibbutz we have a law of equal wages for equal work, for similar work even. And there I won't say there is no problem. There is a problem because sometimes, especially in the factories, the manager tries to pay less to women for the same work than they are paying men, and they always find a reason for it: that women are staying away more than men—a child is ill and she stays at home. And she has a lot of other problems."

"She gets pregnant and has a baby. . . ."

"Yes. They use it as an excuse. But the Histadrut is fighting hard for it, and I think a lot of progress was made in the last years. In politics, in the Labor Party, it was decided at the last convention that at least twenty percent of women should be in all the elected bodies, in the Central Committee in the Knesset, and so on.

"And now, when the Central Committee was elected, in spite of the decision, there were only fourteen percent elected. I tried to find out what happened. The Central Committee was elected in all the branches, and if a branch has the right to elect only two or three, we didn't find a woman who could compete with the man. You had to have five, at least, on a committee to get a woman in on the twenty percent ruling. And women didn't fight for it in most of the branches. In those branches where women really fought for it, they got it. It is a big difficulty for a woman to take upon herself political responsibility and not neglect the family and the house and all the jobs she has to do."

"How did Golda do it?"

"You see, Golda is an outstanding woman, and not many Goldas are around." (This was spring 1977, before Golda's death.)

"But there are other outstanding women, capable women. . . ."

"Yes. But the Goldas always reached the top."

"Those that have self-motivation," I suggested.

"Yes. I am not very sympathetic to this form of fighting for rights. I think it will lead to the contrary. It makes the movement ridiculous. It makes the women in the movement not womanly. Because after all the problems of women getting important jobs and important positions in public life, it has to be combined with staying women, with their very special look at problems as women. And the women's liberation movement tries to make women into men —like men. And this is not the right case."

I was amazed to hear these words from a woman who has held so many "men's" jobs. "They don't want to make women into men at all," I countered. "They simply want a woman to have the possibility of doing whatever job she is capable of doing in spite of the fact that she is a woman and in spite of the prejudices that have existed for so long. And to get equal pay for equal work, to have equal opportunity with the man. But she still wants to be a woman."

"As I told you, I think the right is given to them here, and I don't think that, usually, men are against having women in outstanding positions. But most of the women are not so interested, young women who have to take care of their children. They don't have the time."

"In the kibbutz they have their children taken care of for them."

"Yes, but you have to be out of the kibbutz to take an official job, a public position. And the children come home in the afternoon, and the mother is not here. And the father is, after all, not the mother. And young women are usually not ready to be away from the home and from the kibbutz during those years when they have small children.

"And then," Senta added somewhat inconsistently, "they are

handicapped when they come at the age of forty-four or forty-five and the children are grown up and they are freer to do other things. They are already handicapped because the men have accumulated a lot of experience during those twenty years when they were at home."

"Well, that is exactly why the women's movement in America and other countries feels that the woman should have help in child care, either by having efficient child-care centers established to free her to go to work, or by having her husband share the responsibility for the child so she can develop her own activity or profession. It doesn't necessarily have to be in public life. It can be anything that a woman is motivated to do, according to her own talents and inclination."

"I think you have the best example in the kibbutz," Senta said. "There is all the help in child care. But in the kibbutz, and in all the cities, help is for working hours. After working hours, after all, the mother has to be with her children."

"How about the father?" I asked. "I know of many cases in America, and even some in Israel, in the cities, where the father shares responsibility. They stagger their work hours."

"Yes, he is sharing, but it is not the same. Most of the mothers are not ready to leave the children only with the father. I'll tell you, I think most of the young mothers are not interested."

Although Senta Josephthal has not had children of her own, her more than thirty years as a kibbutz member, builder, and manager-worker should give her intimate knowledge of the role of women in the kibbutz. Her appraisal of the situation is echoed in the book *Women in the Kibbutz,* published in 1975 and written by the Canadian sociologist Lionel Tiger with Israeli kibbutz member Joseph Sepher.

The book argues that the kibbutz experience proves equalization of work roles for men and women to be a failure. Woman's role, they say, has always been and always will be maternal-domestic. An Israeli sociologist, granddaughter of Martin Buber, Judith Buber Agassi, with whom I discussed the matter some days after my visit to Galed (see chapter 4), did a study on "Kibbutz and Sex Roles" in 1976, in which her findings differ sharply from those of Tiger and Sepher.

The book is a polemic against all those who consider the abolition or reduction of the differentiation of the social sex roles, which includes work roles, political roles, and more, both desirable and feasible. Many kibbutz women are dissatisfied and frustrated with their communal work roles of performing personal services to people who are not their family members.

For many, their work roles do not accord with their dispositions. For many, the challenge and possibility for personal growth are too limited. It is those same mothers who are most dissatisfied and frustrated with their communal work roles who demand the widening of their private maternal work role. They are searching for relevance and emotional satisfaction.

What causes frequent soul-searching at kibbutz federation conferences and their commission of special surveys, dealing with the problem of women in the kibbutz, seems to me less the distance between ideology and behavior than the widespread impression of the existence of a social problem in kibbutz society: the realization that the amount of dissatisfaction of women in the kibbutz with their work role is considerably greater than that of men; that this problem is especially serious with young second generation women; that the level of aspirations of kibbutz girls is disconcertingly low; that the self-esteem of younger kibbutz women is considerably lower than that of men; that the level of political participation of second generation kibbutz women is especially low and that there exists a serious problem of second generation women leaving the kibbutz.

Her explanation for the development of "woman's work" in the kibbutz:

Given the acceptance of the conventional norm of child care and consumption services being women's responsibility, the peculiar collective egalitarian structure of the kibbutz, its limited and finite labor pool, necessarily brought about a more pronounced occupational differentiation between the sexes than in the general society.

The upholding of the norm, that service activities are the sole responsibility of women, was in the interest of men as a group, as it has enabled them to obtain a larger share of the non-material rewards from work, such as status and intrinsic satisfaction.

What to do about it? Judith Buber Agassi asserts that the situation is not inevitable, that the existing differentiation of work roles runs counter to the long-range economic and social interests of kibbutz society:

Although there are those who defend the status quo, as conforming with feminine nature, there is a growing number of both men and women in the kibbutz who are anxious to find the way to the declared goal of equal opportunity for full human development for men and women.

Before I left her, Senta and I spoke about feminists in Israel. I told her that women active in the movement had informed me that there is a broad spectrum of women in consciousness-raising groups all over the country, from ages nineteen to seventy.

"They say it. But look at the gatherings," she answered. I've seen them."

I was surprised to hear she had attended any. "I come as a speaker to such gatherings many times," she said. "I always am looking for the young women, but I find very, very few."

"You don't agree with their feminist position, but they ask you to speak?"

"I speak about certain topics I am familiar with: settlement policy, economic problems. And why shouldn't I?" she asked a bit defensively.

"You should," I told her. "And you give them a lot. You represent exactly what they are going to need when their children are grown, or even earlier, and they have to fall back on themselves. Right?"

"Yes," she said, laughing at the contradiction. It was time for me to go, and she accompanied me to the waiting taxi. True to her promise, she helped me pick a few of the delicately beautiful white and lavender wild cyclamen outside her door, nestled under trees she had helped plant so long ago.

As we walked, I said, "It seems to me quite a contradiction that you, women like you and Golda, take the view that you have just described about the women's liberation movement. It is completely contradictory to what you and other women of your stature have accomplished yourselves."

She replied somewhat sheepishly, "I tell you. It's like this. When you have gotten to the top, you forget what the problems are of those who have not arrived."

6 "For the First Time, an Arab Woman Was Something"

"DURING THE WAR IN 1948, we came back to our original village. We had lived for some time in Acre, and in Haifa when I was attending the English high school. My father thought we should stay in our own country and on our own property." Violet Khoury, who has the distinction of being the only woman so far to be elected mayor of an Arab village, was telling me why her family did not flee when the State of Israel was declared.

"My uncles, on the side of my mother, are Lebanese, and I remember that one of them came especially from Lebanon to take us. My father refused on the grounds that nobody can run away from his destiny. Strangely enough, on the same night, when we were still in Acre, a bomb entered our sleeping room. It even broke my bed, and I fell.

"We were six in the same room: my father, my sisters, and one of my brothers. I have two brothers from the first mother. My father was married before my mother. She died when I was ten. None of us was wounded. But this uncle was frightened and said, 'Look, Michaeli, you see what happened, let me take the girls.'

"My father told him, 'A bomb hit the room where six of us were sleeping. Not one was wounded. So it's only that God wants to show us. If we're going to be safe, we're going to be safe in the midst of warring. And if our destiny calls it, we die wherever we may be. So please leave us together. I won't leave my country.' And so we came to Kfar Yassif."

Kfar Yassif, in northern Israel, like many Arab villages, presents a pyramiding of ancient stone houses ascending in steps up a hillside, their sandy color blending almost imperceptibly into the landscape. As we started the climb up winding, narrow roads, the taxi driver, who had brought me from Haifa, asked several men along the way for the house of Violet Khoury. A variety of directions finally brought us to the one-story house, way at the top of the village.

A jolly and pretty woman of medium height, with short, black, curly hair and sparkling dark eyes invited me into her large living room. She was wearing a simple print dress, and had I not known I was coming to meet an Arab woman, I could just as easily have assumed she was Jewish, or of any other nationality or religion one encounters in Israel. The Arab woman on the street is often recognizable by her long, black, beautifully embroidered dress, sometimes unkempt from her labors, and a scarf under a loaded basket on her head.

"You must have something before we start," she insisted. She seated me before a coffee table with a basket of bananas and apples on it, while she went to the kitchen and came back with tea. It was a simply furnished room, with upholstered chairs and sofa, and a large, old-fashioned sideboard-buffet against one wall.

"During the War of Independence," she said as she sat down and lighted a cork-tipped cigarette, "many people left—mostly young people, young men and young girls, but mostly men. The number-one reason was out of fear of war. The second reason was to complete their education in the Arab states, where they could find enough universities. Nobody knew if the war would stop in one month, two months, or a year. So the families preferred to send their young people out."

In speaking of Israel and its conflict with the Arab world, we often forget that there are almost half a million Arab citizens of Israel living peacefully with Israel's almost three million Jewish citizens and not wanting to live anywhere else. Not that they aren't without serious complaints, as articulated by this very bright, lively, and amply proportioned woman. The ambivalent situation of the Israeli Arab started with the establishment of the new State in May 1948, following the United Nations Proclamation for Partition of Palestine of November 29, 1947.

The Arabs rejected partition. The Jews accepted it. When the British Mandate wound up its affairs and departed the following spring, the newly declared State of Israel was attacked on all sides by the five adjoining Arab nations. The Arabs living within the Jewish sector were told by constant radio broadcasts from the Arab nations that their armies would drive the Jews into the sea, that they should leave Israel and return victorious in a matter of days.

Repeated assurances by the Jews through frequent broadcasts and leaflets, urging them to remain in their homes and guaranteeing their full protection, had little effect in countering the mass flight of Arabs from Israeli territory and preventing the subsequent plight of the Palestinian refugees. Notable exceptions were several Arab villages and seminomadic tribes, as well as the entire Druze community of fifteen thousand in the north, which stayed and organized fighting units to defend Israel.

"We were not harmed here in Kfar Yassif," she continued. "I was teaching in the government girls' school in Acre, not far from here, where I had had my elementary education. For my secondary education I had to go to Haifa and live with the family of my uncle, who was then a doctor, while I attended the English high school. The Mandatory regime ended while I was teaching in Acre."

"That, of course, changed everything. Were you able to continue in the reorganized school system of Israel?"

"I applied to be a teacher, but I wasn't accepted. I think for my open ideas then, or my frank opinions." She laughed when she said this. "I was accused to be a Communist. I wasn't. I've never been. And I'm not a member of any political party.

"In 1949 there was a course for Arab social workers. We didn't have Arab social workers then. At most, we had one or two left from the Mandate. And so the new Ministry of Social Welfare of Israel opened a special course, and I was one of the first Arab social workers who graduated.

"I started working in all the Galilee. We were only ten, so ten were divided all over the country. I was given nearly forty villages in the Galilee. In 1949 to 1950 we didn't have good roads and ways of communication, as today. So I had to go to faraway villages. Sometimes I even went on horseback and any car that I could find available. Sometimes I had to sleep overnight in villages because I didn't have transport back.

"The work was very interesting, but it was very, very difficult because, you know, after the war there have been left broken families, many elderly people, since the young people left. There were no breadwinners, only the old people, many sick people, many refugees, people who were displaced from village to village.

"So I had many problems to deal with and the drastic thing was that the government was in a poor financial situation, so I didn't have the minimum of a budget. I don't know how much you know about social work, but you can well imagine a social worker having to cope with all of these problems and having not enough budget. So it was really something very, very serious, very tiring. But because I felt some kind of satisfaction from the work, I really did my best.

"Every year there came more social workers, so I had less villages. I married in 1952, and after marriage I went on working as a social worker." She paused to light another cigarette, which she continued to do, chain-fashion, during our talk.

"What was your husband doing?"

"My husband was a teacher, and then he was elected mayor of the village for some time. I had my three boys in the next years, my three sons. Then, in 1962, I quit social work, and to be home more and for financial reasons, I opened a ready-made clothes shop here in the village."

"Were you born in this village? Tell me something about your early years."

"Yes, I was born in 1929 in Kfar Yassif and have lived almost all of my forty-seven years here. My father was a police officer during the Mandate, and my mother was headmistress of a girls' school in Haifa before they were married.

"At an early age I went with one of my aunts to Jordan because she was alone and she wanted somebody to be with her. I lived with her for three years. My mother died after childbirth, leaving me and three sisters, all younger than I. My father didn't remarry, and I think it was a good thing that we didn't have a stepmother. I felt the responsibility very early."

"What is the population of Kfar Yassif?"

"Five thousand people. There are three communities: Moslems, Christians, and Druze. The Druze and the Moslems make nearly fifty percent of the population, and fifty percent are Christians. I am a Christian. Kfar Yassif is the central village for some other nearby villages, two of which are completely Druze villages."

"When were you mayor of the village? I was surprised to hear that an Arab woman had been elected. My congratulations!"

"Yes. It had never happened before; nor has it happened

since." She laughed. "When I opened my store, my husband was mayor of the village. But then he decided he didn't want to be in politics anymore. So I said, 'Let me take over. I've always been interested in your career.' We had their meetings here in our house, and whenever I brought them the coffee, I had the chance to listen to their talk. Sometimes I would give them an idea, and I was really upset when nobody took any notice of that. I suppose they thought, 'Why, it's just woman's talk,' or something like this."

Violet sighed a big sigh. "Whenever it was proved to them that my idea was the right one and they were wrong, even then nobody admitted it. I had to remind them, 'You see, if you had listened to what I suggested . . .' It seemed to me that it was better for them to go wrong on their own man-ideas than to follow a woman. That was the atmosphere, I felt. So when my husband decided he didn't want politics anymore, I said, 'Maybe you'll let me try.'

"Well, my husband is really modern. He's been educated in a college in Lebanon. He was a teacher. He was the mayor. So he said O.K. But afterwards he told me, 'I said O.K. because I was sure you can't do it'!"

"He was just humoring you?"

"That's it. He said, 'If I knew that you would do it, I wouldn't have agreed.'" She laughed heartily and then explained, "Because of Arab tradition and Arab community, which makes it the man's kingdom, he's the sultan! He's the king!" Violet enunciated her words in sonorous tones. "So I went to the youngsters—the relatives, friends, educated youngsters.

"They accepted the idea, and I ran for the local council on an independent list of Kfar Yassif and, with me, certain educated men from the village. I remember that the people who wanted to vote for me, or who were in the election campaign, used to hear many disgusting remarks, like, 'Hey! You're following a girl. Your leader is a woman!'"

"How old were you at the time?"

"It was seven years ago. I was forty. When we won in the elections, all the youngsters came singing. We made a party here. We stayed until morning. I think it was the biggest feast we ever had, and the happiest people that Kfar Yassif ever saw. For the first time, an Arab woman was something. There was a woman in the local council."

"Were other women working for you, with you?"

"My sisters, the family. But not outsiders, because every woman is still very much linked to the man. During the election campaign, I knew that all the women wanted me to win, to get into the local council. But when I said, 'Look, you have to give me your votes,' they said they can't. I don't know how much you know about the Arab background. It's very sacred, the way a woman has to be faithful to her husband, not to betray him in anything.

"So, though voting is secret, yet the idea that she's betraying her husband is so much a strain—out of her upbringing, of her culture—that she can't do it. So I can say I was very sorry that I didn't have women's backing. I had the backing of families, but not especially women. I had thought that maybe more women would see to it that I am their candidate when the voice of a woman is, for the first time, to be heard. I didn't even get the votes I thought I would get from women because of this idea of betrayal, the feeling of guilt. 'Well, we pray to God that you will win, you'll please be the mayor, but I can't give you my vote because my husband wants to vote for his cousin.' "

The taxi driver knocked on the door and came in, looking for the washroom. Violet invited him to stay in the house, and he became an interested listener, sitting on a couch on the other side of the room. Later he told me he would have much to tell his wife that evening, having heard things from an Arab woman for the first time. He was a sabra, and he knew English.

"O.K.," Violet continued, settling into her chair again. "When I went to the local council, which is nine members, there were eight men and I'm the only woman. When they made a coalition, nobody ever thought of having to negotiate with me, to get me into the administration. After a year and a half of me going down to the meetings, of understanding, discussing, giving my ideas, just hitting the table if I thought I'm right on something, they started to realize, 'Well, a woman can understand something, can do really something.'

"Then one day four of the local council members—men, of course—came here and said, 'Violet, we're going to change the coalition, and we want to elect you as mayor of the village.' When they made the coalition, nobody, it seems, noticed that there was a woman member on the local council, that maybe we can count her in the administration. But after nearly a year and a half of council meetings, really working with a woman and knowing that a woman can be somebody, they came and suggested that, and I was elected mayor of Kfar Yassif!

"I think the hardest part of my career as mayor were the first days when I went down to the local council. It was the kingdom of men, and for the first time, a woman coming to be the head. I remember the first day I came, after they elected me. I saw in every eye of the men there a question mark, and a real bitter one, a question mark of 'We're not used to that. We're not used to a boss being a woman.'

"I knew it was hard for them. I knew it was harder for me, but I knew I could do it. And I knew there is only one way to do it, to work as hard, not equal to the man, but maybe double, to prove that I could do something. I knew that I couldn't fail in giving them authority, friendship, confidence, and really the strength to overcome difficulties."

I don't know what the word is in Arabic, but a *mensch* is the same in any language, for either sex. What a woman! I thought. Gutsy, smart, capable, with a sense of self, even more impressive than for a woman in the Western world, considering the "kingdom of men" she had grown up in.

"I salute you!" I told her. "I can imagine what you had to go through."

She laughed and said, "I was put sometimes into examinations, so to speak. And I was really very alert to what was going on around me."

"They were testing you?"

"Yes. I knew that I shouldn't let my steps falter, because then they wouldn't say, 'Well, anybody can do something wrong, but— oh, she's a woman.' That's what I had to guard against. I worked very hard. I think I made as much effort as I could. I did a lot for my village.

"I know one thing that really satisfied me the most. The first month of my being the mayor, a woman came rushing into the office. She was a very simple, illiterate woman. She said, 'Mrs. Khoury, thank God you are in the local council! My husband used to beat me, but now when he wants to beat me I say, "Look, I'll go to Mrs. Khoury. She's the mayor." ' It was so simply said. But it gave me such a great satisfaction that even this woman saw something, a goal, a woman sits on the local council."

"An improvement in her condition."

"Exactly. So it improved not only one woman's condition, but it made something of a target, something more to be understood. You can't change everything in one year, two years. It's a long, long way. Well, I think I did as much as I could. I met many people. I think many women's organizations felt that it really was something, an honor that an Arab woman can come to such a key elected job. The government offices also honored me very much, tried to help."

Violet went over to the sideboard and took a photograph out of a drawer to give me. It was taken in 1974 at a cocktail party at WIZO House, Israeli headquarters of the Women's International Zionist Organization, in honor of Baron and Baroness Guy de Rothschild. It shows the beautiful young baroness, gowned in long chiffon and bejeweled with pearls and diamonds. Standing next to her is an unidentified officer of WIZO introducing her distinguished guests, and then Mayor Khoury looking lovely in the traditional embroidered Arab woman's dress, with a crocheted shawl over her shoulders, smiling and with a cigarette in her hand.

"How wonderful!" I told her. "You changed it from the 'kingdom of men' to the 'royalty of women'!"

"That's right." She laughed. "Even those political enemies in Kfar Yassif came around. For instance, today I'm still a member of the local council. I'm no longer mayor, but I'm still the only woman member. Even today I say the idea I wanted I achieved. I don't think I can go on because I have many more responsibilities. The children are grown up. They want to go to universities and there are the financial problems."

"How long were you mayor?"

"Until the elections came. After the elections, there was another coalition and then a man became mayor. I was mayor for three years. Now today, in the council, I go to all the meetings. They respect my opinions. Whenever I say I want to quit, I won't go anymore for the elections, they say, 'We don't know how we can live anymore without the voice of a woman knocking down the table!' " Again her jolly laughter.

"That's real success, isn't it?"

"At least they've found the need. I say, 'O.K. I've started the way. It's really shameful that any list of yours doesn't have in it a woman candidate. Just go ahead. I've done my role. It's not nice to be one woman alone on the council. I want to see three or four.' "

"Have there been others now?"

"No. But now before the elections I'm teasing them. I don't want to go back for another candidateship. I tell them every list has to have one woman at least, in a place where she could be one day a local council member. I don't know if they'll do it, but I hope they will. I started teaching in secondary schools after the last elections."

"Had you run for a second term as mayor?"

"Yes. I got one candidate, me, but I couldn't go into a coalition because there was a balance of power that I couldn't take with their conditions. I told you that Kfar Yassif is three communities. It's nearly half-half. For the first time there was a Moslem list, which had two candidates. These two candidates are the balance of power. I'm sorry to say they're not the real face of the Moslem community in Kfar Yassif. They're not so well educated, so they use their fanaticism to strengthen their stand. They have nothing else to show. And so I couldn't do that. I couldn't go on and accept their conditions."

"What are they fanatic about?"

"They want to show the Moslem voter something that he votes for. They don't have anything except playing with religious matters. You can well imagine those ideas. Me, as a Socialist believer, I feel, I believe, a man is a man no matter what his religion is."

"And a woman is a woman."

"Yes! It doesn't interest me at all if he's a Christian, Moslem, Jew, or heathen. If he's a human being, if he believes in humanity more or less, he's much nearer to me than any other Christian who, because he's a Christian, he likes me or I like him. So on these grounds I couldn't go into the coalition, and I stayed in the opposition. I'm sorry for what happened, but whenever they want to contrast it they say, 'Well, Violet did that. In her time, it was really the best.' Because they compare it."

"Do you think you'll run for mayor again?"

"I doubt it. I'd like to run for the Knesset but not for the local council."

"For the Knesset! That would be fine. What are there? Eight Arab men in the Knesset and, of course, no Arab women?"

"Yes. It would be fine. I'm not a member of any party yet. But

I very much appreciate the women's movement which is started now by some Israeli women with Marcia Freedman. Only yesterday I heard that they had seventeen points on their platform. I don't know what they are, but I hope they're satisfactory concerning woman's rights and woman's equality, concerning political grounds of peace, treaties, and so on. I think Marcia and her Socialist ideas are not so bad concerning that."

"Do you think there is much of a potential following in Israel for this movement?"

"It's a new one. I don't know if there's much or not, because the Israeli parties are rooted. They're much older than this movement. They have enlisted women in all the parties. No party is without women, but on a very small scale, I'm sorry to say. There are very few women in the top posts in all the parties, even in Israel, where we're modern and we have some equal rights, but not all equal rights. I don't know if, for the Israeli woman, the best way is to be integrated into the general parties or a concentrated all-women movement where all women's matters can be really discussed, on the welfare of women."

"Does the Citizens Rights Party fill the need as well as a separate Women's Party?"

"Citizens Rights. That's Shulamit Aloni. She didn't put herself only for women. She's for civil rights. It's good. It's general. But I follow the women's movement, the one that Marcia started, as an Arab woman, because everyone sees the points with his own glasses." (Since our conversation took place, the Women's Party received 5,674 votes in the 1977 elections, not enough to put one member in the Knesset, each seat needing 18,000 votes. The Citizens Rights Party got 20,621 votes, just enough to keep Shulamit Aloni in the Knesset, but losing two additional seats from the last Knesset. There were something like thirty-four parties running, which is more or less usual for Israel.)

Violet went over to the sideboard again and came back with some hard candies, complaining good-humoredly, "I always have some chocolates, but my sons find it and it disappears!" Then she went to the kitchen, returning with the traditional sweet Turkish coffee in tiny cups, the standard accompaniment of Arab hospitality. Both the driver, still our interested listener, and I thanked her.

"What do you think are the major points," I asked, resuming

the subject, "that require a Women's Party and pressure from women?"

Becoming very serious, she said in a modulated voice, "There's a very great difference between the standard, the quality of freedom that the Jewish Israeli woman has achieved, and the Arab Israeli woman. There's a great gap. That's why I tell you I see with my own glasses. That's why I feel this movement is really very necessary in point of view of my community, my viewing the need of such a movement for women's rights. If I were a Jewish woman, I don't think I would have really chosen a separate way. I don't know.

"But I know that all women—Israeli, European, American, English—whatever they have reached, they have only reached stages of equality, never real equality. Maybe I can give the explanation that men would like to give: that God made the separation, or God intended that, or it's better that way, or it's healthier that way. Maybe there's something in that, but I don't think any woman has reached real, real equality. She is some way on the ladder. The Arab woman still has much to go. The Jewish Israeli woman has gone gaps in front of the Arab Israeli woman."

"She had a head start."

"Yes. She had more possibilities, according to tradition, Europeanization. I think the Women's Party may be able to help that problem. But I have never joined a party. I never felt that I can be a real member in a political Zionist party. I never felt that's my home. I'm a person who's used to doing the things that I completely believe in. I can agree with some things of the present coalition, but not all. I'd like to go for the Knesset. I'd like to be an Arab voice in the Knesset. But because I'm not a political party member I may miss this career."

"Do you think you may affiliate with some party in the future and then run for the Knesset?"

"I wish we could have a Socialist party where Arabs and Jews have real cooperation, real needs, real points of view. But I can't understand a stepmother. I can't take a stepfather. An Arab going into Mapai or Mapam or any other Zionist party is like going into step-something."

"It doesn't really belong to you, even though it's Socialist?"

"It doesn't really belong to me. I would very much appreciate academics starting a Socialist Israeli party where Arabs and Jews really have equal membership and work for the good of the whole State, for real peace."

"Perhaps you'll have to start that party."

"If I would have the means. I'm not a woman who has the financial means. I don't have enough time. I have to work six days a week to make a decent living for my children." (Since our meeting I have learned that in the recent elections Violet Khoury promised her support to Mapam, the left-wing Socialist party. She announced, "As a mother, I appeal to all mothers in Israel and all lovers of peace, Arabs and Jews alike, to support Mapam for the realization of all our goals.")

"Your husband is working, too?" I asked her.

"My husband is now running the dress shop while I am teaching. But he will soon be sixty-five, and he has to go on pension. And the children are studying, so there's nobody to run the shop. We want to sell it, and nowadays it's not easy to sell shops because people don't know really what is the future of the pound. And with everything that's going on, it's difficult to find a buyer."

"What do you think of the position of the Arab in Israel?"

"Half-truths are always no truths. If I want to explain things to you and to show you the good points only, I'm a liar. And if I want to tell you it's all black, I'm also a liar. As any other state, there's nothing very good nor very bad. It's always taken into percentage.

"History plays its part. You can't say of the Israeli Arabs today they're better than they were in 1948, their condition of life. It's not true, and it's not fair. I think the Mandatory regime, and before it, the Ottoman regime, have only done what they could take away from the Middle East, whether it was from Jews or Arabs. For instance, Arab villages were left in a zero position."

"Which is true of any colonization."

"Exactly. We didn't have schools, we didn't have roads, no electricity, no running water in our homes. We were just left with nothing. We had nothing to be proud of under the Mandatory regime.

"Then the State of Israel, in 1948, had to cope with many, many major problems, beginning with defense, warring with the Arab states, *aliyah,* the immigrants, broken families from both sides, economic conditions, farming, housing, whatever. I don't think any state has had the metamorphosis which Israel has gone through.

"One thing I'm proud of, being an Israeli, are the social laws that the State has legislated. Of this I'm proud. I'm not proud of any contrast made between the Arabs here and the Arabs in the Arab states. Or that now there is a better standard of living. Of this I'm not proud. Because I won't accept it."

"You don't think it's true?"

"It's a half-truth."

"What are the social laws that you're pleased about?"

"Beginning with the compulsory education law, to the law of equality, to the law that protects women's rights, equality in elections, economic equality, the law of social insurance, health insurance, the laws concerning women, especially. For instance, the Moslem woman was always under so much stress, fear for her mere living, for her mere bread, because the man could marry as many wives as he wanted. He could divorce her the minute he wanted to.

"Then came the law of the State, which said, 'No, you can't marry more than one, and you can't divorce her the way you want.' So the woman had a real basis of protection. Of this I'm proud, and I've always been proud. You can't really make any contrast between the condition we are in after those laws and what we had before. We had nothing. Arab women had nothing.

"The religious laws, Christian, Moslem, and Jewish, give more rights to the man, all of them. So the men took advantage of this, especially the Arab man. Bedouin life, nomadic life, *hamula* life gave him the strength."

"What is *hamula?*"

"*Hamula* is the clan, many small families grouping into one big clan with one top man who is the sheikh, or the head of the clan. So he had all the power to have his own kingdom. That's something way back in history. That's why I said everything has its own length. It's way back in history, but its historical fingerprints are on us today. We still suffer traditions. We still suffer the kingdom of the man. We still suffer the inequality, the unfairness—all of that. If it were not for the social laws of the State, I don't think the Arab woman could have had the status she has today."

"I hope you make it to the Knesset," I told her, impressed with her oratorical delineation of the problems. "They'll have to listen to you!"

"The men are listening to me now. I told you that during my first election campaign, the men who voted for me were ridiculed, derised, as though they did something out of common sense. After such a process, after proving that a woman could do something, things changed. But if I were weak enough to be broken, it would have been a tragedy, not only for me but for other Arab women as well. Everybody would say, 'Look, she tried, look what happened to her.'"

"What do you expect of a woman?"

"What do you expect of a woman! And so I go back to the contrast between the standard of living of today and of 1948. It's unfair to say that the Israeli Arabs have come up the ladder. They've been modernized; economically, they're better off. They've been given a better standard of living, it's true. But I think it's true of conditions in the whole world. Most people, most countries, in the last twenty to thirty years have had more or less a better standard of living, ways of communication, radio, television, more education, more social responsibility, the UN, and so on. I go back to the social laws. I really put them as the pillars of the Israeli State, or the community as a whole. This has helped very much to better the standard of living.

"I have to be frank enough and truthful enough to say that if I want to make the contrast between the Israeli Arab and the Israeli Jew, here I say I can't be proud. There's a great gap. As I told you, I know very well that the State faces first-class, top responsibilities. But today, after thirty years, I can't accept any excuse.

"If it's defense, it has to be on me and on Ruth. If it's immigrants, it has to be on me and her. Whatever responsibilities there are on the State, I have also to take part, to share in the development, in the bettering of conditions, in the welfare of the State, Jews and Arabs alike. I won't accept any gaps."

"You are all Israeli citizens."

"Exactly. Now, take a village like Kfar Yassif, which is a very, very old village. They say it was called Yassif after the name of Josephus Flavius. Whether he was after the time of Christ or before, I'm not sure. Maybe two thousand, three thousand years . . .'"

(Evidently Violet's recall on historical dates about matches mine. To keep the record straight, the encyclopedia states that Josephus Flavius, Jewish historian and soldier, lived from A.D. 37 to about 100.)

"That's enough."

"It's enough!" Violet laughed heartily again. "Only until about a hundred years ago, the last Jewish families were living here. Nobody sent them out. But they wanted to be in the cities. During the Ottoman Empire and the English Mandate, villages had nothing to live on. Even many Arabs went to big towns for their upkeep. We still have, until today, the old Jewish cemetery in Kfar Yassif, and we know that in some part of the village there was a synagogue. It is now in ruins. Nobody wants to buy this piece of land because people still hear from fathers and grandfathers that it had been a holy place where nobody can build on it and live on it because it's sacred, holy. There are still some olive trees on the property.

"An old village like this—we got electricity only eight years ago; water we got ten years ago. We paved our roads only two or three years ago. We still have merely fifteen schoolrooms in rented, very bad housing conditions around in the village. We're building schools, but because we don't have the financial ability, and because the government has to give loans and grants, which the government doesn't give on the same scale as the Jewish sector, that's why we don't have kindergartens, no gardens, no playgrounds where the children can play, not enough schoolrooms, no library, no community hall.

"When I was the mayor, by force I brought in a prefab building. We put it up near the local council, and this is the youth club. It's run now beautifully by the youth. They have many, many activities. There's no entertainment at all for our youngsters except for this very nice club. But it's a room smaller than this room, where all the youngsters of Kfar Yassif have to find activities. It is not adequate.

"Local councils have two sources of income: local taxes and government grants and loans. An Arab village gets twenty pounds, about two dollars, per person per year, whereas a Jewish moshav or settlement gets a hundred and twenty to a hundred and fifty pounds per person per year." (With increased inflation since Violet gave me these and subsequent figures, the amount of pounds for dollars must be almost doubled.)

"How is this going to be corrected?"

"I don't know. It is always being discussed and written about, and there are conferences and meetings. We tell them, 'Look, for thirty years we've understood very well—*bitachon*, security first, immigrants second. Today we won't understand that. *Bitachon*, security, immigrants, welfare of the State, duty of the citizen—has to be shared by all citizens, for the benefit of all citizens.'

"I'll tell you one thing. We, the people who were born during the Mandate, we faced two very important ways of regimes. I haven't seen the Turkish regime, but I heard about it from my father. It was terrible. But I faced the Mandate regime and I faced the democratic self-regime. If you have somebody from outside, you know him. He's an outsider. Whatever he did for you, you can bear it. But if he's your own self, he's your own family, your own child, he has to be as good to you as you are to him. You can't accept anything else.

"They can't tell me, 'During the Mandate you were nothing! We gave you something, so it's good.' No. I was nothing during the Mandate. I have something now. But you are the better thing. I want to be as better as you."

"Not more equal or less equal, but equal."

"Exactly. Not more. Not less. There's a very absurd reason for which they say your children don't go to the army. Ruth's children go to the army. Maybe they're killed on the battlefield. My sons don't go to the army. I haven't made this law. Arab men are prevented from compulsory army service. They can go as volunteer soldiers. My son doesn't accept being a volunteer soldier. He goes either as an equal citizen, with equal rights of being an officer or a top general, or nothing. He won't accept going with a Jew, he being his officer because he's a Jew.

"Secondly, the Jew doesn't trust him because how could he trust a person fighting his cousin? That's his cousin on the border. How could he believe that he could fight his cousin? It's a unique state of Israeli Arabs. That's the conflict. It's very hard for both, I know, State and Arabs. But it's harder for the Arabs to tolerate such a condition of affairs. It has to be the State's concern, how to solve such a conflict.

"I know that my State is warring against my people. I know whoever is killed on the border hurts me twice as much as the Jewish woman or the Arab woman on the other side. Because he may be my cousin, or he may be the son of my best friend, whom I work with, live with, I eat with. So whenever I hear of any bombing, whatever names come, if it's an Arab or Jew, it hurts. I can't do anything about it.

"Children who are born in Israel are facing a conflict which is much harder. They don't want to hear about security, about immigration. They say, 'There's only one thing we want. Either we are Israeli citizens, with the same rights, the same responsibilities, or we can't tolerate it. What are we?' You can't translate to them anything else.

"They didn't know any other regime. They don't want to understand that there are some excuses under certain times and certain conditions. They don't want to understand it. They say, 'We are Israelis. It's a democratic State. We want our rights. Why should we suffer because of security reasons? Why should the Jew have more privileges?' "

"Why are the Druze treated differently?" I asked.

"Because the Druze said they were not Arabs. They said they were a special community, which, historically, is wrong. It's only a play of words. Their culture, their language, their history, whatever, they're a sect of Moslems and they are only Arabs. They say their religion is secret. But they chose that they are not Arabs. O.K. The State made service compulsory for them. The Druze go for compulsory service. The Christian and Moslem Arabs don't.

"So I can't, like other people, say, 'Well, in thirty years we have really gone up the ladder.' There is something in that. But on the other hand, it's not enough."

"What do you think is the solution? Is there anything short of peace?"

"After thirty years of co-living, I'm sure the best medicine for this is real peace. Nothing else will change it. Because they are right and we are right. The Jews are right, and the Arabs are right."

"I sympathize with your position. The problem has bothered me for thirty years, too. . . . Tell me something about the attitudes of the young Arab women—how they differ from their mothers concerning modern ways, and the position of women in their communities."

"I think the Jewish woman, even less than a hundred years ago, had the same problems. She wasn't treated well. She wasn't free to marry. She wasn't free to decide. So people are modernizing in some way or other, some rapidly, some more slowly. I think the Arab community goes slower than other communities for the simple reason that it is a traditionally strict community, especially the Moslem part."

"Are some still wearing the veil?"

"No. Nobody. That's finished, even in the Arab states, as much as I know. Many girls are going to university. A larger number are now going to secondary schools. All girls go to elementary schools. And that's why I am proud of the social laws of the State: compulsory education, nine classes. In some cities it's ten classes, without payment. The government covers it. Free education."

"What class do you teach?"

"Seven, eight, and nine, in Acre at the Terra Sancta School, a Christian school. But it has more Moslems than Christians because we get students from all over the Galilee. I teach three days there and three days at the Druze secondary school in Acre. It's a completely Druze school. So I have only Saturday as my free day, which is not really a free day. It's the hardest day because I have to make up all the work of the whole week at home—washing, ironing, cleaning."

"Nobody helps you? Your boys?"

"Whenever I have visitors, the children give a little bit of a hand."

"Your husband?"

"No, no, no! My husband is the king—very European, as I told you. His coffee has to come to his bed. I have to look after his needs. If a shirt isn't ironed. . . . He hates the time that women will have equality. He still is the sultan."

"And you go along with that?"

"I can cope with it." She chuckled. "When I was mayor, I really was on my guard because I didn't want any man to say, 'Well, for this she made you the woman.' And I had to work so hard. I had to look after my house. I had to look after his needs and to let everything go together because I was afraid of the strong tide of the community."

"He has to have coffee brought to his bed?" I asked incredulously.

"Exactly. In the morning and whenever he has friends. I get up very early. I prepare the coffee. I go to school while they're still in bed. I take my sandwich. I leave home at quarter past seven because I have to travel to Acre. I come back at two, half-past two."

"Do you have a car?"

"No. I get there by transportation, by bus. I prepare my food at night for the next day. I have my sister-in-law. She's an old woman. The house is always open. I have to help her, instead of her helping me. I have to bring her meals to bed. I have to bring her tea to bed."

"My goodness! I would have thought you had changed all that by now."

"No. I can't. Even the children. When I say, 'Look, you have to help me,' the youngest boy says, 'Why didn't you have a girl?' I say, 'If I had a girl, I wouldn't let her work more than you do. You would have had to help each other. But she wouldn't have been your slave.' No. That's the community. When sometimes I really beg them to help me sweep the floor, they do it. But then if a friend comes, I can feel that the other boy looks at them as if to ask, Why are you doing girl's work? So whenever the boys' friends come to see my boys, I feel I have to invite them to share in some way. I say to them, 'Will you come and do some sweeping of the floor? It's so nice. It's a sport.' They're a bit shy, but they start helping. So they're equal. They just can't keep on degrading me for what I ask my boys to do. I really make them feel it's a sport, that it's something nice to do, and in this way I make my sons feel that it's not degrading, that they can be proud about it." Pleased laughter accompanied Violet's telling of this achievement.

"That's a real accomplishment. I don't know many mothers who have worked it that well. How about the young Arab marriages? Are the young men sharing any of the home responsibility, or responsibility for the babies?"

"Yes, I think times are changing for the better because the newly married couples are both working, in most cases. Both have studied in the universities or secondary schools. They've seen modern life. They're starting on their own. The good thing now is that youngsters are tending to live alone, not with the family.

"In the past, the parents used to build a room onto or near their own house so the boy would bring his wife and all the family would stay in the kingdom of the father and the mother. Now, no. Youngsters tend to have their own apartments somewhere in the village or in the city. But not together in the same house as the parents."

"Do many of them stay in your village?"

"Most of them stay, in their separate houses, which is a very healthy start, I think. They feel responsibility. They divide the work according to the ability of both husband and wife. She goes to work. He goes to work. He's not shy about giving her a hand. He knows it's his own kingdom now, together with his wife."

"So his attitude differs considerably from his father's."

"Yes, exactly. And the parents understand this way of changing things because they know, with both of them working, they both have to help in the house. She doesn't keep house, teach, and have children all on her own, like my generation. But when she has a girl and the girl can help, then the father doesn't do so much."

"There's no child-care facility in your village?"

"We have a *tipat chalav,* mother and child center, with a nurse, and the doctor comes on a certain day. I think our women are very clever at being mothers. It's hereditary. They learn it in their own homes. You know, the Arab family is a family which likes children, and they have four, five, six, sometimes fifteen!"

"Do the young couples practice birth control?"

"Yes, most of them."

"They get that education?"

"They get it from the women's centers or from their own doctors. There's a center in Acre. The government opened it some two years ago. They give medical guidance and help to all women, from all the entire district, free of charge, which is really a good thing. And then we have Kupat Cholim, the Histadrut government labor-union health service, where we have our nurses, doctors, and where women can get free guidance, free tablets, and so on."

"You have no place where a mother can leave her child and go to work?"

"No." Violet heaved a sigh. "That's something that I really tried very hard to achieve ever since I was on the local council, since I was mayor. I started a women's club connected with the WIZO. I wanted them to help us open a *ma'on,* a place where the working mothers could leave their babies until they come back. First of all, we didn't find a place. I couldn't afford the budget. I couldn't take the responsibility of making it self-service, with the women paying, because I thought that no woman goes out to work except out of financial need. If she has a baby, she won't leave him if she doesn't need the income."

"If she has a profession that she wants to pursue as the baby gets a little older, will she do that?"

"She will, but most of the women just take their three months' birth leave and then go back to work because of the high cost of living. I don't think that they can afford to have just one person in the family working, especially when they get married, build their house, and all that on installments. They get loans, so both of them have to work hard to pay back and to live.

"She gets pregnant and has her first child, one or one and a half years after marriage. She can't leave her work. They still have large debts. So she has to find a place for her baby. What happens? Years back the granny or the aunt used to care for the babies, especially when they used to live together. The woman went to work. The old mother at home looked after the baby. Since the young couples don't want to live under the control of the parents, they choose, and rightly so, to live alone. So now granny says, 'O.K., I've done my job. Now I want to have my own life. Why should I go on bringing up babies?' And she's right, too. She has to live her own life."

"She doesn't want to be a baby-sitter."

"Exactly. And it's only right. After bringing up fifteen of her own, with all the terrible conditions she suffered, we owe her something—to sit two or three years without doing much. So it's really a problem that we don't have a day nursery. We can't afford that, the government doesn't help, the local council has no resources, and the mothers can't afford it.

"I made a budget three years ago. It had to be nearly five hundred pounds, about fifty dollars, for each baby per month. Five hundred pounds today isn't much, but if I would want to start such a place today, I think it would cost us a thousand a month for every baby if we would want to make it on a modern, healthy basis."

"What do you think of the new abortion law that's been passed recently?"

"I think it's not so good, as far as I understand, because they made all kinds of restrictions. A woman can't get an abortion without going before a committee of three doctors, and so on. Why should she? I believe the woman has the right, if she wants to have an abortion, to have an abortion. Nobody is having the pregnancy but her. Why should a man decide for her?

"I'm not satisfied. I want a state of affairs in which the woman herself can decide for her own body. It's true her husband is sharing, but what trouble does he have? She's the person who suffers. He gets only the luxury, the glory of being a father, of having a good time. If she wants to get rid of it, if she wants to have an abortion, she has to decide alone."

"Do you have any particular thoughts you would want to express to American women?"

"Yes, very much. I helped start a movement which we call the Bridge for Peace, with Jewish women here in Israel. Maybe if I would give you the idea of getting this into the heads of the American women, to try to make an International United Women for Peace, that throughout the world we could unite to forbid wars. Because, after all, we are the people who suffer. We lose our men, our children. We are the people who really bring life. So we are responsible for it. I think if women were united in this way, they could stop wars. We still have the Shalom movement."

"Is that the Bridge for Peace?"

"Yes. I don't know if you've heard about Ruth Lys. She's a Jewish woman; her son was killed in the Yom Kippur War. She wrote to Jehan Sadat, the wife of Egypt's president, beginning a now-famous correspondence with her. She got an answer in which Jehan said she's also interested in peace. After some meetings, I suggested that we write to a country where both Arab and Jewish women can meet in an international conference.

"But I had an operation. I went into the hospital last year. So I couldn't go on. I don't know what happened afterwards. But I think it has to be stronger than Israeli and Arab women. Arab and Israeli women need it very badly, but I don't know how much we can do because in the Middle East it's too much the man. It's not like Europe and America."

"Have you been able to travel abroad?"

"Yes. I have visited a doctor uncle in Oklahoma City some time ago. I saw that there the woman is really much more equal with the man. Now, with Mr. Carter new in office, I, as a woman, as a mother, really have something to say to him. I don't know if all those deadly weapons are the answer to the needs of humanity. Much more is the cooperation between women needed.

"Instead of fighter airplanes, refugees could be settled. If we make accounts, the Palestinians, if in those thirty years of bombing and killing, if they were given a very small part of all this expenditure, I don't think there would have been so much bloodshed. I know many Israeli politicians don't agree with me. They think it's a political question and not an economic one.

"I think economics and politics go together. There's no policy without economy, and there's no economy without policy. So what I want Mr. Carter to set as his goal is more peace, less airplanes, less deadly weapons. I think he's the person to be the real negotiator between the Arabs and Israelis, to bring them to peace, to bring them, not to let them play about peace. But to bring them to peace."

"He can try to bring them, but the Israelis and Arabs have to sit down together to make their own peace."

"Exactly. When he doesn't give weapons to both sides, they will sit. So don't let him give weapons to both sides."

"I'll tell him."

"And not Russia. I don't accept that Russia gives weapons to the Arabs and that Israel doesn't get from them. I don't want any weapons in the Middle East. I want them to have one single weapon. They have to sit for peace. Nothing more and nothing less."

Violet Khoury's peace formula came to pass. Will Sadat's going to Jerusalem and Carter's efforts at and since Camp David truly bring that peace she longs for?

7 Dream into Nightmare

THE WONDER AND JOY of sitting at home and watching the Olympic Games by satellite were unimaginably shattered by a terrorist action so brutal and murderous that, of the 1972 Olympic Games in Munich, no other memory remains. For Esther Schahamorov Roth, a member of the Israeli team, the shock and horror of the slaying of twelve teammates, plus a deep personal loss, is something that will never leave her.

"At Munich I lost the man who at that time was the most important to me, Amitzur Shapira. He was a teacher at Wingate. He was my coach. He was like a father to me."

I had gone to meet Esther at the Wingate Sports Institute, on the Mediterranean near Natanya, about fifteen miles north of Tel Aviv on the main road to Haifa. Walking up the incline from the road where the bus from Tel Aviv stopped, I was surprised to find extensive lawns and gardens, dotted with modern buildings and sports areas of all kinds.

The institute, named after Major General Orde Wingate of the British army, was established in 1957. During the Mandate, Wingate, a quick-tempered, Old Testament–quoting maverick, displayed open sympathy with the Jewish community and, on his own, organized and trained the first strike forces of the Haganah, the self-defense organization of the Jewish population. For these actions he was removed from his post. He died in a plane crash in India during World War II. Wingate is deeply remembered in many ways, the institute being one of them.

Its sixty-five acres contain a Physical Education Teachers College, a School of Physiotherapy, a School for Coaches, and the

Army Physical Training School. It also boasts a research department, a Center for Sports Medicine, a Department of Instructional Media, a library, and a Training Center for National Teams. Having been enlarged over the years, it has three gymnasiums, a stadium, an Olympic-sized pool, and various courts and fields for other sports.

Seeing a sign RECEPTION, I entered the building and asked a young woman in one of several offices where I could find Esther. "She's waiting for you at the hotel," she said in good English. "I'll take you there."

So Shoshana from San Diego led me up the continuously sloping terrain, saying in answer to my usual query, "My husband and I came to Israel eight years ago. He's a psychologist and works in a mental institution. At first, things were so tough I was ready for the institution myself! But everything straightened out and is fine now. We have two children, two and four."

She left me at a rather large modern building, a few stories high, which, she explained, is a hotel for visiting athletes and Israeli athletes in training. In the lobby, a handsome, olive-skinned young woman with long black hair parted in the middle came over to me with her three-year-old son, Yaron, in tow. A beautiful smile exposed perfect white teeth as she said, *"Shalom.* I'm Esther. You are Mrs. Stern?"

There was no doubt she was an athlete. Though not in running shorts, her yellow flared corduroy pants and burgundy ribbed sweater revealed a tight, beautiful body with slim hips and narrow build. "The translator was here," she said in hesitant English, "but she had to leave. I don't speak English. All I learned in school was some Shakespeare!"

"Could Shoshana help us?" I tried to maintain an attitude of confident expectancy in the face of this major obstacle.

"I'll see." She left with her boy, to return not with Shoshana, who was busy, but with Dikla Yarkon, a bright, sandy-haired twenty-one-year-old kibbutznik from Revivim, near Beersheba.

"I'm just a student here. I am not a champion in any sport. I just want to teach different kinds of sports," she said. Her English was surprisingly fluent. I'm a sabra; my parents are sabras. Their parents came from Poland."

"You're very nice to help us. How do you know English so well?"

"I spent some months in the United States, and I have an American boyfriend."

"That's the best way in the world to learn a language," I told her as the three of us walked down the hall to an empty classroom, where we installed ourselves, Esther having left her child with the hotel receptionist.

"Munich is the one subject that I really try not to talk about," Esther began. "I know it interests all the journalists who talk to me. But this is for a book, so it's different. Maybe it should be printed." She spoke in an animated, energetic way. "It was really such a big shock, and this is why I don't like to talk about it that much.

"At the last Olympics, in Montreal, everybody was talking about Munich, everybody was asking me about it. It really contradicts my feelings to talk about it, after losing a man who was so important to me. The shock was so great that I don't like to make it a routine, because it becomes a routine when you constantly talk about something, even though it was a great loss."

"I don't want to press you," I said.

"I want to tell you, and I will tell you. The first thing, I was expecting a great deal out of Munich because I didn't participate in the Mexican Olympics, and I was training and training and I got to Munich because of the records I got. So I really was expecting to win. This is the dream of every athlete, to get to the Olympics. It was all like a dream for me to be there because I was very young and the atmosphere at the Olympics is incredible. You meet people of all colors and all nations, which is different from a European competition. You meet just everybody, and I was walking there like in a dream. I'm telling you all this because this was such a dream and then it turned into a nightmare, all of a sudden. The contradiction is so great.

"I slept in a room with another girl, a swimmer from Israel, Shlomit Nir. The rooms of the men and women are separated at the Olympics. This is why I wasn't where the disaster took place. I was about five hundred meters away from there. I was participating in a one-hundred-meter sprint, just to get the feeling of the Olympics, not to get any record. Just because I was very inexperienced in Olympic Games.

"In this sprint I almost reached the finals, although I didn't expect to. I just expected to run once and get out. I almost got into the finals, but another woman who had—" She and Dikla started to giggle. Then they let me in on the joke. "The other woman and I had the same results. But the photo finish showed that her breasts were forward more than mine. She was probably leaning more, or had a bigger chest, and this is how she got ahead of me. But for me this wasn't the main thing. I was there for the hurdles. I just did it to get the feeling of it.

"This was really a surprise. In that running I broke some Israeli records, and it was like amateur running because I hadn't meant to run for the medal. After that, we had a day of rest and then we started training for the hurdles. I only ran once for the hurdles, and I went up to the second stage. This was something that nobody expected me to do, so it was the greatest joy. And for Amitzur, my coach, he said it was the happiest day in his life because he really didn't expect it. He was very worried and didn't sleep the whole night. And then I went up another stage. But this was the day before the massacre.

"The reason they didn't expect me to go to the other stage was because the people I was running with the first time were the girls who were expected to take the first places, the strongest girls of all the runners. When I passed to the upper stage, Amitzur was so happy he said to me, 'Esther, this is the happiest day of my life,' because before that he was really very unsure, he didn't know whether I could do it. He said, 'You made me the happiest person in the world.'

"The night of the massacre they organized the show *Fiddler on the Roof* for us in Munich. Amitzur, as a personality, was a man who was devoted to sports. Sports was the most important thing in his life. This was the first time that somebody really made him proud, when I passed to the other stage. That night we went to watch the show, and he was very happy. He translated the show for me because he spoke Yiddish. After the show we went up to talk to the main actor, who was Shmuel Rodensky. We drank *'L'chaim,'* 'Cheers,' and when we said good night, we separated after that. It was a very pleasant evening. That's when we said good night, and after that . . ."

Esther leaned forward in the chair, her arms on her knees, her hands clasped, and continued intently. "We were going to meet each other in the morning, near the dining room. But in the morning Shlomit Nir came in and screamed that something happened to the Israelis. When she came knocking on the door, at first I was upset because I was supposed to run that same morning and I wanted to continue sleeping. But when she said that, I realized that something must have happened. She wouldn't just come banging on the door like that.

"Then I had strange thoughts. I thought to myself, 'What could happen? It's just an Olympic Game.' But then someone said somebody got killed, and there was shooting. But we really didn't know. Then the guards of the building—each building had guards —they came and took us to a room. But we only felt something had happened. We really didn't know. We knew as much as the people in Israel knew because we didn't see anything. It was just being in all this mess.

"A few Israeli sportsmen succeeded in running away. What was most upsetting to us was that we didn't know what was happening. We were terrified. We knew our people were getting killed there. But for the rest of the sportsmen from other countries, for them it was like some big event, something out of the ordinary. They started taking pictures. It was like something interesting was happening, like a show.

"It was a terrible moment to be in a room, especially when we started noticing who wasn't there yet. We knew two people got killed. We all knew each other. Of course athletes know each other. But we didn't know who the two people were who got killed. We just were sitting there guessing, not knowing anything."

Since our translator, Dikla, was hearing this account from Esther for the first time, she was having noticeable difficulty in interpreting the monstrous happening for me while focusing on the nightmare that Esther was reviewing. They both kept going, possibly from fear of breaking down if they stopped.

"They put us in a room, brought us training suits and a hell of a lot of food, and we didn't know what to do so we started eating. It was all guessing. We just knew two men got killed so far. But when we heard the first name of the men who got killed, this is when I couldn't help myself anymore and I started crying. Even two men getting killed is already a tragedy, but you don't realize it until they say a name. You never believe that it's really happening until they say, 'That's it. This man got killed.'

"That night, I just didn't know what to do. We were watching television. We knew fighting was going on inside. Sometimes they said they released the men. Sometimes they said they didn't. They wanted me to run that day to prove that even if two people got killed, Israel will still not give up and Israel is going to participate.

"So there was the possibility, with everything finished and only two men killed, I would run. This was the decision, although I knew I couldn't do it because I was already broken mentally. The doctor gave me two sleeping pills, so I slept all that night and I didn't know what was happening. This is the night when they killed everybody else.

"Before I went to sleep, they announced on television that they were released, that they ran away, so I went to sleep feeling that everything was going to be O.K., except, of course, for the two people that we already knew were killed. In the morning, while I was still sleeping, everybody in the delegation already knew about it. They didn't want to wake me, but when they came into the room and started standing near the bed, I just knew it.

"This is a moment that is very hard for me to describe." She put her hands to her eyes and tightened her lips. "I can't describe the feeling of coming. . . . Of course we didn't run. . . . We just left. We came on the plane with all the bodies of the people who were murdered. We brought our sportsmen friends home with us.

"They continued the Olympics, and where I was supposed to run, the track was empty. They didn't put anybody there. They read my name. There was an empty place. Everybody knew, of course." Esther took a deep breath and was relieved to have finished.

"I can understand," I told her, "how very difficult it is for you to talk about this. It is most difficult for me and Dikla to hear about it."

She smiled and said, "The dream, of course, is to get to the finals, the dream of small Israel. It's not so much for the gold medal. But in Asia, I got three gold medals, three months after I had a baby. The first thing I felt like doing after the massacre in Munich was quitting completely because it was such a big dream for me before, and all of a sudden I felt there was no value in it. If this is what happens at the Olympics, massacre and murder, it meant nothing to me. I just wanted to leave it and forget about sports.

"The second thought I had while I was sitting at home—I had a boyfriend, Peter, who is now my husband and my coach, and he was helping me a lot—I started thinking: In Israel we have many wars, but in a war you expect death, and you don't expect death at the Olympics. That's why it was such a great shock. You don't expect the team to come back in coffins. Then I started thinking: If I quit sports, what am I gaining? That's what the terrorists want. They want us to stop, and they want to disrupt life here. So then I decided to continue. The main thing is to continue for the memory of all the people who got killed there.

"In Montreal, at the '76 Olympics, I felt that I was the only one who kept the memory of these people who cannot talk. I was the only Israeli who was at Munich who continued training for the Olympics. I am the only one who can talk for them, by keeping on doing the sports—especially for Amitzur, whose entire life was dedicated to sports. Now we have new ones going into the Olympics, but none of the people who participated at Munich. Some dropped out. Others didn't qualify.

"For Montreal I only had two years to train, while others had four years, because in two years I got married, I became pregnant and had a baby. I had a Caesarean, and although I had that, I decided I was going to go back to the same fitness I had before, in three months. This was like a world record"—she laughed—"and I did it."

"That's an achievement! What are your measurements?"

"I am one meter, sixty-five centimeters [five feet, four inches]. My weight is fifty-four kilograms [one hundred nineteen pounds]. As I said before, I was more in the center of what was going on because of Munich. My main purpose was to fulfill what I couldn't do there. At Munich I only ran once and got to another stage. In Montreal I got to the finals, and I won sixth place in the hurdles. The thing we were happiest about at Montreal was that we all came back alive and in good condition."

"It took a lot of courage to return to Olympic competition. When did you start competing?"

"In 1970, when I was eighteen. I had my first big competition, in Bangkok, in the Asian championships. I got two gold medals and one silver, which was a very great win for Israel, and for me. It was a national and personal victory. I won the gold medals in the pentathlon and the hurdles, and the silver medal for the distance long jump [running broad jump].

"Before Bangkok, I was unknown. Nobody had heard of me. That was when people started thinking of me as putting money on me or starting to develop me as a runner. I was supposed to go to the Mexico Olympics. I passed the minimum requirement for that. But I strained a muscle in my leg and I couldn't go. Than I started training with Amitzur Shapira for the Munich Olympics.

"A year before the big Olympics there's the small Olympics, which took place in Munich also. It was like getting prepared for the big Olympics. I participated in this and took third place in the pentathlon. But for Munich itself I only trained for the hurdles and the hundred-meter sprint. As part of the training, we used to go to different places in Europe. If there was a girl who was the best in the world in hurdles, I used to go places with her and compete so that I could train."

"Did you encounter any problems from Israel's political situation?"

"The first time I confronted the political situation was at one of the competitions in Sweden. There was an Arab who was second-best in the world, and he said he wouldn't compete if I was there. Although I was unknown at that time and he was very famous and very good, the organizers said, If he doesn't want to compete he can withdraw. At the last moment he called his embassy and then said he would compete. He was a long-distance runner, and they let him go ahead because he wasn't in the same event that I was.

"In Greece I also came across the Arab relationship with Israel when some Egyptian girls came into the competition. This was very rare because their girls are usually not participating in a lot of sports. It's not as developed as it is in Israel for women. When the girls came from Egypt, they said they will not participate in the competition if the Israeli girls participate.

"We Israeli girls just wrote our names down for the different events, and the Egyptians dropped out. There were two other Israelis with me. They were training for eight hundred meters.

"One thing about training before the Olympics, I didn't have much competition because in Israel I was the only one who was doing it on the Olympic level and I didn't go abroad much compared to girls from other countries. For example, a girl from abroad would participate in twenty-eight international competitions. I would participate in five."

"Why was that?"

"Because Israel is farther away from Europe than most other countries and it's very expensive. Israel doesn't have that much money for sending us abroad. The reasons are technical and financial. Those were the reasons before Munich, but now there are other ones, political ones. Now Israel has to push itself into competitions.

"People really don't like Israel to be in competitions because they have to supply a lot of security and guard the athletes. I am passing the minimum level for all the competitions that are taking place in Europe. It's just that you really have to push your way into it.

"I feel that foreign countries want me for the results, for the competition itself, but then I feel unwanted when it comes to providing security. Right now I feel they would rather give up the whole sprint than invite me into it, although it could do their athletes a lot of good because it's more competition and they can advance better."

"You were born in Israel, weren't you? And your parents?"

"Yes. I was born in Tel Aviv in 1952. I'm twenty-five. My parents came from Bukhara, in Russia, forty years ago. My mother works in a clothing shop, and my father works for the municipality. He used to make shoes for boxers and wrestlers. We are four children in the family. Three are married, and one just finished the army."

"Did you serve in the army?"

"No. I didn't go to the army because I studied in the Wingate Institute for three years and after that I got married and had a child, so I didn't go into the army. I was exempt. My older brother used to be a wrestler, and he also taught wrestling. But then he quit, and now he wants to be a singer.

"My brothers all have a talent for sports, but they left the hard work to me. They didn't keep at it." She laughed. "I started taking athletics seriously at the age of fourteen and a half. Until then I was just very good within the school framework. Then I started training at Hapoel.

"In Israel we have two main clubs or organizations for sports. One is Hapoel and the other, Maccabi. I trained in the Hapoel organization. As a child I didn't know which one to belong to, so

I just went straight to Hapoel. It didn't really matter, and that's where I remained. I was sent to the coach, not the organization. Every sportsman has to belong to an organization."

"It may interest you to know that in America we would say 'sportsperson' if we didn't want to designate sex," I said.

"You mean it's part of women's lib?"

"Yes, that's part of the change since the development of the movement. A woman wouldn't say, 'I was the only sportsman.' She'd say, 'I was the only sportswoman, or sportsperson.'"

Esther was obviously interested in the subject. "I feel that women in America need women's lib because they feel that they're being neglected or they don't have equal rights. As a sportswoman in Israel," she said, picking up the word, "I think the situation is the opposite because men train until the age of eighteen, for example, and then they have to go to the army for three years, which is something that stops their training and disrupts their ability to advance. As a woman, I didn't have to go to the army. We are exempt if we are in physical education. I could go and study physical education and continue training twice a day in order to get better results.

"It really doesn't matter if you're a woman or a man, as a sportsperson." Here our translator had a bit of difficulty in adjusting to the new terminology but smiled triumphantly when she said it. "What's important is the results you're getting. I don't get any better or worse conditions than a man. So I don't feel any discrimination. Maybe in other sports there is a difference. Maybe, for example, in basketball. You never hear about basketball for women. It's never talked about on television, and not much in the newspapers. The reason could be that they're just not as good. They don't get as many good results."

Her son, Yaron, ran into the room to check up on his mother. Esther laughed and hugged him, gave him a pat on the behind, and sent him out again. "Has having a child changed your life very much?" I asked.

"It's a lot harder being a housewife and a mother and a sportswoman. We have an apartment in Herzliyah to take care of, just north of Tel Aviv, and I have a problem, if I'm going abroad, what to do with my child. Who's going to baby-sit? One thing that's good is that my husband is also my coach, so I can go with him. It all depends on the way you organize it."

"The baby goes along sometimes?"

"The baby is the real conflict I have. If I go for a long time, like I went to the States for two months, I take the baby with me because I really hate to leave him, even if it's with his grandparents. Because now he's at the age where he feels it and he misses his mother. I didn't take him with me to Montreal. I left him with my parents. He was two and a half then. Now he's four. He may go with us next time abroad.

"After Munich I had to choose a coach and I didn't know whom to take, and I couldn't really get attached to anybody else because I was so attached to Amitzur. But then it really helped that I found Peter. I can be attached to him as a husband and as a coach. Peter was the one who really pushed me into going back into sports."

"Is he a runner, too?"

"His specialty wasn't athletics. He was in gymnastics. But he gave it up in order to help me get to the same place I was before. He went along all the way with me, and he was also with me in the Montreal Olympics. This is something that is interesting. Because here you have something—maybe you can call it 'families.' Because the man who is supposed to be making a career wasn't following his career. Here he gave up his career in order to push mine, to help mine."

"You're a very lucky woman. I don't imagine many women athletes are that fortunate. Is there a large number of women athletes in Israel? Are they encouraged by the athletic clubs?"

"They are. But they have to be very good. So far, nobody got to a high place. There was one, Chana Shazifi, a runner who also trained after she had a baby. But besides that, nobody else."

"No swimmers? Tennis players?"

"No. We have many girls in sports in Israel, but it's not on the international level."

"Are they encouraged in the high schools?"

"If they're good enough, they are. In the beginning of a career in sports, like in schools and clubs, there's no difference between the boys and the girls. They both get exactly the same treatment. At Wingate now we take little kids for gymnastics, groups of girls and boys who are very gifted, higher than the normal, and we train them. They prefer investing money in the girls because they don't have to go into the army if they are in physical education or special university courses. They will be able to continue and develop more than boys. After all, generally, women in Israel like sports, maybe as much as American women."

"Do many foreign athletes come here to train?"

"We would like very much for other sportswomen and sportsmen to come to Israel. This is the ideal place for training all year round, because of the weather. The climate is very comfortable. Wingate is the main place for people to train, but the main problem is that we don't have a Tartan track. Athletes like to run on Tartan, which is synthetic, and this is what big competitions run on. We usually run on a cinder track.

"Another thing is that there aren't that many people here to compete against. If foreign athletes come, there's not much competition for them. One of the problems is that we don't really belong to Asia. They don't like to accept us Israelis. And also, I personally —my level is more the European level. And as I said before, we have the problem of security when we go to European countries for competitions, and this hurts me as a person who has to compete."

"How about new immigrants? Are there good athletes among them?"

"We have many newcomers, and the purpose is, if they're athletes, to allow them to advance and develop and to help them if they have any absorption problems. There are a few men who are weight lifters and wrestlers. I don't know of many women, but there's one girl from Russia I heard about. She's running eight hundred meters. She's training somewhere in the north."

The thought suddenly occurred to Esther that she had been talking for some time, and she laughed. "I'm not a talker. I'm a runner. But it seems like I have to talk more than I run!"

Her decision after Munich has not changed. A few months after our meeting, I read: "Esther Roth, Israel's Olympic sprinter, collected her second Maccabiah gold medal last night when she won the 200m. in record time in Israel's International Competitions at the Ramat Gan stadium."

8 Madam Justice

I DON'T KNOW what the protocol is in America for interviews with justices of the Supreme Court. I discovered that in Israel the Ministry of Justice controls such interviews, and permission is rarely granted. I came upon this bit of incidental intelligence the day after I arrived in Israel, in March 1977. Miriam Ben-Porat had just been appointed to the Supreme Court, the first such appointment in any country. This was something to celebrate, and of course I wanted to meet her.

Friends took a dim view of my chances, but Bella Diamant, my persistent helper and expediter in the Government Press Office, said, "Why not try?" Six weeks later, a few days before my departure, she called me triumphantly from Tel Aviv to report that permission had been granted and to give me the new justice's home phone number in Jerusalem. There were no secretaries to go through, only her husband, who called her to the phone readily after I'd stated my business.

A gentle-voiced woman, Miriam Ben-Porat was expecting my call and asked me to come to her office in the Supreme Court building, in the Russian Yard near the Russian Church, at 11 A.M., two days later.

"What bus do I take to get there?"

"I'm not sure, but you'll know when you're there. The church bells are ringing most of the time. It is across from the Central Post Office."

"I know where that is. I'm sure I'll find it."

After I had hung up, I was amazed at the question I had asked her. But this sort of informality in high places is fairly typical of Israel. I certainly wouldn't have asked a United States Supreme Court justice what bus to take to his office. I suddenly realized that, after my many visits, I had absorbed certain Israeli mores.

Usually quite profligate with the use of taxis in foreign countries, my husband and I had decided, since we were in Jerusalem for an extended stay in a period of high inflation, to use buses as much as possible. But often, after getting minute directions for the bus, we lapsed into taxis.

The morning of my appointment, the phone rang about nine o'clock. "Here is Ben-Porat. My ten o'clock meeting will last until eleven thirty. I don't want to keep you waiting. Shall we make it another day next week?" I told her I didn't mind waiting if it was convenient for her, but I would be leaving the following week. She agreed to see me at eleven thirty.

I left for my appointment, fully intending to catch a bus in front of our Jaffa Road apartment. It was a Friday, the day before Passover, and Jerusalem was in a frenzy, the population rushing to get things done before the Sabbath. It's a serious complication for religious Jews to have to prepare the Seder meal on the Sabbath, when they can neither ride nor light stoves. In our apartment building there was a special "Sabbath elevator," which was set to stop automatically at every floor so the religious tenants wouldn't have to push a button. When the elevator for heretics wasn't free, the trip to our ninth-floor apartment was rather prolonged.

I stood at the bus stop. After two buses, filled to bursting, had passed, I hailed the first free taxi and got in.

"Where do you want to go?" the driver asked.

"To the Supreme Court."

"I can't take you there. I'm from Tel Aviv. I'll drop you on Jaffa Road."

"You'll take me to the Supreme Court, please."

"No. I'm not from Jerusalem. I don't know Jerusalem."

"I'm not from Jerusalem, either. You shouldn't have stopped for me. Take me to the Central Post Office. Do you know where that is?"

"Yes. Then you'll know where the Supreme Court is?"

"Yes."

When we reached the Central Post Office, the driver mysteriously also knew where the Supreme Court building was—in full view, up an incline across Jaffa Road. He drove into the Russian Compound and even made sure I was at the right entrance. He was directed to the back of the huge ancient stone building, to the offices of the justices.

The compound was built to accommodate nineteenth-century Russian pilgrims to the Holy Land. Today, it is occupied by the Israeli law courts, the Jerusalem police station, and the Russian Orthodox cathedral. Herod's Pillar (surrounded by an iron fence) stands in the compound between the police station and the cathedral. It is thought to have been brought to Jerusalem for inclusion in Herod's Temple. (I gleaned all this from the tourist office's *Guide to Jerusalem,* which concludes with Bus Nos. 2, 3, 5, 6, 7, 15.)

A security guard at the entrance searched my purse and tote bag. In answer to my question: "Miriam Ben-Porat?" I was directed through several long, narrow, high-ceilinged halls, then up two steep flights of ancient and worn stone stairs, at opposite ends of the building, until I arrived at the top floor. While traversing these venerable corridors, I felt somewhat awed by the thought of the pilgrims, with their icons, who once passed here.

I was concerned, too, that Madam Justice had to make this sizable trip to and from her office every day. I had had the same thought, as well as disbelief, when I'd mounted four flights of wooden stairs, years back, to the temporary office of the then Minister of Labor Golda Meir.

A woman was walking along at the far end of the hall. I discovered it was Miriam Ben-Porat, finished with her meeting and ready for me. A pleasant, motherly-looking woman of medium height, trim figure, and well-coiffed short dark hair, she put out her hand, greeted me warmly with a smile, and led me to her office nearby.

"Did you have any difficulty in finding me?"

"No," I said, "but the church bells weren't ringing."

She laughed. "I'm sure it's the one time they didn't ring all day." As she spoke, they rang out wildly.

She sat at an immaculate desk, with me across from her. No wood-paneled luxury here. Her black judicial robe, in contrast to the gay print dress she was wearing, hung behind her in the small room that was so simple and unadorned it might have housed a clerk of the court. There were no bookshelves, no books, only a few wooden chairs to complete the decor. A large window looked out on the compound.

When I placed my tape recorder on the desk, she said, "Oh, my English is so bad! You won't use this for broadcasting, will you?"

I said, "No, not at all. This is just for my own notes. Please don't be concerned. Your English is fine."

"Then let us begin."

"I understand that in order for me to have this appointment with you, permission had to be given by the Ministry of Justice. Is it usual that Supreme Court justices do not meet with people who want to write about them?"

"We try to do our work without much ballyhoo and what would seem to be self-made publicity. We talk only through our decisions, usually. But as the first woman, a fact that cannot be totally ignored"—her eyes lit up with amusement—"I was permitted to meet you." Her speech was thoughtful and measured.

"I'm most happy about that. I was sleeping off jet lag at the time of your appointment, so I missed the newspaper that day. I imagine there was quite a bit of excitement about it."

"Yes, yes, to say the least. The women consider me an asset, you see. They feel more sure of themselves because a woman is regarded as good enough to serve on the highest level of the judiciary and equal with the men serving in the same court. And that gives them the feeling, 'If she can do it, we can do it.'

"So I received many letters and telegrams of congratulations and, of course, 'the right woman in the right place,' and so on. I'm not sure whether it is I, or they, or the feeling of 'oneness'—that we are part of the world of women, and this is another step, and not an unimportant step, ahead."

"A very important one."

"For me."

"And for women, in general, all over the world."

"I don't know. We're all persons. I'm not a representative of women, and men are not representative of men. We are mankind and human beings. We have to enhance the belief in ourselves. Men are born of women. I think we are very much alike. We only have to believe in our possibilities and abilities, develop them, and make others believe in us."

"Did you always have confidence in yourself? Could you imagine that you would be where you are today?"

"Not in my wildest dreams! Quite the opposite."

"What brought you to this office?"

She sighed, "I'll start at the beginning. I was born in Kaunas, Lithuania, in the middle of 1918. My parents were Zionists, many rabbis amongst them. We were traditional. I went to Hebrew school, and I finished the secondary school, which included high school. Then, in the fall of 1936, I came to Israel—then Palestine. A greater part of the family remained in Lithuania."

"Did you come with a group, a youth group?"

"No, alone, with a certificate. Two years later, World War Two broke out. I had to support myself, but it was helpful to me that a sister and brother had already come here. I was the youngest of six children. Part of the family was killed during the Nazi occupation. I don't know if it's interesting. To me, it is."

"Very."

"Yes? I was even told how my father was killed, by eyewitnesses. He was gathered with thousands of Jews on a certain mountain, Green Mountain. And it was green. Afterwards, it was red. They were all told to lie down, with their faces downward. My father was not only a religious man, and a person I very much respected, he was also a proud man, and he did not want to kneel down before the Nazis or anybody that is not God. So he took the Bible and stood up, and then one shot killed him. A brother was also killed. My mother was taken with a group of women and children, and they were all exterminated.

"One sister was in South Africa, where she died of cancer. So here we are, two brothers and one sister, two of them engineers, one an architect. Now you would like to know why I chose the legal profession, wouldn't you?"

"Yes, I would." I was grateful for her prompting me. The horrors of the Holocaust always leave me speechless.

"First of all, I think the reason was in my childhood. I was about ten years old. One of my aunts, very dear to me, helped my parents to bring up the children. My parents went to Lithuania, where I was born, from Russia, after World War One. They were very rich in Russia but lost all of it and had to start again, to make a new life. My aunt was childless and a bit crippled, but she was a great person, a great soul.

"One of the neighbors brought proceedings against her about a plot of land, and each time when she returned from the lawyer she was always in such a bad mood. Of course, she was not very objective about me. I was the youngest, and she saw in me her own child.

"One day, when she was upset about the proceedings, she muttered to me, 'If you had been a lawyer, you would have saved me from all my troubles.' I think that subconsciously, somehow, that was when I made the decision. I'm not sure, of course. A more practical decision was made later on, especially to break the line of engineering in the family. We were all good at mathematics, the same with me. But somehow I wanted to vary it. So I chose the law profession, and I didn't regret it."

"Was your father an engineer also?"

"No, my father had a rabbinical title. He was an educated man. He was almost an engineer. We had a garment factory, with all kinds of machines to weave the material and to make the garments. When a machine was out of order and the specialist didn't know what to do about it, my father managed, somehow, to fix it.

"But what I liked best about my father was his moral standard. It was a standard that was very hard to live up to. He was a very just man, an honest man. He was loved both by Jews and Gentiles. That saved him for some time. My mother was just a good soul. She was not so educated, less of a personality. But she had feelings for everybody.

"What else?" She searched for more. It isn't easy to lay out the past for a stranger, just like that. "I eventually entered the law classes here. The examination papers were sent to England, so I was told. That's how we finished the law classes. But it was not a very high standard. It was even less than average."

"The classes were under what auspices?"

"It was called law classes, and I think the Mandate had the teachers, organized it, and paid for the teachers. They were local teachers."

"You said you had to go to work and earn a living when you first came here. What did you do?"

"I worked at the Jewish Agency, and that's why I received my license only in 1945, although I started my studies in 1937 and finished in 1942."

"What did you do at the agency?"

"I was a secretary in one of the departments. When I received my license, I was not sure enough of myself to start in the legal profession as a lawyer. It was too great a responsibility, in my eyes. And then I couldn't imagine myself taking on a case that I did not believe in, or to please a client. So I continued my work in the Jewish Agency until 1948, when the State was born. By then I was already married, and my husband influenced me, talked me into trying my profession."

"Whom did you marry?"

"He was a poet at that time, but he was also a businessman."

"Was he also from Lithuania?"

"No, from Poland. I followed his advice, and I went to the Kirya [Civic Center]. The state's attorney was then Haim Cohen, now a Supreme Court judge, and he gave me the opportunity to make a start. I hoped to be able to sit at a desk and to prepare the material for someone else to do the job.

"To go to court, appear, plead—I couldn't imagine myself doing it because there were almost no women in this profession. So I didn't believe in my power to appear against an opponent who was a man, who had much more ability. Then one day Haim Cohen decided, 'You have to appear in the magistrate's court in a certain case.' It was a small matter, but I regarded it as a great tragedy. 'What am I doing? How can I take that upon my shoulders? Impossible! The responsibility of representing the State of Israel!'

"I went to a small courtroom, with old walls, the floor was— I don't know how to describe it. I couldn't imagine myself standing before the judge. I just wanted to get used to the place where I would have to appear. Oh, well, it was not so bad after all. And after that, I had greater cases, bigger cases, and in two years' time I was deputy secretary of the court, a legal appointment."

"Did you win that first case?"

"Yes, but it was a small matter, and I prepared it so well, so . . ."

"Elaborately?"

"Yes, elaborately. I didn't sleep for two nights, so there was not a gap or a hole that I left open. So I succeeded."

"Did the judge hear all of it?"

"Yes, he did. Then I had the good fortune that one of the high officials, one of the prosecutors, had to leave suddenly for another country. I knew the case by heart, having worked on the material. It was a murder case. Before he left, he told me, 'If you are offered this case and you do not take it, you will have yourself to blame for many years. I tell you, you can do it!' "

"That was the push you needed to give yourself confidence?"

"Yes. I think I owe him very much. I was offered the case and I said yes, but in a very low voice." Madam Justice laughed in recalling her early fears. "So I prepared it—very elaborately, as you said. And I even told the judges that it was the first serious case that I was appearing in, so they had to put up with my shortcomings. They were very nice about it. And I think I did quite well. I'm not sure if I could do it better today. I don't know. Because I wanted it so much."

"You probably went into more detail at that time."

"Exactly. And there wasn't a problem that I could possibly imagine that I didn't deal with beforehand in order not to be taken by surprise. This was in 1950. So the case went well. Much better than I expected."

"Apparently you didn't expect much of yourself at that time."

"No, I was not sure of myself at all. In fact, Cohen, the state's attorney, was in Prague when I was offered the case. When he returned, I knew that he would be very angry that such a case was left in such young hands. So I thought it would be better for me to approach him and not wait until he came to me.

"I told him that there was no choice, that I tried my best. I knew it was daring, but I'm sure he would be glad to hear that all went well. He was very glad and very nice about it. Then he said, 'Well, if you can appear in a murder case, you can also appear in the Supreme Court.'

"Of course, I learned a lot. I gained experience. The first time I was very nervous, and I remember that I spoke like a machine. When one of the judges distracted my mind by asking me something, I was confused for a moment, and I heard his fellow judge say to him, 'Leave her alone. Can't you see that she is excited?' I still thank him for it. He was very considerate and understanding.

"Well, the next time I was less nervous, and then I felt very much at home. The judges even felt how much respect I had for them. They felt it, and they appreciated it. But I prepared my cases very carefully. I don't think that, on the spot, I can find a very good answer to things."

"Do you find them in the middle of the night, like I do?"

"Yes, yes, I think so. Well, of course, experience does something to you, and some answers are ready because I know them. But if I have to find the answer, I have to search for it. I'm not one of those who can take it out of their sleeves. That's why I worked hard. I didn't take any case lightly, even if it appeared very simple. In 1958, I was appointed judge of the district court. In the meantime, I had many cases—murder, rape, security cases, and so on. You wouldn't be interested in special cases."

"Yes, I would, especially today—the incidence of rape, and how it is dealt with."

"Yes. One of the cases was about a small girl of five years old. She was found in a red overcoat, lying in one of the sabra trees in the vicinity of Bar Ilan University, not only dead but also raped. No suspect could be found. Then a man confessed to the murder. How did it happen? One day he told his wife that he had done something terrible. She said she would tell her father or go to the police. 'If you go to the police, I will kill you,' he shouted. He tried to suffocate her, but the neighbors heard the commotion and called the police.

"He was schizophrenic, it turned out. He was taken to a mental hospital, where they took down his personal history. He was asked whether he was a good student, and he said, 'I was never a good student.' Why? 'Because the other children always ran after me and called me bad names.' At the time, I think he was about thirty-five. He was also the father of a small child. His answer was suspicious because the newspapers were full of the story about the child that had been raped and murdered. Often, people who are not mentally sane put upon themselves the blame for something they have not done.

"He seemed to have special confidence in one of the doctors, which the others sensed, and they left the room. So he was tête-à-tête with the doctor, and he said, 'I'm glad we're alone because I can tell you: perhaps it is I who killed that girl. You see, I'm Dr. Jekyll and Mr. Hyde.' He actually used those words. It amazed me. 'And Dr. Jekyll is not responsible for the acts of Mr. Hyde, and that

162/ISRAELI WOMEN SPEAK OUT

is why I tried to kill my wife when she said she would tell her father.'

"The doctor didn't know what to make of it. He didn't know if it was pure imagination or whether it was true. So he gave him an injection of truth serum, which worked in a very strange way. Apparently, earlier he had had the urge to tell the truth, but when given the injection, he concealed it. It worked the other way around. Then he had the strength to conceal, while the sane man didn't have it.

"When he was insane, without the injection, he told the truth and wanted to show the place, the scene of the murder. So he was taken there. It was a very difficult case because afterwards he claimed he didn't remember anything. Amnesia. But I proved the case. It was not easy. At that time, the sentence was death. No, no, just a moment. A short time before that date, we did away with the death sentence, and it was only life imprisonment.

"Irresistible impulse was not considered a defense in those days. In the meantime, there were two other cases. I'm not allowed to talk about them because I didn't appear in those cases. Again, Haim Cohen, the attorney general then, agreed that I could try to persuade the judges that irresistible impulse should be regarded as a defense. So I wrote two or three articles and prepared myself especially well for this case. My argument was accepted by a majority vote, and since then, irresistible impulse is regarded as a defense in Israel. The man was sent to a mental hospital, where treatment expelled the 'wicked murderer' or, rather, put him under control."

"Congratulations! They had to put you on the Supreme Court."

"I must say I was very pleased about it."

"What do you think of the status of women in Israel? Are rape cases treated fairly, for instance?"

"They are difficult cases because it's done mostly in private. On the one hand, you don't want to send to prison someone who has had intercourse with a woman with her consent, and afterwards she turns to the police for God knows what reasons and tells a story that has no foundation. On the other hand, we have to take into account the fact that it is not done in the presence of witnesses, as a rule. There are exceptions sometimes.

"So we have to find some solution that will make it just enough for both sides. We take into account the behavior of the woman immediately after the rape. If she's hysterical, or she shouts for help and so on, all these can be corroboration. But if she keeps it secret, perhaps because she's ashamed, and she doesn't turn to a doctor, then, of course, there's no proof. And if there's no proof, then her testimony alone would not be enough.

"In most cases, I think, there are signs of violence. If she goes to the police immediately, or to someone who can testify in court, I think that we can usually get to the truth. I think we are well advised in the rights of women, but men do not believe in women here as equals."

"Apparently you have had no serious problems in your own career, in competition with men in the field," I commented.

"No. None at all. I told you that but for my husband I wouldn't have turned to the profession from the start. Then it was the attorney general, now Supreme Court Justice Haim Cohen, who made it possible for me to make a start. Then several women joined their office, and there are even a few judges."

"Are there many women lawyers?" I asked.

"Yes," she replied and added, "Why not?"—the Talmudic response that is a favorite among Israelis. "I can see, every year, more and more women joining the group in my lectures at the Hebrew University, some of them very good. Some judges are very good. Even here I'm the only woman, the first woman to sit on the Supreme Court. I was also the first woman who was president of the district court. There I was the head of eleven men who worked for me." This she said quietly, but with obvious pride.

"How are you appointed to the Supreme Court in Israel?"

"There's a committee of nine members. We're eleven on the court, but the committee is not only from the court. There are two members of the bar association, two ministers, two members of parliament, three Supreme Court judges, and the president." This was the first time I had heard the word parliament used instead of Knesset, an obvious influence from her British Mandate law classes, as was the use of "whilst" and other words in her very good English.

"It's not a political appointment, like in America, chosen by the president but subject to the advice and consent of the Senate?"

"There can, by chance, be some combination that expresses

political bias, but I think that generally it works well. And you are appointed for life."

"Where does the division come between the secular courts and the religious courts?"

"The rabbinical court has limited jurisdiction in the sense that it handles only cases of marriage and divorce between Jews who are permanent residents of Israel. It can also handle personal matters such as alimony, custody of children, by consent of all parties concerned. All other matters go to the secular courts. In some cases, there is parallel jurisdiction between the rabbinical courts and the secular courts—for instance, custody of children or alimony. If the parties agree, they go to the rabbinical court. If one of them doesn't consent, it's a matter for the secular courts."

"So many women I've spoken with are dismayed and frustrated at the continuance of the restrictive and discriminatory religious laws that govern marriage and divorce. Since the beginning of the State, I've been troubled by this anomaly in a democracy. Do you anticipate in the near, or maybe not so near, future that there will be civil marriage and divorce in Israel?"

She was slow to respond, then said, "That is not for me to say." It was clear that I had touched on a sensitive subject for a Supreme Court justice to be quoted on. I changed the subject.

"You are quite an exception to the experience most women have in trying to get ahead in a man's world, despite your timid start."

"I was timid because there were so few women. If I had found a crowd of women, I wouldn't have hesitated so much."

"In almost every field, all over the world, it presents itself as a problem to women."

"Yes, of course, but a woman has a very important role to play that men cannot fulfill: to have children, to raise children, pregnancy, and all that."

"Do you have children?"

"Yes, I have one daughter, who was born in 1955."

"By that time you were quite advanced in your career."

"Yes. It was no hardship for me to raise my child. I was a happy mother. I hope she was happy. She now has a year-and-a-half-old child. His name is Ilan, after a young cousin of mine who survived the Yom Kippur War, a pilot with decorations for his bravery, only to be killed later, in one of those unfortunate accidents, in military exercises. He was a marvelous fellow, twenty-four years old."

I shook my head in sympathy; then I asked, "How did you manage when your daughter was a baby? Did you have someone stay with her while you worked?"

"When she was a child, I devoted quite a lot of time to her— in the afternoons, evenings. I had someone stay with her the rest of the time, but she was an independent child and there were no problems. She is now studying at the Teachers' Seminary.

"I have discovered that I am something of a teacher myself. I told you that I lecture at the university. I started there in 1964. I change the subject from year to year because I want to cover another topic, to learn it better, deeper, to understand it better. I love lecturing because I like the contact with the students. The lectures are on various subjects: civil procedure, the law of bills of exchange, promissory notes, research, assignments, contracts, torts, and so on. I'm still continuing."

"Do you ever think back on your aunt who said if she had you for a lawyer she wouldn't have had so many problems?"

"She has been dead for many years, but she's still alive in my memory. She was like the first mother to me."

The phone rang, telling Miriam Ben-Porat that a car was waiting for her. We left together, and she guided me down stairs and across corridors, but not the ones by which I had come. Mysteriously, we emerged from the maze, this time at the front of the building, to find the waiting car. I accepted her kind offer of a lift.

The workday was finished. Virtually everything, including the Supreme Court, stops early or in midafternoon on Friday, to prepare for the Sabbath. On this occasion, the departing justice wished the guards and attendants, *"Shalom. Hag sameah"*—"Happy holiday" added to the usual *"shalom"* for the approaching Passover. The young driver gallantly held open the door for us, and we were on our way.

"This is one of three cars at the disposal of the eleven justices," she told me. "They are used by appointment and, understandably, are not always available." No black Cadillac, this, or even one of the new Mercedes used as taxis, under a reparations agreement with Germany. In keeping with the modest appurtenances I had

already observed surrounding a justice of the Supreme Court, it was
a small inconspicuous car, not new.

As we drove through beautiful, bustling Jerusalem, my favorite Israeli city, where too many poured-concrete skyscrapers are
imposing themselves on century-seasoned pink stone buildings,
Miriam Ben-Porat offered these addenda to our talk.

"Although Israel's laws are largely English parliamentary laws,
we also have new, original laws. As you saw, I wear a robe in court,
where I am addressed as 'Your Honor' or 'Madam Justice.' " In a
relaxed, carefree mood, after finishing the task of reviewing her
life, she added, "I do not wear the British judicial wig, nor do the
men.

"I must come to America or England for at least six months.
I'm sure my English would improve. I sent my daughter to the
United States and Mexico as a Bas Mitzvah gift, but I have never
had time to go abroad. I better do it now, before I get much older."

"Your English is very good," I told her. "Fifty-nine is not so
old, but I hope you will come to the United States. I never envi-
sioned, when I wrote my first book about Israeli women, that I'd
be back twenty-five years later to do another. Then I was forty-five.
You're good at mathematics?"

"Impossible!" was her generous response. Then she said,
laughing heartily, "You'll be back here in another twenty-five years
again."

A few days later, I received a personal note on this letterhead
—"The Supreme Court of Israel, Jerusalem, Mrs. Justice Miriam
Ben-Porat"—in both English and Hebrew, with the seal of the State
of Israel. The following editorial from the *Jerusalem Post,* dated
March 6, 1977, was enclosed.

SUPREME COURT'S NEW LOOK

With the appointment of Judge Miriam Ben-Porat along with
Judge Shlomo Asher to the Supreme Court, Israel has scored a first
—the first woman to sit on the supreme judicial body of any country
with a common law system.

It may well be asked why it has taken nearly thirty years of
statehood before the appointment of a woman to the Supreme
Court. The answer is two-fold. Despite the example of a woman
Foreign Minister and indeed Premier, there has been a certain

amount of traditional resistance to the idea of feminine representation in one of the most distinguished and prestigious institutions of the State. But the main reason is simply that, till now, there has not been a woman suitable for such a high office.

Judge Ben-Porat has qualified for her promotion because she is an excellent jurist. By her energetic and passionate devotion to the legal profession, and by her manner of conducting her court—reinforced by the fine record she scored as acting judge on the Supreme Court during the past five months—she has proved herself capable of filling the exacting demands made of the highest judges in Israel. In short, she has all the qualities that are required of anyone who aspires to sit on the bench of the Supreme Court. She is *pars inter pares,* and if she were not truly "equal" she would not have been eligible for the Supreme Court, whatever her sex. And no one would want it otherwise.

Now that women have started taking an active, and full-time, role in the Israel world of law, and particularly in the Attorney General's and State Attorney's offices—in which Judge Ben-Porat, too, received her legal training—we may expect more of them to reach the top of the ladder and thus provide a future source of potential Supreme Court justices.

9 A Woman Is a Woman Is a Woman

IT WAS JUST BEFORE the May 1977 elections, when she was totally preoccupied with doing everything she could to assure top place for the Likud Party, that I met Geula Cohen. It is now history that Likud was the winner and that Menachem Begin became prime minister.

I would love to have seen Geula when the returns came in. There is nothing moderate about this woman. Everything she believes, she voices passionately, reiterating her views in poetic cadences. On this occasion, her former comrade and commander in chief in the underground Irgun had made it. What a celebration! She was sixteen when she joined up in 1942 as a freedom fighter to rid Palestine of the British Mandate government and to establish a Jewish state. As a member of the Knesset the past four years, she had made it, too.

Despite this busy period, she had agreed to an interview. A tall, well-filled-out woman with flowing black curly hair, she greeted me warmly at her office in Tel Aviv, in Jabotinsky House. Geula has the big brown eyes of the Yemenites, and she looked impressive in blouse, vest, corduroy skirt, and black boots. Jabotinsky House, named for Vladimir Jabotinsky, founder of the militant Zionist right-wing Revisionist Party, of which Likud is the successor, is a striking-looking building of fourteen stories, with continuing balconies circling each floor. Geula's thirteenth-floor office has a magnificent view of the Mediterranean and all of Tel Aviv.

"Please excuse me a moment. I will be right with you." She left me with her secretary, who proceeded to tell me that Geula is the greatest woman in the world and handed me *Woman of Violence, 1943–1948,* the book that Geula wrote in Hebrew, which was published in English in the United States in 1966. As I was leafing through it, Geula returned, looking somewhat harassed.

"I'm so busy! Will you interview my book instead of me?"

"Sorry. Absolutely not. I want to speak with you."

"I have so much on my mind!"

"Perhaps it will relax you to talk about other things," I suggested.

"I have only a half hour." This was a new predicament for me, but in fact we talked for more than two hours.

"My English is very bad," she apologized. Although I thought her English excellent, I asked if she wanted a translator. She refused. As we spoke, I helped her, from time to time, to find the word she wanted in English. I wished that we could have done the interview in Hebrew. The Yemenites have the reputation of speaking the purest and most beautiful Hebrew in the country. I started to study the language years ago, but soon realized that unless I were living in the country and attending an ulpan full-time, I was a hopeless case. In her book—which I understand is an excellent translation—the language is so beautiful, colorful, and at times even elegant that I regret even more not knowing Hebrew.

Despite her apology, Geula expressed herself fully and emphatically in her own brand of English. When checking the Jerusalem transcript against the tape of the interview, I was appalled at the liberties the transcriber took. Apparently she felt she should set Geula's sometimes exotic phrases into her own pedestrian English. I have restored it to the original.

"My father came from Yemen," she started, lighting the first of successive cigarettes, "when he was five years old, in 1905. They came on foot most of the way from Yemen to Israel. My mother was born here. On my mother's side, I'm fourth-generation Israeli. All were born in Jerusalem, but originally they came from Morocco. I was born in Tel Aviv in December 1926. Our home was very traditional. My father was very religious, and I think my entire ideology came from him and from his traditional home."

"Do you continue the religious tradition?"

"No, and I'm sorry about that. So, more and more, I see to it that, although it doesn't come naturally for me, I try to force myself to do some things, to be more religious, because more and more it's in my head how right and how beautiful our tradition is. It's not only for the Messiah to bring it to mankind. I think wisdom is there, justice is there, and beauty, in our tradition."

Another Yemenite woman, whom I met a few years after Israel's dramatic Airlift Magic Carpet that brought fifty thousand Yemenite Jews to Israel, once told me, "We had letters from Israel saying the Messiah had come and that Israel was for the Jews. They said that the Arabs were out and that the Jews had made a *medina,* a State. We sold everything and came together with three hundred people. About a hundred were on asses, and the others came by foot. Some women carried their children on their backs, but we had an ass that my little daughter and I rode on. My husband walked next to us.

"It took us twenty days over the desert. We started at five every morning and traveled ten hours every day. [It is two hundred miles from Yemen to Aden, on the Red Sea, where Israel's planes awaited them.] We made hard-baked bread on the way so it would not spoil, and we cooked the meat well so it would keep. The day before we arrived at Aden, we stopped while, with the help of my husband, I gave birth to my baby." This she said without self-pity, glad to have left Yemen, no matter how hard the journey.

Geula's grandparents, two of those few Yemenites who made the difficult journey to Palestine in the early days, were, no doubt, among those who wrote letters that the Messiah had come, signaling the mass exodus of Yemenite Jews and delivery from their Arab oppressors. For two thousand years since the dispersion, they had been deprived of schooling or medical attention, compelled to live in ghettos and to wear only black outdoors, and forbidden to sit on an ass higher than a Moslem's. They never saw knives or forks in Yemen. They had no toilets or beds. They clung to the Torah in a determined effort to retain the only culture they knew. Most of them spoke only Arabic. The boys who learned Hebrew from their elders sometimes learned it upside down, as several of them surrounded one of the few leather Torahs that later were carried over the desert to Israel.

Five- and six-year-old girls started to learn embroidery to help their mothers decorate garments for the Arabs, while their fathers made delicate jewelry and articles of leather for their masters. It was from this background that the Yemenite Jews arrived in Aden.

"We were exhausted and filthy," the woman told me of their arrival. "We were sick and thin from our journey, and full of lice. My husband's feet, and the feet of the others who walked, were bleeding when we got there. At Camp Hashed [set up by the American Joint Distribution Committee], they cleansed us, gave us food and clothes, and tried to make us well. My baby might not have lived in Yemen, he was so tiny and sick, but the nurse there helped him to live, thank God. The wind from the sea never stopped blowing the hot desert sands into the camp. But we were thankful to be out of Yemen and on our way to Israel. And then, at last, the airplane, like a mother, took us all home."

Though they had never seen a plane, as the huge airships swooped down out of the sky, the people of the Bible recalled that "God said to Moses, 'You have seen how I bore you on eagles' wings and brought you unto myself.'" Fifty thousand went home on the wings of twentieth-century eagles.

"We were ten in our family," said Geula, proud descendant of these people, "but all the good parts of myself are dead: my mother, my father. My husband died two years ago, and my first son died when he was three, both of illnesses. Only one son is left to me, and he is now in the army, in the paratroopers, a wonderful boy."

"What was your life like before the establishment of the State?"

"The spirit of our tradition and my national awareness, which I got from my home, was the best schooling, and has remained with me all of my life. It was not by accident that I was born in this house and got this education. The roots are there from my home.

"I joined Betar, which was the Revisionist movement for youngsters. Afterwards, when I was sixteen, I joined the Irgun Zvei Leumi, or Etsel, National Military Organization. In those days I was studying to be a teacher, in the Teachers' Seminary. But my mind wasn't on my studies, and I became more and more involved in the activities of the Irgun. This was in 1942, when the Irgun made an agreement with the British Mandate government that they would stop fighting them for the duration of World War Two. They would cooperate with them until after the war.

"But one of the leaders, Avraham Stern, thought we shouldn't make arrangements with the British except under terms that they would help us: that after the war they would establish a Jewish homeland and Jewish government, as they promised they would do. Otherwise we would continue fighting them.

"And that's how it was. You've seen my book and the story of how I became aware of the Stern group. I was in the Irgun and didn't know anything about the other. I was young and not politically minded then. I was moved only by feelings and tradition. But when I read the propaganda of the other group, I was convinced they were right. I left the Irgun and joined Lehi, the Freedom Fighters of Israel, which became known as the Stern group." She did not say "Stern gang," as it was commonly called.

"After a while, they found out that I had a good voice for broadcasting. My pronunciation is very Hebrew, and I was chosen to broadcast for the Stern group. For me, that was really something, like a present from God, because my temperament is so anticonspiratorial, antiunderground. The things I believe in I want to shout in the streets. And to whisper to someone, even to a man, is very difficult for me.

"So if I could stand near a microphone and say what I think about the Jewish people, the British, the things that were happening, that for me was a luxury, a *mitzvah*. I did it with all my heart, and as they say, things that come from the heart enter the other's heart. This was a very good front for us, especially since we weren't known. They heard my voice, and they thought, 'Who are these gangsters?' And here was a voice, a woman's voice, the human touch, and it was very important in those days. I fought with the microphone much more than my friends fought with guns.

"My male comrade's voice was strong and incisive, but my voice was a call from within me, and if that call should ever stop, I would be voiceless. I believed in that voice and abandoned my body to it, letting it rend me, burn me, char me to ashes if necessary. After every broadcast, the smell of cinders was in my nose! Something in me was being offered up on an altar." (It is clear that Geula didn't, and doesn't, subscribe to anything British, particularly their penchant for understatement. She throbs; she vibrates; she burns.)

"Where did you broadcast from?"

"In Tel Aviv, in our hideout, an attic in the Carmel souk, the market here in the center of Tel Aviv. It was a 'dirty' place. What we called 'dirty' meant it was not known to the British. We thought it wasn't considered a conspiratorial place, and we didn't have anyplace else. As it was, we decided that would be the last time we would be broadcasting from that place.

"I always loved that market. It hummed with human voices. I loved the bargaining, loved to watch the hands sort the good from the bad. As soon as I was old enough to carry my mother's shopping basket, I would be dragged along to where the Arab vendors kept their stalls. To me these stalls always seemed to be the soul of the market. The lemonade man who adorned his head with colorful feathers and decorated his small cart with lemon boughs hung with tiny bells, the butcher with the handlebar mustache—all this entranced me. Most of all, I loved to listen to the bargaining that went on between my mother and the vendors in earthy Arabic. It was art, not business." She laughed, fondly recalling childhood memories.

"Is that where they caught you, in the souk hideaway?"

"Yes, in February 1946. They came in while I was broadcasting. My sister had told me the British were looking for me at home. It's a wonderful story, what my mother did. She stood in the doorway and told the officers, 'Get out of here. Get out of here at once! You've made my life hell for me. Do you expect me to serve you tea and crumpets? Wormwood is all you'll get from me. Because of you I've lost my daughter. Because of you she's afraid to come home. Because of you I haven't seen her for months. Because of you I can't sleep at night. Get out of here, all of you!' " Geula thoroughly enjoyed the retelling.

I asked her family name, the name of this woman whose fearlessness, as well as her rhetoric, had molded her daughter. "My mother and father were Cohen," she said. "My married name is Hanegbi. Even when I married, I kept my maiden name because I was already famous.

"It's a long story how they caught us. They put me here in the Jaffa jail. After two days, I tried to run away and to make contact, but I failed. Then they sent me to Bethlehem. That is a city near Jerusalem with no Jewish population. The only Jewish population there were those in prison.

"There were two prison buildings. In one, you were freer, when they couldn't pin anything particular on you, a detainment camp. The other was for after trial. They put me in the detainees' camp, and again I tried to escape. I succeeded in jumping all the fences, but they ran after me and captured me half an hour later while I was running on the hills. They shot me and wounded me. Here, on the thigh, I have a scar." She indicated the spot. "So I couldn't continue running.

"I stood up, and I think this was the most difficult moment in my life. I was a young girl, just eighteen, standing like that on the Judean mountains, wounded, all bloody, with hands stretched up, and with many, many soldiers running to catch me." Geula's hands were up, her voice breathless.

"So they caught me, and this time I was put not in the detainees' camp but in the heavily guarded building, in a small cell, in solitary confinement. After a month, I was brought to trial.

"At the trial I told the judge, with his curly wig, 'I do not recognize your authority to judge me, and so I do not owe you an account of what I did or did not do. I, a Hebrew fighting woman, a member of the Freedom Fighters of Israel, consider you to be intruders who are subjugating our homeland. There is only one body of law which I have accepted of my own free will, and that is the law of the Hebrew underground.'

"The courtroom was in an uproar. The judge leaped from his seat and shouted, 'Make her stop! Make her stop! Make her sit down!' The entire audience was on its feet. The judge threw down his gavel. 'If the defendant insists on proceeding in this manner, I shall be forced to close the case.' But I insisted," she continued dramatically. " 'There is one more thing I have to say concerning the role of women like me in the underground. When a Hebrew fighting woman is brought before you, you judges are in the habit of thinking that she must have been enticed by others to do what she did. I would like to point out to you that when it comes to fighting for one's freedom, it is not necessary to entice anyone. The ideal for which one fights is enough. From time immemorial, women have been ready to sacrifice themselves for the creation of a new, free life.'

"My voice was the only weapon left to me. I raised it as high as I could. 'Do you really think that by imprisoning me and my comrades you can crush our spirit? It is not we who gave birth to that spirit, but that spirit which gave birth to us, and our death will not diminish it.' "

As for the outcome of the trial, Geula told me, "When they caught me, I had a gun with me. The judge said I would be getting seven years for the pistol and two years for the broadcasting. I laughed to myself and thought, How stupid you are. It should have been seven for the broadcasting and two for the gun. What could I do with a pistol? Nothing! But with the microphone . . . !'' Her excitement was as high, and the scene as vivid, almost thirty years later, as it was the day it happened.

"I, and all my friends before and after me, changed the situation in the military court. We were the prosecutors, and they were the defendants. We turned it around. We stood up without lawyers, without anybody, and said, 'That's right! We are members of the Stern group. We are fighters. We're born here, and we want to kick you out of here. You don't belong here. Go back to London! Jerusalem is ours!' ''

Geula heaved a sigh and put her hand to her head, as though it were too much to live through again. "I don't know why they don't teach these things in the schools. You don't need Zionist propaganda anymore to be a proud Jew. Only to read all the history. If a camera would be there, or if you'd look with the eyes of a poet or an artist, you'd see that I was prosecutor and he was the defendant. Not only because of what we said. We changed the reality at those moments, to the reality that they, in fact, were the defendants.

"I remember my mother was sitting there with my baby brother, five years old. She took him with her to the trial, which lasted from morning until afternoon. When the judge said nine years, all of a sudden I heard a voice from the side of the room where my whole family was sitting, the journalists, and everybody. I saw my mother standing up and singing 'Hatikvah'!

"Ecch!" This was a pained exclamation that came from Geula's throat from time to time. "I'm telling you—forcing the judge, the whole military court, and all the soldiers to stand up! I'm sure when the judge and all the others saw this, they knew it's not what I said, which could be called propaganda, but what she did that was the proof. They must have felt their administration would not last. That if there are Jewish mothers like my mother, they can never conquer this nation.

"I was in prison for a year and a half, and the whole time I was looking for a way out, for a hole here or there. My last attempt to escape was a success. I was the only girl who escaped.

"I tried to become ill in order to be taken to a hospital in Jerusalem. I knew that I couldn't run away in a non-Jewish population. It's a fact that for half an hour I was running in Bethlehem, looking for someone to help me, but no one would. First of all, I wanted to do it in Jerusalem. There was a prison for men in Jerusalem, and in this prison there was also a hospital which served the civilian Arab population. When a prisoner was put into this hospital, he was guarded by soldiers.

"I tried to become ill by many artificial means. For example, if you want to know, if you eat a cigarette, the tobacco causes your temperature to rise. If you put some pieces of onion here"—she pointed to her armpit—"a half hour before placing the thermometer there, it makes it hot. And there were many other tricks."

"You were taught all that?"

"Yes, everyone was. But they didn't take my temperature just at that moment. I cried I wanted my temperature taken, but I didn't succeed. Then God helped me. I really got sick. I was so ill that I didn't even think about escaping. I had pneumonia, and they had to take me to the prison hospital because they didn't have facilities in Bethlehem.

"I remember for four days a Jewish and an Arabic doctor sat near my bed, all night, with an oxygen tent on me, and early in the morning the crisis passed. Of course, all the time the Arab woman warden and soldiers were next to my bed, too. As soon as I felt better, I began thinking how I could escape from this place.

"At that time, our policy in the underground was not to help prisoners run away because what did you need them for? The British would search for them. They would have to be hidden. They were no longer good for the purpose. 'Ecch!' they said, especially with girls."

"Were there many girls in the movement?"

"Not so many, but mostly fighters. I didn't have any complexes about being a girl, about doing what the men were doing. So I was happy when they gave me the broadcasting job. I am a woman and I wanted to be a woman, to do what women could do. As a woman, I had special talents that no man had, and he can't conquer me in that. I have to be very much a woman to conquer him, not to be like him. I have to be myself, and only then can I win.

"There were some girls who went out with guns or pistols, but

I didn't like guns. Of course, I wanted to be involved in every action, but I wasn't so crazy about guns. I had a friend who was very good with them, as good as the men. But you have to have a special character for that. It wasn't for me, and I don't think it's for women.

"I managed to get word out to my comrades that I wanted to run away, and because it was the third time I tried to escape, they decided to help. I told them that I was still a little ill, but I could manage, and they would have to help me. They planned it; my husband too. He was one of the very top commanders of Lehi, of the Stern group."

"You were already married?"

"No, but he made the plan, and he planned it with Arabs from a village near Jerusalem, Abu Gosh. They were very friendly with the Jewish kibbutzim, and helped the Haganah, and they also helped us. There were some Arabs who were members of the Stern group. One of them was Yosef Abu Gosh, and there were others.

"I told you that the civil Arab population was in that hospital. So they made out that they came to visit an Arab woman who was from Abu Gosh. They planned that they would bring an Arab dress and veil and put it in the bathroom and the two Arabs would pretend to have a quarrel in order to distract the soldiers who were on guard. The Arab woman warden, who was always with me, started to go into the bathroom with me. So a Jewish girl, dressed as an Arab, who was supposedly the wife of one of the two Arab men, distracted her attention so that she wouldn't be near the bathroom door when I would come out, dressed in my costume. Everything was arranged like clockwork. And I escaped!"

Geula threw her arms out triumphantly. "In half an hour I was made over into a blonde, and because I was ill I was taken to a convalescent home. When my mother came to see me in a month's time (they didn't allow her to come sooner), she didn't recognize me. You see how dark I am. And I was only looking forward to the day that the British would leave Palestine, so that I would be able to come back to my original color. I had a very good personal reason. I stood at the microphone as a blonde, but I spoke as a dark woman."

"You were again broadcasting for the underground?"

"Yes, I continued broadcasting. My escape was a sensation, a very big story. That's why I told you I didn't change my name, because Geula Cohen was already a name people recognized. So from that time, I did the broadcasts until I was able to broadcast the good news that the British were leaving.

"I got married shortly before the British left the country. My husband and I knew each other, we were friends, for three years prior to that. The wedding ceremony took place in a small room. I was still blond. We used other names. We didn't know the British would be leaving so soon; otherwise we would have waited. But I didn't want to live with him without being married, because my parents knew that we were together.

"The high command of Lehi didn't want the men and women to get married because tomorrow there's a child and you would be out. They were right, and so sometimes they separated lovers, sent one to Jerusalem and the other someplace else. They also separated me from my future husband. It was a very rational policy, because first of all you had to love the country, and then you have your personal life.

"After the British left, it was very difficult to get used to civilian life. The first thing I did was have my hair dyed black, to my natural color, like the black roots. I looked at myself and said, 'It's me again! Thank God.' Then I entered Hebrew University. I had been kicked out of Teachers' Seminary because I was a terrorist. The last month of the last year, when I went for one of the exams, the principal called me in and told me that I would have to leave because I belonged to the Stern group.

"Though we were not accepted by the establishment in those days, afterwards Ben-Gurion wrote about my book, 'Holy is the pen that wrote this book.' He wrote a very exciting letter, and because of the book he began to change his attitude towards us. Not that he thought we were right at the time, but that we were patriotic and that our motivation was good.

"I studied philosophy at the university because we had many, many questions, and we thought that the books and philosophers would give us some answers to our many, many questions. I came back to my Jewish treasures, and only there I found my answers, not with Kant, Aristotle, Heidegger, and all the others. After I studied these philosophers, I had many more questions, instead of answers. In the questions of our sages, there are more answers for me than in the others' answers.

"What I'm doing now, since I have been in the Knesset, is to bring this Jewishness to the students of Israel. I interrupted my studies at the university to give birth to my two sons and went back to complete my studies. All this time I wrote for a monthly publication of our political and ideological ideas. We sold it in the streets. I didn't finish fighting the war. I was in the front all my life.

"For me, journalism was another front. I only exchanged the pistol and microphone for the pen, and afterwards, in the Knesset, with my mouth, because the job isn't yet finished. The war is going on. We haven't yet all of Palestine. We haven't brought all the Jews in yet from the Diaspora. These are the goals of Zionism. To be a Zionist is to give Eretz Yisrael back to the Jews and to bring the Jews back to Eretz Yisrael. More than that, we're not only fighting for the continuation of the Zionist revolution, but even for securing what we've already achieved.

"And I feel that this is *the* revolution in the world now. There is no other revolution which is at the same time also a spiritual one. It's not only a physical one. It's not only a political one. Because a nation, in her history, decided one day it has to bring a Messiah to make another world. Now she has to go on or to diminish. Because no one can stop us, only us. *No one!* Not Egypt, not the Palestinians, not Syria's Assad, not the PLO. *No one* can stop us; only us, if we give up our goal, because only this has kept us.

"All the other nations that didn't have any challenge, any Messiah, to live for disappeared. Russia will disappear; America will disappear. Every one will disappear as they disappeared. Because Persia of old disappeared, and other great nations. They were not less great than Russia and the United States of today, and the other great powers. If you have something to live for, you will live. It's the same for a nation as it is for a man or a woman.

"If Israel decides one day we no longer believe in bringing the Messiah, or in going on in this revolutionary Jewish pattern, we will be like others, and we will die like others. Either we will live only like Jews and go on living, or be like others and share the rules of men and nations, with all the laws of life and death of nations."

"What do you think of the condition today of the Yemenites and other Jews who came from the Moslem countries?" I asked. "A Yemenite social worker who was brought here as a child told me, shortly after Airlift Magic Carpet, of her difficulties in trying to help her people 'grow up two thousand years,' as she put it."

"I think the government made all the mistakes they could have possibly made regarding them. From the material point of view, they weren't provided for equally, because that would have meant giving them much more because they were so far behind. The government's policy completely failed because of this. That's a fact because the gap has become larger instead of becoming smaller. From the spiritual, cultural point of view, they wanted to make them like them, to take on European culture, and they took from them all their integrity, their authentic culture. It was a big mistake, because spiritually there are differences, and we have to keep these differences in order to be one nation. They took them all and dressed them in khaki, only to symbolize what I mean. That was a great mistake.

"What's more, it was from the standpoint that our European culture is higher. That's not right and never was right. What is culture? Culture is due to your past and your future, and our past is the tradition of Judaism. And our future is Eretz Yisrael, the land of Israel, and Am Yisrael, the people of Israel. That's our culture. It's not technology and all these things which are only the means. The future is your feelings towards Eretz Yisrael, Ahavat Yisrael, love of Israel, your feelings towards the people of Israel, the values of Israel. That's the future as well as the past.

"And the culture of these people, of these tribes, was much deeper than with the Western Jews. The Western Jews lost their roots. But the Jews from the East kept these values all the time, in authentic ways, in Yemen, in Morocco, in Iraq, and in many other places in the East.

"The Eastern Jews were always in the ghetto—in Yemen, in Morocco. They didn't go to the universities and didn't learn mathematics, technology, and everything that they learn nowadays."

I told her I had recently read of a case in which a Yemenite family resorted to *alfesht* because their seventh child was weak and fearful while his older brothers were "strong heroes." The mother told the Israeli doctor that this would have been all right in Yemen, but in Israel everyone must be an achiever, and so her youngest child, who was a poor student, had to be "cured." She had been called to the school to explain what had happened to the child.

"Yes, that's just what I'm telling you. They didn't have anything, even doctors. As you probably read, the *alfesht* is a traditional Yemenite ceremony, a 'cure' for mental difficulties, including phobias. The ceremony consists of cutting the 'patient's' back with a razor blade until a 'black spot' is reached. Superstitions! It is based on the belief that fear makes the blood black."

"I accompanied a doctor, some years ago," I recalled, "while she attended Yemenite babies in a clinic. She was terribly frustrated in trying to reeducate the mothers. I understand that the Kupat Cholim has been making an effort in reeducation."

"Yes, this is very much needed. From this point of view they are still very, very low. But from the Jewish point of view, authentic Judaism, they remained with their roots intact.

"So instead of respecting these authentic values, the government ignored them altogether. Now another process is taking place. The youth of these communities are now frustrated with the Western culture, and they're coming back to their traditions. That includes Kurdistan and Iraq. Each has its specific tradition. They want to put back what was taken away from them. The government made all the mistakes, I think, from the materialistic point of view, as well as the cultural, spiritual, and value point of view.

"Now, I think, what should be done is to change all the policy, and that's what we want to do. That's what I want to do if I'll be in the Ministry of Education. There are two things that have to be done. Jewishness has to be taught to all the children in school. Not to be religious, but to know, to come back to our history. Because otherwise, we won't be here anymore if we won't be connected with our roots. We are living now in a contradiction. We are living like non-Jews, like all the other nations, but we die here only like Jews. And this is a contradiction that shouts to heaven!" She shook her head in dismay.

"The other thing is to break these gates between the communities. Sixty percent of our population comes from these communities, from Arab lands. It shouts for correction. The government is Socialist, and I'm not a Socialist. I've never been. I'm a Jew, and for me it's enough to be a Jew, to be good and be right and to do justice. I don't need any socialism."

"What happens when these children go into the army? Do they adjust to other ways and learn new methods? Is the army an assimilator?"

"It's not good because nowadays in the army you have to deal with very sophisticated and modern equipment. You need some mathematics, and you need to be much more educated. They don't have enough of it. Even from the security point of view, it's an evil. It's very hard to change things, because objectively they came from a very low standard. But they're here thirty years!

"Thirty years ago the government could say, 'We're not to blame.' The government of Morocco has to be blamed, the government of Iraq. But we're now thirty years later. We are responsible if their standards and conditions are still very low."

"Are they qualified to go into the army, to carry arms and do what they have to do?"

"Not all of them are now on a very low standard, only some. There are many jobs in the army."

"Did you serve in the army?"

"I served only for some few months, after the British left, because afterwards married women were not taken."

"Let's talk about women."

"No, we can't!" We had now talked for almost two hours, instead of the half hour she had allotted.

"Just briefly."

"No, we can't."

"I have to hear about women—very briefly."

"I'll tell you in two words my belief. I think that a woman, like any human being, has to be different. I'm not for equality. I'm against equality. Because when you talk about human beings, and I'm a special human being, I'm talking about justice, not about equality. It's not by accident that in the whole Bible there's not one word about equality as a value. Equality I need only in a material sense—housing, jobs, everything like that. Material things can be divided in the middle, half and half. But in character, integrity, in the spiritual world, you can't divide things. There are different integrities.

"So I'm a woman, and I look to the society for justice as a human being, not for equality. Because if I have to go at twelve o'clock to nurse a baby, they have to let me go and give me the same salary as the man who can't go. That's only to symbolize the difference. This is justice. Sometimes I need more rights, sometimes I need less, not equality, not equality in everything. So as a human being I think we have to fight for justice."

"Do you think women are getting enough justice?"

"We're getting more and more. Here and there are things that still have to be corrected, such as a woman in her household has to be treated like a woman working outside her home."

"Should she be paid for her work and have all the social benefits?"

"Not paid, but all the fringe benefits—pensions, vacations, and all these things. For instance, we have here behind you"—she handed me a piece of paper—"here we've written down special points that have to be for women, for our election platform."

"Do you have it in English?"

"No, you don't have a vote, a voice for us, so I didn't put it in English." Geula enjoyed her little joke, as did I. "But the points are mostly what I've been telling you. From the human being point of view, we have to fight for justice. As a Jewish woman, I want to contribute like the man, in all fields of life, and I think I can do it in politics, in security, and in the economy. There's a very nice saying in Hebrew, *isha v'em b'Yisrael,* a woman and mother in Israel. There's no such thing in any other language in the world. Every woman in Israel is at the same time a mother in Israel. That means that you have to care not only for your family but the family of all Israel at the same time.

"So I think a woman can function in every field of life, like the man, and sometimes even better. In the municipalities, for instance, I think women can do even more, and I think many more women must function in the municipalities. Women have to contribute in politics, evenly with men, depending on personal inclination and motivation. Not every man is involved in politics; it depends on his temperament and his wants.

"It's very natural that fewer women are interested in politics, because it's mostly not in their character. They are more involved in everyday things, things they can touch, and not so much in abstract thinking and planning for the larger community. In the present government there is only Golda Meir and perhaps two or three others that you can say are political creatures, although it's the party that has been in the government for thirty years.

"They say they have given women all the opportunities to advance in politics, but I think that they did not give women all the opportunities. I think if we make women more and more conscious that politics is not ending at the door of their house, but in the streets, all the dangers that she tried to keep her children away from, and she made sure her children would grow up healthy from the physical point of view and the emotional point of view, all of these dangers are still in the streets.

"She can't throw her child to the street without looking afterwards what happens to him. This is what I always say now. She can't leave him to these dangers. She has to go out from the house. For eighteen years she is running after him with a banana, with this, with that! You know."

"You mean, *'Ess, ess, mein Kind'?*"

"Yes. *'Ess, ess, mein Kind.'* It's not enough. What I'm saying is that she has to deal with politics, because dealing with politics is dealing with her house, with her husband, with her children, with herself, and she has to deal with politics."

Geula's promise to give me her opinion on the subject of women in two words was going along very well. "Do you think that women should do all this in a separate political party?" I asked.

"No, not at all. A separate women's organization should only deal with very special things, like the existing women's service organizations. That's another thing. Politically, of course not. A Jewish woman much more so, much more so, because our politics is very, very hard. We are one great family, this nation, and we are responsible for one another. It's not only a symbol that our history begins with four mothers and three fathers—you know, in the Bible, the founders of the people of Israel: Abraham, Isaac, and Jacob; Sarah, Rivka, Rachel, and Leah. Sarah, the wife of Abraham, was the first one who dealt with politics. She told him that 'our son, Isaac, will not play with the Arab boy, Ishmael.' "

"Wouldn't it have been better had he played with the Arab boy and become friends?"

"No, it wouldn't. Then we wouldn't have the Jewish people."

"Don't you have to live with the Arabs?"

"Yes, of course, but what she was aiming at was against assimilation. You have to stay with your own people, not to give up your identity, not to give up your country, not to give up your security. Of course, *shalom* with everyone, but first of all, *shalom* on Israel. That's the basic. Otherwise, with whom will you make peace? With the Arabs and no Jewish people anymore? *Shalom* has to be done between two. We can survive only if we have our terms of survival.

"As I told you, a woman, as a human being, has to have, first of all, justice, not equality. Then, as a Jewish woman, like the man, to contribute exactly like the man. And a woman being a special thing, we have to be different. Different!" Geula repeated the word emphatically. "Because I don't want to be like a man, to take a nail and to flex my muscles! No, because I need my hands to be very soft in order to embrace my little child, in order that my husband will embrace me and won't run away to another woman. My hands have to be soft and not muscular, not tough—only to symbolize my point of view. Yes? I want to be different, and I have to be different. And that's my philosophy about women."

But she thought of something else. "I think we have to change another thing. Society has superstitions about women, not to do this and that. Society has fixed ideas about the woman. Now there are many new feminist groups to release the society from these fixed ideas. How do you call these parties, parties for the realization of the woman?"

"Women's liberation, to liberate the woman."

"Oh, my English!" Geula threw up her arms in frustration. "I think that the real liberation of women will be when she will liberate herself from the fixed ideas she has about herself. That's the real liberation, because she thinks about herself, that she is nothing, and she has to be freed from these ideas."

"To give her a sense of self, of her own capabilities, not to feel that she is just the wife of her husband, the mother of her children," I said.

"Yes. When she will be free from these fixed ideas, the society will change. If we will be honest with ourselves, if you have to choose between a woman doctor and a man—I don't know you, but I'm sure that most women, if they would vote, would prefer the man, not the woman."

"I'd prefer the doctor who is best qualified."

"You think so! You think so! But if you have two who are both equally qualified?"

"Some women in America today will go only to women doctors."

"O.K., because they are best."

"Because they like the way they are treated by women doctors. They feel that many male doctors talk down to them and are not

186/ISRAELI WOMEN SPEAK OUT

as considerate, as sensitive to their problems as a woman doctor."

"O.K., so they are liberated from this point of view. But most of the women now . . . I'm telling you . . . me, take me, take myself, I would have to think much more about going to a woman. It doesn't come naturally to me. If they have the same quality, the woman and the man, the same quality, I'd prefer the man. Why? Because for many, many years they've educated me that the man is the better doctor. I have to analyze it in my head and not in my feelings. And to overcome some superstitions . . . no, that's not the word."

"Prejudices?"

"That's the word! Prejudices! I should say to myself I'll go to the woman if she lives near me, and not prefer, immediately, the man. It's the same thing with advocates, lawyers. Every woman will prefer the man when they have the same qualifications."

"It's a question of reeducation."

"Yes. So now we have to liberate the women from these prejudices, to care for herself. That's the first and most important thing to do. And that will help us free the society from these prejudices. That's the only liberation that I'm looking for. I don't want to be like a man. I'll cry the moment the world will be equal in this way. No child, I think, will be born. As long as I have a womb . . . someday this might be changed, and women nowadays are doing everything to change it, but as long as we are different, long live the difference!"

The interview was over, almost. When we finished, she said, "You were right. It did relax me. I'm glad you came." She asked her secretary to phone for a taxi to take me to Allenby and Rothschild, to the *sherut,* the public taxi that would take me back to Jerusalem. It had been a perilous ride that morning coming down to Tel Aviv through the Judean hills, with the driver collecting fares from the seven passengers as he maneuvered around the few remaining hairpin curves at breakneck speed, regardless of signs clearly marked DANGEROUS CURVES. The beauty of the forests and the fields and the smell of orange blossoms in the air were welcome distractions.

"I'm sorry you're leaving soon and that I'm so busy before the elections," Geula continued. "I'd like you to come to my home for coffee."

"I would have liked to. Do you live near here?"

"Not far. And my house is very oriental. You would like it." She took my address, to visit me if she comes to the States again. She's been here a few times.

"Please send my book back to me at the Knesset. I only have two copies, and it's out of print. I will be in the next Knesset."

"You know that before the election?"

"Yes, because I am high on the list. I hope to have an appointment in the Ministry of Education. That's what interests me very much."

We were still in her office. "Do you ever look out the window at this marvelous view?" I asked.

"Never. I never get time."

"Are your relatives in the Likud Party? Do they consider you their leader?"

"Some are. But they don't consider me their leader. They are patriarchal. Only a man can be a leader. That is my brother." As she walked me to the elevator, she said, "I want to make the woman the core of the family. The family structure has broken down. It is weak and must be strengthened. The woman must realize she has her own strength."

Geula's expressed wish to be in the Ministry of Education was briefly realized when Prime Minister Begin made his first appointments and named her deputy minister of education and culture. The appointment ran into difficulty from Zevuln Hammer, whom Begin had already named as minister of education. His complaint was that Begin had not consulted him and that he had his own deputy in mind. The incident was, no doubt, highly distressing to her, but Begin subsequently appointed her chairman of the new Knesset Aliyah and Absorption Committee.

The problems of this committee being very close to her heart, she has already characteristically stated, "Too often the officials and bureaucrats involved in aliyah and absorption have been untalented and untrained people. The job should be given more status. The new committee's formation was long overdue. The Law of Return, which passively welcomes Jews to come here, has to go further. We must provide a psychological boost to *olim* [immigrants] and make them feel like full-fledged citizens."

I was not surprised to see Geula Cohen on television news, September 25, 1978, when Begin opened the debate in the Knesset on giving up Israel's settlements in the Sinai, in accordance with the Camp David agreements. Her fiery nature in full blast, she demanded that he resign because of the agreements. A member of his own party, Likud, she kept interrupting him, shouting, "Stop cheating the nation!" until she was asked to leave by a vote of the Knesset. She reflected the hard party line, seeking all of Palestine.

10   Growing Up Improvising

WE HAD SAT at the welcoming corner fireplace in her small Arab house on the outskirts of Jerusalem six years earlier, my husband and I, chatting over tea with Ruth Levin. We then spoke mostly about her painting and mine, Milton's sculpture, and mutual friends in New York. This time was different. When I told her what I was doing back in Israel, her lively, intelligent face lit up. In an urgent, staccato voice she said softly, "There are so many remarkable women here. I may think of someone for you."

Although we had met twenty years earlier when her husband, now dead, was cultural attaché at the Israeli embassy in Washington, we had seen each other only a few times. I suddenly realized, sitting there with her again, how very little I knew about her, other than that she painted, ran a small graphics business from her house, had a grown son and daughter, and, since last we met, had gone to Denmark when Harry Levin became ambassador to that country.

It occurred to me now that I should know more about this "old friend." My knowledge of her was hardly more than sketchy. Was it all embassies and exhibitions?

"How about you, Ruth?" I asked.

"Oh, I don't know that I'd be interesting for you," she answered, but then added, "My origins are far away and long ago. I've had so many reincarnations in the course of my life, and one stage doesn't have much to do with the other."

"That makes it more interesting," I said.

"Yes, and more tiring, I suppose."

"You're exhausted?"

"No, I can't say I'm exhausted. No, I'm not exhausted."

"You look very lively."

"People say I'm insufferably lively. That actually is our family trait. I come from Sudetenland. I never let on. Usually I say I come from Prague. I came in 1935 when I was fifteen. My brother was already here. He came to Prague to fetch me, and we set up housekeeping together for one year, which was very stormy."

"Your parents didn't come?"

"They were divorced and both remarried. My stepfather was a Zionist. My father was a completely assimilated Jew. But at the very end he wanted to go to Palestine and made all the preparations. But he was caught by the Nazis, and he and his wife perished in the concentration camp in Theresienstadt."

I interrupted. "Ruth, can we set a time when you can talk at length? I'd like to hear more." She agreed to "sit" for me, and I returned a few days later.

Ruth is an attractive woman of medium height, with a trim figure, considerably younger-looking than her fifty-eight years. Full of nervous energy, she is outgoing and has an easy smile in a handsome face that bears a suggestion of the Asiatic. Having little time for beauty parlors, she pulls her slightly graying brown hair back casually into a knot at her neck, with strands falling loosely over her forehead. Large glasses rest on her small nose.

Her house is in the sparsely populated Nefe Yof area, near the Herzl Forest in the Judean hills and not far from Yad Vashem, Israel's stark and moving memorial museum to the victims of the Holocaust. A car must enter through a clearing in a rocky, empty lot to reach the little garden at the entrance to the cottagelike house.

The interior, with Ruth's sensitive, large, abstract paintings, mostly in pastel tones, on the walls, oriental throw rugs, an eclectic assortment of antique tables, cupboards, and chairs, plus a collection of objets d'art from everywhere, and a wall of books, gives a sense of warmth and a well-ordered life focused on the cultural. Her studio is off to one side of the small L-shaped living room; kitchen and bedrooms are on the other.

"As you probably know, at that time you could only get to Palestine if you had a certificate," Ruth said, resuming her story. "I had a student's certificate for the Bezalel Art School, which just opened, and it was a whole *balagan* there, completely chaotic. It was an art school, but there were no teachers, there were few students. It was all very difficult, completely disorganized. After one year I dropped out and also got married.

"I met my first husband in a *mitatich*—that is, where a family would cook midday meals for all the poor people who were here alone, and most of us were alone in those days. There were few grown-up immigrants from Europe here. None of us had any parents here. We all came alone. Most of my parents' generation perished, like my father, most of my friends' parents."

"Did anyone help you get here? Any organization, like Youth Aliyah?"

She explained that her stepfather gave them the money for the trip and continued, "My first husband was a policeman. A Jewish policeman in those days was a young man who was recruited by the Jewish Agency, which was sort of our underground unofficial government at that time, to counteract the British and Arab police forces. This police force was sort of a spy concern. The British police were the *Herrenvolk,* the rulers. The Arab policemen and Jewish policemen were intriguing and spying against one another.

"In '36, the Arab riots broke out and the situation became very difficult. The Jewish policemen fulfilled a very important role. Those who spoke English, like my husband, were in the CID, the secret intelligence department. They tapped phones—officially for the British, but unofficially all the information they managed to find went to the Jewish Agency. He was very poorly paid, and we were extremely poor.

"He was sent to Matza, a village not far from Jerusalem, to guard a sanatorium which was opposite two Arab villages very hostile to the Jews. He was in charge of the watchmen who came every night, so we moved there. I was supposed to cook for those watchmen, which I did very badly. We were shot at and sniped at almost every night. People were killed, but we didn't take it too badly because we were all very young. I was sixteen. He was a so-called older man. He was twenty-six." Ruth laughed and explained, "He spoke English quite well, as he had learned it from the British here. He was of German-Russian extraction, but an orphan, here alone.

"We weren't married yet. Although my mother was a very emancipated woman, she thought there was a limit to everything and that her sixteen-year-old daughter should actually get married. She was in Prague, and we would correspond. So we did get married after six months, when we came back to Jerusalem. Having no profession, I started to work as a maid. I had studied in a commercial art school in Prague for one year, but that was hardly enough to enable me to earn a living."

"You knew at an early age you wanted to be an artist?"

"I always wanted to be an artist, but I was afraid to approach Art—with a capital A. I was brought up with the idea that I ought to make a living, even though at that time we didn't need it. My mother worked all her life, and all of us children had a profession that we wanted right from the beginning. I, to be an artist. My brother always wanted to be a teacher, and my sister wanted to work in agriculture, as a scientist. All of us eventually did those things.

"As a maid, I was shocking. I had no idea about anything at all. I forgot to tell you that during the riots we were stationed in various outposts around Jerusalem, where I was also supposed to cook. Actually, I joined the Haganah because I wanted to shoot and to carry arms and to do all sorts of romantic things. But the famous equality of the sexes hadn't reached the Haganah yet, so I was told to cook.

" 'But I can't cook,' I said. They wouldn't believe me. 'Every woman can cook,' they said. So they just had to grin and bear it. One of our commanders is now our President Katzir. He was a dashing young man. He won't remember, but he once tasted something I cooked and his face was very sour. He survived it, thank God!" Ruth was enjoying her review of those days and went on in her very clipped English, which she speaks fluently as a result of her marriage to Harry Levin, a South African, and the time she spent in America and England.

"I worked as a maid in three or four different places on the same day because in those days people couldn't afford to have a full-time cleaning woman. I would just work an hour or two in each place, then run to the next one. In one place the woman was a nurse and would leave before I came. She expected me to shop and cook, so food would be ready for them in the evening.

"Again I said, 'I can't cook.' So she said she'd write it down for me. I couldn't read Hebrew then, but I wouldn't admit it. I rushed with her long list to the grocer. He would read and translate it, give me the stuff, and I would rush back to the house and try to follow his directions. It was a disaster!" She laughed heartily and added, "It was terrible, really.

"Our joint earnings were so meager that we had a very difficult life, and at the end of the month we would pawn the few things we had. Then, by chance, there was a competition for a children's game. I didn't win it, but I got second prize for designing a game where you have a long snake full of numbers, one to one hundred, and you throw dice, et cetera. Through that, I got to work in a small factory where they made printing blocks.

"I worked there with men only. It was very hot in the summer and they wanted to take off their shirts but didn't like a woman there, so I left after a while. Through that job I got into the graphic design department of the Jewish National Fund. There I made inscriptions in the *Golden Book,* by the piece. Every designer from Europe knows calligraphy from left to right. If you do it from right to left, it doesn't come out in the middle. Knowing nothing, with lightning speed I would read the inscription I was supposed to copy on the certificate and start writing from the end, backwards. People who saw it said, 'My God, she must be mad!' "

Ruth's eyes sparkled with amusement as she poured more tea and said, "In all those early years, we had a very gay life. It was a difficult life, but full of hope and romance and danger. I don't believe that I completely took in what it was all about. For me it was a terrific adventure."

"It's too bad youth is wasted on the young." I offered Shaw's worn but valid truism.

"It certainly is," she agreed. "But it wasn't only that we were young. Palestine, Israel was young. We were all young. The whole thing was a wonderful, wonderful time. I'm not just saying this because it was long ago. Everything was new. Everybody was kind. Everybody was nice. There were no locks on the doors. Everything was wide open.

"When I worked as a maid, I was as good a person to be with and to entertain in the evening as anybody, as the people who employed me. There was no class distinction, no money problem, probably because nobody had any. We were all poor except maybe a very few families of the old Sephardic indigenous community who had been here for many generations. They were wealthy.

"They were also very much connected with the British because the few high positions which were filled in those days by Jews were filled largely by those families, originally from Spain and Portugal. But we were not in those circles. We were immigrants. We were all young. We were all poor, and we all had a wonderful time. Most of us were of European origin because at that time the oriental community was either very wealthy and didn't mix with us or very poor and didn't mix with us either.

"The wealthy ones were very cultured people with a long, long family background, whereas all of us had lost our family background. We were standing on our own two feet here. We had nobody to back us, nobody to help us, nobody to bother us, nobody to account to, and that was, in a way, very, very nice. That was the big adventure. If I think today that my daughter would be in such a situation, I am horrified!

"I would never, never, if anybody would ask me, permit my children to live the way we lived. Some of our friends died in the riots. They died of thirst when they went hiking to God knows where in the desert. There was nobody to say anything, no restrictions, nothing except for our own ideology, which was very, very strong. We were all red-hot Zionists. But I don't believe it was a political Zionism. It was a dream Zionism, and we didn't quite see how it was going to become real."

"Had you experienced anti-Semitism in Prague, in school, or in any way?"

"There was no real incident, but I was the only Jewish student in the Czech school. In the *Gymnasium* I was with two others in the higher classes. Of course, we were different. Also, my background was partly German, so that made me doubly different. Later on, I went to a German high school, and there most of us were Jews. The German cultural background was Jewish in Prague, so the Jews were not liked by the Czechs, not only because they were Jews but because they were German-oriented.

"I went back to Prague once for medical reasons because I had no money to take care of myself here. My husband and I went back to visit my mother, and also my father, who still lived in Sudetenland. It was just a few months before it was taken over by the Germans, and of course it was extremely unpleasant, with direct incidents against Jews, which was not yet the case in Prague at that time.

"It was when we came back to Palestine that I started to work in the Jewish National Fund, writing those inscriptions and doing some graphic work. And there I met Harry, whom you have met. He was a South African by birth and had been here since 1929. He came from a very Zionist family, and he already belonged to quite a different social group than I did at that time.

"He was close to the British Mandate population here because his mother tongue was English. He belonged to the so-called Anglo-Saxons, which means nothing, but that's what people are called whose mother tongue is English. He worked for the Jewish National Fund in charge of the department for England, America, and South Africa. He was a journalist by profession. We fell in love, and I divorced my husband. I left him. I took one carpet and one lamp under one arm"—she laughed—"and two chairs in another arm, and I went off. I took a room in Jerusalem. Harry was also married at the time." Ruth said this so matter-of-factly that I asked her if her marriage had deteriorated.

"I wouldn't say that our marriage had deteriorated. We had had a wonderful time. Apart from our jobs, we were dog trainers. We had a broken-down apartment on a flat roof, and on that roof we had about fifteen boxers. At that time they were trained for self-defense because during the British Mandate, as you know, Jews were not allowed to carry arms. Only in the most extreme cases would people carry a revolver. But if they were caught, it would mean prison for a long period.

"So a lot of people, a lot of watchmen, people in kibbutzim and moshavim, and even in town, used to have dogs which were trained against Arabs. They were extremely fierce dogs. If someone would touch the owner, the dog would attack. Or if you would give a command, almost inaudibly, he would know to be on the alert and would go for anyone who would rustle in the bushes, for instance.

"My husband and I had passed a course with a couple who had emigrated from Austria. Both were doctors. They brought the first boxers to Palestine and gave courses for young people who wanted to train dogs for themselves or for others. We enjoyed doing it, but we parted good friends. It was just that we had no children and my aspirations in life were different. He was a very nice fellow, but we had grown apart.

"I'm still very friendly with my first husband. He is here in

Jerusalem. I visited him yesterday. He had an accident and has a huge plaster cast around his torso. I painted a sort of Botticelli scene of three naked ladies gamboling about, and in the background I painted everything abstract. He wanted me to do it and said that when they cut it off he will hang it up."

"What happened to him?" I asked.

"He's now a photographer and was photographing Israel Bonds people who came here. He climbed on some kind of excavated column and slipped off. He practically broke his back. It was terrible!"

"How long were you married to him?"

"Ten years. I was all of twenty-six. I left the marriage just as poor as I started it. But that was O.K. I had a profession by then. I had gotten into graphic design, but I hadn't painted yet, even though I very much wanted to. In those days people didn't approach art as simply as they do now. Art—painting—was something very serious. You just didn't buy paints and start. I took it more to heart. I was afraid, and it was a big hurdle. So I stuck with commercial art, which was the easy way out. And there was the money, of course.

"That was during World War Two, and I want to say something about it. I think young people today are more aware of what goes on around them than we were. Maybe I'm a particularly egocentric person. Maybe all artists are very egocentric. But I must admit that in World War Two, even though my father was in Europe and I never heard from him again, and knowledge came back to us of what was going on, and we helped illegal immigrants come to shore—we saw the ships, we saw the people—nevertheless I don't believe it penetrated until much later. The war, and Hitler being practically in front of our door in Egypt, it didn't bother us. I don't know. I think today people know that war is very serious. Maybe because we've had so many wars in the meanwhile. I know that my children are haunted by war. For them it's a daily occurrence. It's part of their lives.

"For us it was something that we never expected, even though there were a lot of the Free French, the Free Czechs, the Free Poles stationed here because they were fighting in Egypt. They came on leave here, and they were all around us. It was such a disaster, but it was too far away for us. As you know, there were not too many people here who fought. The British didn't want a Jewish army. Only at the very end did they relent.

"And we were still gay and young and adventurous. Retrospectively, I often think about it. And I feel very badly about it, that in my life I missed the awareness that young people have today. Maybe it protected us also. It gave us a much better life. With all the opportunities that kids have nowadays, I think they have a lousy life. I think they have a horrible life because of this extreme awareness that they have. Everything has come so close to them. Maybe it's because of TV. It could be that when you see a war right in front of you on the screen, you can't escape it. We didn't see it. We only heard about it."

"Have the Israeli wars been on the Israeli TV screen?" I asked.

"Oh, yes. Not always. Not the Six-Day War. We didn't have it then. Our first TV broadcast was the victory parade on Independence Day in '68, celebrating the Six-Day War. It was fantastic. We couldn't believe the victory parade, and we couldn't believe the TV. It was surreal.

"Well, I've gotten off the track," Ruth said as she got up to stir the fire. "I wanted to tell you that when Harry and I fell in love, that was in the last days of the Mandate. At that time we had an underground broadcasting station here in Jerusalem, from the Haganah, and Harry was the English announcer. The station would move somewhere else every night because the British were after it. I was enchanted by Harry. He sounded wonderful on the radio with his wonderful deep British voice, which I could never achieve. I could never achieve that fantastic accent.

"I lived in a room in the middle of town, and there was curfew all the time because every day there were incidents against the British and against the Jews. Things were being blown up, railway bridges, cars. It was Götterdämmerung. It was the end of the Mandate, and everything was absolutely chaotic. Jerusalem was full of barbed wire. This area, every other area, was cordoned off, and everybody was against everybody. Harry had a curfew pass, and he would roam around the empty streets to see what was happening.

"Again, maybe not every person feels this way, but there was a glow, a romance over everything. I think it was the lack of immediate contact, even though I was present when people were killed. I was present many times when things were blown up and cars would fly sky-high. But today when I'm present, as happened to me not too long ago when I was on Ben Yehuda Street, it's different. An abandoned car, which was fixed up with explosives, blew up. I wasn't hurt, but I was traumatized. I don't think it was just because I'm older. Maybe it was because I had no children before. It was only your own life. Who cares, anyhow? I think you become aware of your surroundings and of the danger only when you have children, because until then nothing matters very much.

"Well, in the midst of all the chaos of '46 I went to England. I went to a real art school for the first time. That was a big day. I packed a little valise. I left Palestine—again without money, again without anybody to do anything for me. It didn't matter. I came there. I hardly spoke English, but I had been accepted to an art school in London. The city was completely bombed out. London was in pieces, but again people were nice. People were wonderful."

"How did you arrange the school acceptance in the midst of all that?" I asked incredulously. The answer was simple.

"I wrote. I sent some samples of my graphic work, my commercial art work, and they accepted me. There were a lot of people at that time whose credentials were even less than mine because there were many ex-servicemen who'd come back from the war, and many of them studied art, some seriously, some not so seriously. Anyhow, everything was sort of wide open in those days. I left Palestine knowing that I would come back here, but again it was an adventure to go away."

"Were you divorced?"

"I was divorced. Yes."

"Was it difficult to get a divorce, with the problem of the religious laws?"

"No, as long as we had an agreement and we were friends. We married, he and I alone, and we divorced, he and I alone. We had no family here, no problem. We had no money, no property, no children. We just decided it would be a good thing to divorce. It sounds better than it was. Of course, it was heartbreaking for us to leave each other. But we came to the conclusion that we had had a good life for ten years. I was in love with Harry, and I simply didn't want to be married to my husband anymore, and that was that."

Mystified by Ruth's seemingly uncomplicated approach to the

problem, I asked if Harry went to England with her. "No. He stayed here and I went alone. I had no idea if I would ever see him again. We were lovers and we were very much in love, terribly in love, but he was married and had a child. I didn't know what his plans were, and I didn't ask him either.

"I went to England by ship, through Beirut." Here her exposition of the carefree romantic took a shocking turn. "I had a horrible experience in Beirut. I was raped by an Arab, which I never forgot or forgave. It was my fault, absolutely my fault. I was a silly girl."

"How did it happen?"

"I traveled third class on a very poor ship. It came from Marseilles to Haifa, and it took two nights to sail to Beirut. It was very, very hot. All these young kids in third class were standing around, looking at the first class, where they were dancing and having drinks. Then some fellows came out and asked the girls to come in and dance, and we did. There was one Arab who asked me to dance. It was quite pleasant. The next morning we were coming to Beirut, where he got off. He asked me, 'Do you know Beirut?' I said, 'No.' He said, 'Shall I show you?' I said, 'No, no, thank you very much.' And he went off.

"We had no money to go to town. We were stuck on the ship. It was boiling hot. The ship was loading. It was sailing again the next morning at four o'clock. In the afternoon that chap came around again, in an open car. I had never been in an open car. It was white with red upholstery. Look, I was a silly girl. I had no experience in life except the riots. That was my big experience. And I had been married, but I was very young in my outlook. I was this mixture of European sophistication and complete ignorance in other ways, naïve and absolutely oblivious of danger.

"Anyway, he came and pestered me with 'I'll show you this, I'll show you that.' I said, 'No, no, no.' He said, 'I'll drive you up on the Lebanon, on the mountains, on top of Beirut.' "

"Did he live in Beirut?" I asked, trying to get this terrible story straight.

"Yes, he did. That was something, to see the Lebanon, so I went with him. It was already afternoon, and we drove up and up, up, up. And then I said, 'Let's go back.' He said, 'No, let's drive here and there. I'll show you.' It got dark. Then we came to a place. It was closed, and he knocked. An Arab servant opened the door.

By that time I was feeling very, very queasy. But this man served us some coffee and some *arak*. Nothing happened. There was nobody in the whole place. Until this day I don't know what kind of a place it was.

"And then we drove back. I was already congratulating myself that I got away without a scratch. By that time, it was night. Then he stopped and said, 'O.K., now let's—' And I said, 'No, please, let's not.' 'Look,' he said, 'there's nothing you can do.' I tried to get out, and he opened the glove compartment, took out a nice little gun, mother-of-pearl, and said, 'Look, one more squeak out of you. . . . Nobody will ever find you here on the Lebanon, and the ship is leaving tomorrow at four o'clock. Before you'll be missed, they'll be halfway to Trieste, or to Marseilles.'

"So I struggled some more, but then I said to myself, 'Look, it's not worth it.' Afterwards, we silently drove down to the ship, and I crawled up there with my blouse torn and my trousers torn. He had given me his card before that. I kept it for many years, but then I thought, 'Ah, the hell with it.' I suppose somebody shot him by now, anyhow, in Beirut."

I was amazed at her story and realized more and more how little I knew about her. To have overcome what must be the most horrible experience for a woman, and not let it destroy her. I wondered if she had gotten pregnant.

Ruth shrugged her shoulders. "No, but I thought I might have gotten sick, I might have gotten something. I went to a doctor in London right away. It took over two weeks before he managed to tell me that I was all right. I didn't think that I could have any children. I had been pregnant when I was very young, but lost it. I started very early, before I came to Palestine, while I was still in Prague.

"My home life wasn't very brilliant, with my stepfather. I was left very much to my own devices. My mother believed in it. She was a great feminist and felt very frustrated by her upbringing. Her older brother died when he was eighteen, and her parents never forgave her. If somebody had to die, it should've been the girl. She really got a lasting trauma from that.

"It was my generation that was a lost generation of European Jewry. Young European Jews, between the ages of fifteen to twenty-five, who were completely uprooted, came here without family, without language, without money, without background, without supervision, without anything. We just had to make the best of it. It made us into extremely self-reliant people, all of us, who could improvise and find our way anyplace, in any circumstance. But of course, many of us got knocked about a great deal in the process of living like this and growing up like this. . . .

"Anyway, I was in London," she resumed. "I was in art school. Harry came six months later. We spent the most marvelous year together. He was at Oxford. I was in London. We had a wonderful, wonderful time. Then he got his divorce, came back here to Palestine, and four months later I returned. We knew that war would break out. The British had left, and there was utter chaos.

"I came back just before the outbreak of the War of Independence in 1948, and we got married, Harry and I, in the final days of the Mandate because there was nothing else to do, the way Harry was brought up. He was not an artist. He was not a bogeyman. He was very well brought up. He was a very proper Anglo-Saxon. He didn't think it was right to live together without getting married. I'm sorry that we married. I thought we had been much better off and happier not married." Ruth's abiding honesty was refreshing. "But he very much wanted to, and I didn't want to lose him. At the time, everything was so chaotic here, and again, I had no money at all, and I had no place to live, and he didn't want me to live with him without being married. So we married.

"The rabbi who was going to marry us lived on Ben Yehuda Street, and the day before the marriage, Ben Yehuda Street was blown up. There was a huge explosion, you remember?" Yes, I did. "The British soldiers left a mined truck on the street, and on a bright morning, when Ben Yehuda Street was full of people, the whole thing blew up. The rabbi's apartment, where we were to be married, was destroyed, and he sought refuge in a German hospice here in Jerusalem. So we were married by him the next day in the chapel of the hospice, with Jesus Christ and Holy Mary and whatnot all around us." Ruth laughed. "He was a Reform rabbi from Germany and afterwards became chief rabbi in Sweden."

"Wasn't it unusual for a Reform rabbi to be allowed to perform a marriage here? I thought only the Orthodox could."

"In those days, nobody cared about those things. It was the last days before the war. Everything was disintegrating. If people wanted to get married, O.K., they got married. If they could find a rabbi, O.K., he married them. We had no witnesses. Nothing. We went on our honeymoon to Beit Hakerem, near this area here. And then the war started.

"My husband's nephew was killed in the first days of the war. He was an eighteen-year-old boy. Just straight from school he went to the Palmach. He was killed in one of the first battles, in the Galilee. So my introduction to Harry's family was very unfortunate. They were sitting *shivah* at the time I met them. It took years before I got to know them. They lived in Tel Aviv. We went to see them when they were sitting *shivah,* and we got back to Jerusalem just as the siege of the city started.

"Did you ever see Harry's book on the siege?" I told her I hadn't. "I'll give it to you. It's very interesting. It tells the whole background. During the siege we were here in Jerusalem. We lived in Harry's apartment, which was full of the former Mrs. Levin, and I was very unhappy there, after that marvelous time we had had in London when we were just alone. You see, my whole background made me alone all the time. I was never used to having either a social background or a family background. And Harry was very conscious of having backgrounds. It was very important to him. I was not very happy at that time because it turned out his being proper shocked me very much."

"You weren't aware of that in England or when you had been together before that?"

"No, not at all. It really knocked me sideways. I was completely confused. But we lived through the siege. You can read about it. It's a diary—about him, about me, about the whole situation. It's a very good book and was extremely successful at the time.

"We never believed that we would live through the siege. We never believed that we would last, that Israel really would happen. We were hungry, thirsty. We had no water, no food. We lived from day to day, and shells were raining down on us night after night. We slept in the corridor down below in the house where we lived. All the tenants slept in the corridor. It was the most sheltered place. We lived on the top floor. Once a shell dropped into our apartment, but it was a dud and didn't explode.

"At that time we had a young American couple living with us. They had been staying in a very exposed area. Those were the first

Americans I had ever met, and we had a very good time together. Unfortunately she was pregnant, and the doctor had ordered her to stay in bed to save her baby. She was getting along fine. But that shell dropped right in her bedroom. It came with such a tremendous roar and crash, ripping holes in the ceiling, that she lost the baby from shock.

"The siege was a tremendous event in our lives because not many people remained here. Even today, people have not forgotten who left Jerusalem before the siege because they were afraid. Nobody talks about it. It's not a topic for conversation. But in the back of your mind, it's something that one remembers. The people who stayed here were like those in Britain's 'finest hour.' This really was one of our finest hours because everybody helped everybody and we were one big family. We thought that maybe we wouldn't live through it. When the convoys of food got through from Tel Aviv, it was unbelievable—the joy, the happiness that food came, that we were not forgotten, that relief came. It was fantastic!"

"Was Harry in the fighting?"

"No. He was on the radio, which broadcast every night, as long as there was electricity—news, encouragement, songs, and whatnot. I was in the Haganah. I was drawing maps, very detailed maps, which would help in the fighting."

Harry Levin's book, *I Saw the Battle of Jerusalem,* gives a most moving report of Jerusalem under siege. He speaks of the difficulties of getting around unlit streets cordoned off by barbed wire, of friends and acquaintances being killed, of narrow escapes from bombs, and of his overriding concern for Ruth, who had lost considerable weight from lack of nourishment.

In one passage he gives this fond appraisal of her:

> Ruth was full of excitement when I met her for lunch. She and Rivka R. went painting this morning. People must have thought them brainless. One passerby did remark, "Nothing better to do in times like these?" They chose a protected spot in the lee of a large building. Ruth's picture is well conceived, with fine sense of colour and vivid depth. She's gifted, but paints with so much passion that it leaves her exhausted for hours. She kept brimming over all through lunch, talking even faster than usual. How she loves life and the world, and what a concentrated, intense vision she has of it! When she is happy it's hard to be gloomy in her company. But these days

she is looking thin and pale; I am very concerned about her. Tomorrow she starts on her new *tafkid* (duty) in the map-drawing section.

The courage of the Jerusalemites is legend. With the road between Tel Aviv and Jerusalem blocked by the fighting, only two major convoys of food came through from November, when the war began, until the end of April, when the road was taken by the Jews in the war's bitterest battle. Food supplies had been cut off almost immediately, with only small convoys getting through occasionally. There was little kerosene, no electricity. The pump station and the pipeline for water supplying Jerusalem were cut off by the Arabs.

Jerusalem's women joined the men with firearms to answer shooting at their border. Children helped their parents gather twigs, papers, old boxes—anything that would make a fire to cook their meager supplies. They resorted to picking weeds to eat, notably the *hubeza*, a small heart-shaped edible weed found in every garden. The two convoys of food came after Purim, in March, and before Passover, the end of April. *Hubeza* leaves have since been added by many Jerusalem families to the bitter herbs of Passover.

"Then the State was declared, which, of course, was an incredible, incredible event for us," Ruth continued. "It is something I remember as one of the greatest moments; that, and after the Six-Day War. Of course, we lost the Old City. We lost half of Jerusalem; the Western Wall, everything was gone. But we survived, and there was a State, and we started to live all over again."

Ruth did not dwell on the extreme hardships that she had lived through at that time. It seemed characteristic of her to minimize the bad experience and to remember the joy and the triumph of survival.

"Harry was one of the first people recruited by our first foreign minister, Moshe Sharett. He was in a group of diplomats who were recruited from all walks of life. That's why the diplomats in those days were all so brilliant. They were not people who were brought up in the diplomatic circuit. They had no diplomatic school. They were outstanding professors, journalists, writers, artists, politicians, and kibbutzniks. They were people who were considered able and worthy to represent Israel.

"In 1950, Harry was appointed to be the first representative of Israel in Australia and New Zealand. And there we went. I must say that by that time I had adjusted to Harry's being proper. I saw that he wasn't quite that proper after all. We managed very well. But then came another crisis. And that was that I was suddenly in public life, which was a very great crisis for me because I had been always a very private person and Harry had not. For him, public life was a stimulus and a challenge. He was a very, very good diplomat and a wonderful public speaker.

"For me, it was rather difficult. First of all, I was very young. I looked very young. I don't know what the Australian Jews expected. But there was that little girl coming out of the plane who was supposed to be the wife of the consul general. He was twelve years older than me. That means he was close to forty and I was all of twenty-eight. I think we were a success, but half the time I didn't know whether I was coming or going. I didn't know how to handle the situation.

"I want to come back for a moment to painting. I had painted in London. It was a great thing for me, and I had started very well. When I got into the diplomatic life, I continued to paint. But diplomacy is the exact opposite of art. One is completely external. The other is completely internal. One is extrovert. The other, introvert. One is mask. The other is the only truth that you have to dig out of yourself as best you can. It presented a great conflict for me.

"During the twenty years that Harry and I were married, we lived in Australia and New Zealand and Washington, then back in Israel for four years, and then in Denmark, where he was ambassador and where he died. All this time my painting, at which I think I got better and better, had to take second place. There were endless interruptions and always this to do and that to do. It meant traveling, seeing and meeting people whom you'll never see again in your life, expending all your energies on making contact with somebody and making an impression for Israel and explaining it, and so on.

"But it was a wonderful time. It was a great thing to be in the group of the first representatives of Israel, because Israel was a super country at that time. Everybody loved Israel. And everybody loved us, these 'super Israelis.' We were, most of us, modest, naïve, forthcoming, eager to help, eager to explain. We were enthusiastic

Israelis and Zionists. And it came all from the heart. So it was all a wonderful thing. But as far as my own development was concerned, that was another story.

"After being in Australia for one and a half years, we were transferred to Washington, where Harry became consul for the cultural and information department in the embassy. And there we stayed for seven years. I had a child, my first child. He was premature. He lived for three months and then died a day before the brith. I didn't think I could have another child. After all these years, this was the first one. We tried and tried and tried, but it didn't work. And I went back to Israel and adopted my son."

"You went back without Harry?"

"Without Harry. He couldn't come for two months. So I went to find a child and to be with him. David, my son, was one of the first, if not the first, legal adoptees in Israel. Because at that time we had no laws about this at all. There were many orphans from the war, from the Holocaust. People took them and had them and kept them and brought them up. But we had no legal framework for that.

"When I returned to Israel, I went to the WIZO home in Tel Aviv, where they told me there were a few children. They brought me a child. That was David. I said, 'This is the one I will take.' I never looked at another child. I felt, really, an immediate closeness to him, and I didn't believe that that was a thing one could shop around for. And the more one would look at children, the more confused one would get. If I hadn't liked him and loved him, of course, if I hadn't felt this sympathy for him, I wouldn't have taken him. He was exactly the kind of child that I wanted. It may sound funny. But he was a very manly, sturdy, and serious child."

"How old was he?"

"He was three months. I played with him. I had no idea what to do with a child. I had never held a baby in my arms. After three weeks I took him to Washington. The trip was a disaster. I didn't know how to hold him, to handle him, to change him. He howled and howled and howled for hours on the plane. Then I gave him a tranquilizer and he fell asleep. Then I shook him awake because I thought he was dying. It was terrible! He came to Washington looking like hell, to his new papa. But after a few days, he looked all right. And then I got pregnant."

"What year was that?" It wasn't easy to keep up with the chronology of Ruth's life, so filled with unexpected turns and surprises.

"It was '52. I got pregnant just about three days after I came back with David. I just couldn't believe it. My daughter was born seven and a half months later. She was also in an incubator. There was also trouble. But she was well. Michal survived, and she is a wonderful girl. What upset me was that I had three kids within fourteen months. I didn't know where I was at all.

"Washington was a wonderful time. My life was wonderful, but it was very hard. I was very upset by those babies, and it took me some time to adjust to the fact that I had children. I had never been a particularly motherly type of person. And I never particularly wanted children. But then, of course, when I had a child and he died, suddenly there was this terrible emptiness." Ruth spoke passionately and painfully, a woman starkly honest with herself, yet always acknowledging the "wonderful time" along with the pain and frustration. Her *joie de vivre* and sense of humor were irrepressible.

"We came back to Israel in '58. Harry went to the Foreign Office. I took care of the children and started to work as a graphic designer and, to some extent, a painter. The sad fact is, the truth is, I don't know how many women manage a professional career with being a mother. Maybe nowadays they do. It is possible. This generation—my daughter's generation—manages, although I know she has a hard time about it, as well. A very hard time.

"My generation didn't manage it. My painting, my career, my development was always, willingly or not so willingly, subordinated to Harry's work. It was his life, and I went along with him. We had a fine time. We loved each other. We fought each other. I developed intellectually with Harry, and I became a worldly person. But my own inner development was subservient. I fought against it, but not very hard.

"When I was in Washington, I had two exhibitions. I also had one in Boston and one in New York, and I did some book illustrations. It was not halfhearted. But it wasn't as good as it could have been, for sure, because it was always done by the way, when there was time. It was very serious, but it wasn't primary.

"I had a moderate success as a painter, but it was always the 'wife of the Israeli diplomat' who was exhibiting. I was allergic to this whole diplomatic syndrome right from the beginning, certainly when it was coupled with painting. A painter and diplomat just don't go together. It's not serious. It can't be. When people said to me, 'Why do you do it? Why don't you devote yourself to your children—they are so young?' I said, 'Look, after all I must have some life of my own, and I don't believe that children have to have a full-time mother dancing around them.' My children certainly proved that it's not necessary.

"Fortunately, I didn't completely neglect my own life and career. I would have been in very bad shape when Harry died if that had been the case. We went to Copenhagen in '61 and we were there for five years. I think we were a great success for Israel, because this was a couple that was a bit different from the usual ambassadors, because Harry wrote all the time and did some painting, too. And I painted. Our friends were writers and artists, apart from the politicians who were Harry's professional contacts. The Danes very much appreciated that Israel's representatives were a couple who had something more to say than the comparatively narrow and circumscribed conversations that go on in diplomatic parties.

"In Copenhagen I started to paint seriously for the first time. It was still against the embassy life, but there was more time for me to devote to painting. I didn't exhibit in Copenhagen because I didn't believe that, as the wife of the ambassador, I should mix these two things up. I would never know when the painting would be reviewed, criticized, written up because I was the wife of Harry Levin or because I am Ruth Levin. That was one thing I couldn't really stand."

"The children were with you in Copenhagen?"

"Our children were with us, yes. And they had a hard time. Diplomats' children have a terrible time. It affects children differently, depending on the mentality of the child. For instance, my daughter, even today, has a deep-seated suspicion towards people. She had never been treated except with the greatest niceness and friendliness, because she's an extraordinarily nice and sweet and clever and vivacious girl. But she doesn't believe it.

"When she was a little girl, she heard me and her father have a quarrel, or we might have been in a bad mood or tired. Then someone would come. We might have a party, or visitors, and we would appear with big smiles painted on our faces and say, 'Oh, hello. How are you? How lovely to see you. How wonderful, this, that, and the other.' And there was this little kid looking at us with big eyes. She couldn't believe it. After a while, she would come down to the living room and start making conversation. I was horrified! But I couldn't stop her, because that's what she saw us doing.

"I think it had a disastrous influence on her. I have to say, with terrible sadness, that only after Harry's death did our life become normalized. The children developed a straightforward sense of values only after I came back here with them and they went to an ordinary boarding school. I couldn't help them. I had to reorganize myself. I took extreme care never to say one thing that would not be true and never to make one phone call that would be phony. No hypocrisy. I felt so strongly about that.

"You see, when you have a couple of people who are as strong-minded as Harry and I were, we had our differences of opinion. Let's take education, for instance. Here was David, an adopted child. Harry always felt that David had to be particularly well-treated and kindly treated and indulged. I didn't think so. I felt, what the hell, if this boy annoyed me—and he annoyed me terribly sometimes—I was jolly well going to do something about it. It had no bearing on the fact that he was adopted. I felt no difference whatever between him and my daughter.

"David reacted to Harry's conflict. And, as children do, he manipulated it. He manipulated that, and Michal, my daughter, manipulated something else, our social syndrome. And the whole thing was not good. I thought the children were in not too good a shape. They had no friends. They spoke Danish only so-so. They went to an international school where kids came and went and nobody cared anything except that they should be quiet and happy and not bother the parents.

"After we had a Bar Mitzvah and Bas Mitzvah together, because they are just one year apart, they went to a boarding school in Holland. Three weeks later, Harry died from a heart attack." Ruth threw up her arms in dismay, reviewing that most difficult period in her life. "I had had a hysterectomy and had just come out of hospital. I have total amnesia about everything at that time—

about the operation, about the children, about the funeral. You know, it's a terrible thing"—she heaved a very big sigh—"if that happens in a foreign country. It is more terrible than I want to go into, because you are alone. I had Danish friends, better than acquaintances, but so what? What could they do for me?

"I was in this huge embassy, four floors of it. My children went back to the boarding school after the funeral, which took place here in Israel. I returned to Denmark and rattled around in that embassy like a pea in a shoebox. Harry died in November. Christmas came, and the children came home for vacation, and we had a terrible time."

"Why did you stay in Denmark after Harry's death?"

"The children had just gotten into this boarding school. I didn't want to upset them once more. Also, I hadn't collected myself. I didn't know what I was going to do. People said, 'Why don't you stay in Denmark? You have very good friends here. You can stay here.' I had a very good friend whose husband died just a few weeks before, and after the Christmas vacation, I moved to her place. She's a doctor, and we are still extremely good friends. She will be here to visit me in two weeks. I stayed with her for six months, waiting for the children to finish the school year.

"Harry had a heart condition when we married, and I knew it. When I was in hospital, he felt pretty bad. I'm never sick, and all our life we had been taking care of his heart and an ulcer. I said, 'For once, let's just concentrate on my hysterectomy.' The day before he died, he came to the sanatorium where I was, and we had dinner together. It is good to remember that we had a very gay and flirtatious dinner, as if we had just met. He died the same night.

"You know, when a husband dies, some people are nice and some are beastly to you. I was in a complete daze. I started to work in Danish TV, because Israel's TV had just started and I thought when I went back I could become a designer for TV. But it was terrible in Denmark. There was this TV town where everybody spoke only Danish. People didn't stop talking the language when I came around. When I was the wife of the ambassador, people spoke English to us. But now everybody spoke Danish, and I only understood about half of it. I was very unhappy."

"I didn't realize, at a death, when a woman loses her husband, that people are so beastly," I remarked.

"Look, some people may love you and some people may hate

you. When something like that happens to you, those who love you are nicer and more loving, and those who hate you let you feel it. That's what I discovered after Harry's death.

"I had been very much looking forward to coming home. But when I did come back to Israel with my children, it was much more difficult than I anticipated. This is an immigrant society, and people who come to Israel are new. If you are abroad for four, five, six years, you are new all over again. The population changes here so rapidly that people who are away for a certain number of years come back to a new constellation.

"It's not like a Dane who comes home to Denmark after six years and finds the furniture standing in exactly the same place, the same ballet playing, the same theaters, the same parties, the same everything. Here it's completely different. Society in Israel changes extremely rapidly, partly because of immigration, partly because of the wars, because every war transforms Israel. While we were in Denmark there was no war in Israel, but there was a very severe recession and that completely changed the constellation here. I had been away for so many years, except for the four years we were here in between appointments. And then we knew it was temporary. I had really, all my life, never been in one place for more than eight years at a time. The longest I had ever been in any place was in Washington. So while I was certainly very much an Israeli and had been here right at the beginning and had lived through many things, timewise I had not been here very long.

"When I came back I was very disoriented, and, this being an immigrant society, people expect that immigrants are going to take care of themselves, more or less. I'm not talking about the Jewish Agency helping Russian immigrants, et cetera. That's another thing. That's official help. Immigrants here complair very much that Israelis are not very nice. Now why are Israelis not nice?" Ruth both asked and answered the question.

"Israelis are very, very hardworking, very poor, very nervous, inwardly nervous, very easily upset, falling from one crisis into another—political, social, economic—constantly. You've been here a few weeks. Every day there's some major catastrophe. So there is not too much time and energy left over for making a great effort for newcomers. Nevertheless, we know that newcomers eventually manage.

"I came home, and I was like a newcomer. I had, once more,

no money. I had this house, fortunately, which was the one safe place to come back to. But it looked like hell. It had been rented and half destroyed. It was in terrible shape. I sent the kids to a Youth Aliyah boarding school because I didn't feel that I was in a condition where I could help them to integrate. I was new myself here."

"Did they speak Hebrew?"

"Oh, yes, they spoke Hebrew. Of course, so do I. But my Hebrew is not good enough to help children of high school age in homework."

"Didn't Harry leave any money, any insurance, anything? Pension?"

"Pension, yes. But the pension is minimum. Anyway, I also felt it would minimize our daily conflict because David, in particular, who had again lost his father, was extremely upset by Harry's death, and he took it out on me." Again I felt Ruth's stark honesty in probing her problems. "It would have been easier, if anybody had to die, it would have been easier if I had died and not Harry. David was very close to Harry, more than to me, and I fought for two years to regain the children's confidence.

"I always thought that Harry was a more decent person than I, a more proper person than I, a more respectable person than I, and a more reliable person than I, so in many ways I deferred to him even if it was often against my better judgment. But I gave in because of the feeling that he was a better person. Now I was alone with the children, and I had to convince them that I was a good person as well."

"You had to convince yourself," I suggested.

"I had to convince myself. Yes. That's a very true observation. Now, eleven years afterwards, I am convinced. I've convinced myself. Yes. The thing that helped me here, really, was the Six-Day War. The Six-Day War was for me a great event. That made a place for me in this country, a permanent place.

"You see, I had been present at the birth of Israel. Then I had been abroad, representing Israel. My contact with Israel was secondhand during all this time. The next thing that happened was the Six-Day War, where I was again present. That was my great good luck, because I realized for the first time, consciously, in a completely aware manner, that Israel was my country, that I was an

Israeli, that I was a Jew, that Jews and Gentiles are not equal, as I had claimed all my life, that there is a difference, that there is a common language between Jews which is achieved immediately, which takes years to achieve with a non-Jew.

"They don't have a common language. We can only feel sorry for them in that respect because we have something, a common experience, on which we can call for the sake of communication and getting closer. That I felt extremely strongly during the war and afterwards, and it was that that integrated me here, for good. For the first time in my life I felt I had a place where I was definitely at home, where I could play a part, and where I could, for the first time, not be an outsider. I could be a member of the community and contribute.

"As a painter, for instance, I could find something that I had to say here which was my own personal experience about Sinai or about the desert, Judea, the mountains, about Jerusalem. It may not be an outstanding contribution, but it's my own." Her paintings of the Sinai are very beautiful, lyrical, sensitive large canvases.

She went on, "It's a sad thing to say that, in some ways, my life had become, after my husband died, much simpler, much more difficult, much less rich. Of course, I miss him terribly. But from being half a person—he was half, and I was the other half—now I'm on my own, and for better or for worse, and willy-nilly, I have to be a whole person. The main part of this is Israel, really. I've never been so much at peace as I am now, at fifty-eight. At last, after all these years—a few years here, a few years there—of living out of suitcases and having half the things in another place—my books in another place, and the paintings that I'd do would be completely irrelevant and out of place in the new place—now everything is, at last, together in one place.

"My children and myself are together in Jerusalem. We all have our separate lives, but we see each other frequently and have as good a time together as strong-minded individuals can have. They are both at peace here too. They have no desire to be some-place else, except to go on a trip. Many young people here have a sort of claustrophobic feeling about Israel. They can't get out. There's the golden paradise somewhere abroad, with the most marvelous things—money, possessions, travels, et cetera—that are out of their reach.

"My children, young as they were when they were abroad, know that abroad is just another place, a nice place, maybe an easier place, but it has its drawbacks. They know it's there. It's within reach, but they have no particular urgency about going there. And I'm happy about it, because this urgency in young people here very often leads them to take steps which they regret and are difficult to repair. If they leave, the longer they are away the more difficult it is to come back again. And it poses enormous problems.

"My kids, touch wood"—and she tapped the coffee table—"fortunately don't have that. They got over this schizophrenic feeling about life being only half real when they lived in embassies and went to foreign schools and were in an international environment. It's possible that they have become more parochial. It's possible that they have become more limited. I don't know. I hope not. At least I try to do my best to keep their horizons open. But too much choice can be destructive.

"This is really a wonderful country to be at home in, if you make a living, as I do now by having my graphic design bureau, which I'm very fond of. It exasperated me very often. But I started it ten years ago, and it goes very well. I have nice clients, good relations with my printers and platemakers. They are my friends. I like making enough money to lead a decent life. And I like making it myself."

Then, for the first time in our talks, she mentioned Amos, the man she has lived with for several years. On other visits she had asked if he would come out to meet us—he works with her in the graphic design business that she conducts from the house—but he had declined, as she said he usually does with strangers. "I live together with a man who is an unusual kind of person," she said with a sigh. "He's very eccentric, and he's very solitary. But probably so am I, even though I look like a social kind of woman. I think, the older I get, the more glad I am to be on my own, and with only a few people, in an environment which is familiar to me, like Jerusalem or like Sinai, which I can explore in depth.

"I don't just look at them, as I used to travel around the world to see Australia and New Zealand and the Grand Canyon and Denmark and Sweden and God knows what else. It was all from the outside. I'm content to be in one place where I can see things from the inside. I can do something with it. I have no desire to see any new things. I've seen enough, and I want to utilize what I've seen and what I've experienced in Israel, which has at last assumed its proper place in my life.

"It has always been a problem to me because I belonged and I didn't belong. I was coming and going, and I was representing Israel without being part of it, in a way that always made me very insecure and gave me a phony feeling. Now I feel that I am much more of one piece. I'm very sorry that Harry didn't have the good fortune to experience this for himself, because I'm sure that it must have mixed him up also.

"Everybody must get mixed up by that kind of a life, having to make your home temporarily in a new country and meeting people in an unreal background. In this country I know exactly what people are saying to me. When somebody talks to me I can evaluate exactly what he means. That doesn't mean that I'm enchanted with everybody that I meet here. Not at all. People are rude and unpleasant just like everywhere else. But at least I know where I am. This is one thing I always missed in my life, to know where I am.

"Being here for the Six-Day War, which came out very well, and then the '73 Yom Kippur War, which came out not so well, finally gave me the feeling of belonging. But then my son was already serving, and of course I was as worried about him as everyone is with a son in a war. I hope to goodness there won't be another one. But I suppose it's too much to hope for.

"I would wish for anybody who comes here as an immigrant that eventually everything should fall into place and that they should be content. I was born under the sign of Libra, and Libras are always in great need of balance. That's their sign, the Scale. I don't say I believe in it, but there is something about people's attitudes, mentality. It very often fits, and it certainly fits in my case. Balance and tranquillity and peace are terribly important. I want to express this in my paintings.

"I don't want to use big words, but what is in Sinai is an eternal feeling. The silence there is so eternal that you can hear the silence. It's as though you've been there before." Ruth spoke intensely and passionately about her feeling for the Sinai, where she and Amos would be going soon again for the Passover holiday, with her friend coming from Denmark. They camp out under the sky, and she sketches the landscape for her new paintings. She speaks frequently of her attachment to the Sinai with a mystical fervor. Her paintings reflect this. "It's a place where you really belong," she said emphatically. "I don't think I've ever belonged in any other place!"

As our talks progressed, Ruth became deeply involved in unraveling the emotional layers of her constantly changing experiences for her own clarification as well as mine. From time to time, something occurred to her that she wanted to be sure not to omit. "There's one more thing I want to mention about being alone," she said emphatically, on one of these occasions. "Now it all sounds so great. I seem to be content. It took me many years to become content.

"This is a Middle Eastern society, and in the Middle East a woman without a man is still only half, or even less than half. I think it's more difficult to be alone here than in Denmark, for instance. I know many widows in Denmark, and they are working in their professions. They go out to parties, and nobody thinks about having them around or not having them around because they don't have an escort.

"Here, this is still a problem. I know that many of the war widows, young women, have a terrible problem about it because some women think they are after their husbands. Then, too, the trouble is that if they do go out, people think it's wrong because they should mourn. And if they do mourn, then they're a nuisance to everybody, and that's also bad. In spite of all the war widows here, there has still not developed a norm for how to act.

"Amongst the oriental communities, mourning is accepted. If you lose your husband, you mourn. You make a terrible fuss. You cry. You weep. You shout. You are terribly and obviously and clearly and visibly unhappy. That's the way it should be.

"Our upbringing was to restrain yourself and to control yourself and to put up a good face. I think that's the best way because eventually, through controlling yourself, you get over things. Other people say it isn't so. Psychologists who have studied the question of widowhood, which is so prevalent here, say that obvious mourning is better for your psyche. You release it. I wish the very new feminist movement here would deal with this problem."

"Is the feminist movement dealing with other problems effectively?"

"Effectively? No, I don't think so. But the problem here is so vast. I don't know if we've become more Middle Eastern–oriented, but I think emotionally women here have regressed. Maybe if you look at the outstanding women in the professions, it seems all right. But when you look at the emotional attitude of men towards women and women towards their place in society, I have my doubts if we have really progressed—at least, not as much as we should have. In this new society we could have made much greater steps in that direction. We didn't."

"Do you envision that the feminist movement will take much of a hold in Israel, in time?"

"Israel has a good explanation for everything that goes wrong here or isn't done in the right way. We have other problems to think about, and that's a fact—other priorities. It's true that this is not one of the major problems here. It's maybe a major problem for each woman concerned. But it's not a general problem. One has to accept the fact that this is not the first priority. I hope that eventually, if and when we have peace, that it will be a priority. It may not be in my time, but maybe in my daughter's time. I know, for instance, she lives with a young man who is a doctor, a psychiatrist. She's a student of philosophy, and she works as a social worker in the evenings. These two have endless problems about who does what in the household—what's your role, what's my role."

I wanted to meet Michal, and she took time off from a busy schedule to talk with me over tea in our apartment. She's a charming young woman, beautiful, small, with tousled curly hair, large glasses like her mother's, and a ready smile. In staccato words and a soft voice, similar to Ruth's, she said, "I think a very important part of my life was in Denmark. It's not easy for children whose parents are diplomats. They have to go out a great deal, and it was very, very difficult without them. It's a cold way of life, very sterile. And I remember my mother used to have sleepless nights worrying about us. I'm sure she told you.

"All those cocktail parties. We had to stand at the door and shake hands with three hundred people. I remember thinking then how these people are like on a stage. It affected me. It was so artificial. It's very, very important for me to have sincere relationships with people as a result of that."

On the subject of feminism: "Unfortunately, women's liberation has not invaded the university. Most of the women there say frankly that they are there to find a husband. It's a product of our society that still considers a woman on the shelf if she isn't married when she's twenty-three or twenty-four. I don't agree. I'm serious about my studies and will go on for a master's. I'm very involved in the work I do with disadvantaged adolescents, outside of school. And I can see my mother manages very well without being married. Of course, she needs someone next to her, which I also have.

"I've been living with my friend for two years. We have our differences, but we try to work it out. Look, I'll give you an example. I used to work as an artist's model. He, being from Argentina, has the macho psychology. For him, a woman is a woman, and he objects very much to my stripping nude in front of a group of strangers. I explained to him that for various reasons I wanted to continue. I find that it gives me something, and it should not be questionable.

"I know it was very difficult for him. I continued for a while, but afterwards I quit out of consideration for him because I knew that he had really made an effort, for quite a long time, not to say a word about it. If you can communicate, it's a way to happiness. That's what I really think you should teach people." It's a wise mother who has a wise daughter, I thought.

"My son and his wife, who are both on the square side"—Ruth laughed at her frank evaluation—"they also have problems. She's a teacher, and he's a computer technician. He's a very sort of patronizingly masculine kind of young man. I think she's not entirely satisfied with the situation as it is. I know very few women who are what you would call in America liberated. They fight for it, but I don't think they've achieved it."

"How do they resolve their differences? Does your son contribute to some of the household work? Where there are no children, of course, it's much simpler."

"That's true. But even so, what he does is always under great pressure. He says, 'I'm stronger than my wife. I'll work in the garden. Let her work in the house.' But that's not the point. It's not a question of measuring strength. She has to work more in the house than he has to work in the garden. One is necessary, and the other is not entirely necessary. I think they have great arguments about it. And my daughter has endless arguments about it with her boyfriend.

"My daughter and daughter-in-law are in the feminist movement—my daughter very actively, and my daughter-in-law less so. They have small groups where they discuss."

"A lot of women in America feel these consciousness-raising groups have been helpful to them in looking at their problems objectively and in throwing off the woman's-role stereotype that they've grown up with."

"Then how in the world does this awful book that I just read about in *Time* magazine, *The Total Woman*, get a following?" Ruth asked in utter amazement. "I can't understand it. I think it's terrible. I can't comprehend it. Most men to whom I've mentioned this *Time* article, including Amos, would you believe it, say, 'Why not? She's right. At least she's right for two million people who bought her book and who like the idea. It's up to her, and it's a free country,' and all this nonsense.

"What is this woman going to do when she's fifty-five? Is she still going to dress up in a Gypsy costume and seduce her husband under the table? I mean, what is she going to talk about? It's absolutely outlandish! And what has the feminist movement done about it in the States?"

I couldn't help laughing at Ruth's outrage. "Obviously, they can't control what this woman does, or her followers. She's got a whole system of groups meeting all over the country," I told her. "It's shocking and discouraging that she's gotten so many worshipers at her shrine."

"Just imagine!" Ruth went on. "A man comes home. He's nervous, tired. He's worked all day. And he's greeted by a woman attired in a sexy black nightie. Suppose he doesn't want to be seduced? What then? I was really outraged by this thing. I was very sorry to read it. I absolutely got upset about it."

Ruth and I agreed that, having gotten around to this subject, our talks had covered just about everything. But, most unexpectedly, we were to see each other again before I left. We were staying through Passover and had accepted an invitation for Seder from Jerusalem friends shortly after our arrival. The afternoon of the Seder, our hostess called in great distress to say that the doctor had just diagnosed her two ailing children as suffering from scarlet fever and had advised the family to go into voluntary quarantine. No Seder.

We had refused an invitation from relatives in Tel Aviv, but it was too late to make the trip, especially in the heavy holiday traffic. Milton and I looked at each other. This year—not "next year"—in Jerusalem, and here we were with the option of scrambling eggs in our apartment or of going across Jaffa Road to a lavish public Seder at the Hilton. The former seemed less objectionable.

"Ruth and Amos are having a joint Seder at their house with two other couples," I said. "The room is small, but I wonder if they could squeeze us in. I have a feeling Ruth would want to know our predicament."

"Do you think you should?" said Milton.

I phoned.

"Oh, how terrible," Ruth lamented. "Michal just phoned from the Old City. She had bumped into a couple from Amsterdam that she knew. They had no place to go for Seder, and she invited them. We're seventeen now, and it's a big squeeze. But . . ."

I told her not to hesitate to say no, that I would understand completely. But she wouldn't let it stand. "We have to do something. I'm going to consult with my co-hostesses and call you right back."

The answer was, "We all say you must come. We have more than enough for everyone. We've raided Mahane Yehuda market. It will be a *mitzvah* to have you."

If it was a *mitzvah* for them, it was a super-*mitzvah* for us. On the way to Ruth's house, a little later, we passed the market, which was not far from our apartment on Jaffa Road. Milton and I had enjoyed a few sorties into its wonders. The market is an experience in itself. The ancient site of the Judean encampment, it's a Middle East traffic jam of people, carts, baskets, noise, heat, dust, and trucks. This torrent flows around the maze of ancient cobblestone lanes and stalls, pursuing fruits, cheeses, candies, baked goods, meats, vegetables, fish, olives, salamis, nuts, and flowers. Vendors, with carts full of pita breads, hot from the market's ancient pita factory, shout their wares.

Innocently wandering into the market two days before Passover, we were overwhelmed by the crowds buying armsful of long green-stalked garlic, baskets filled with dozens of chickens, and strawberries as large as plums. Buyers line up haphazardly to have their purchases weighed on old-fashioned hanging scales. Their shopping finished, they queue up outside the market, waiting to get onto buses with their unmanageable loads. We came through relatively unscathed on this madhouse day.

It happened that two of the Seder guests were delayed and arrived towards the end of the Seder, which eased the seating. And the hosts decided Elijah would understand if his place was occupied in the emergency. Milton and I are still talking about that Seder—the flavor, the depth, the variety, the Jerusalem ambience, so different from our American Seders, which we often sit through impatiently until the point in the service that says, "The meal is served." The evening lasted until midnight, and we were enthralled and transfixed during all of it.

The service was led by Scottish-born Nathan Bar-Josef, recently retired from the Foreign Ministry and former ambassador to Norway when Harry Levin was ambassador to Denmark. He luxuriated among cushions, in a thronelike chair, to simulate the required reclining position for the occasion, and wore an elegantly embroidered velvet headpiece that resembled a fez more than a yarmulke. The service was mostly in Hebrew, but for the benefit of us and the Dutch couple, he spoke English with a Scottish burr from time to time. We were given elaborately illustrated English Hagaddahs. The other guests had a variety of Hagaddahs in Hebrew, which caused them to energetically discuss occasional variances in text and meaning.

The guests ranged from ninety-year-old Malka Locker, poet and widow of Beryl Locker, who was for many years head of the Jewish Agency in Palestine, to an eleven-year-old girl, daughter of a Jamaican father, her seventeen-year-old brother, son of an English father, and their attractive magazine-editor Israeli mother. Others were Bar-Josef's wife Lois, from Scarsdale, New York, who teaches English literature at Hebrew University, where she is working on her doctorate; their daughter, on leave from the army for Passover; their son, a student of mathematics at the university; Ruth's son, David, with his wife; Ruth's daughter, Michal, with her psychiatrist friend from Argentina; a woman from South Africa with the National Broadcasting Company in Tel Aviv; and, at long last, the evasive Amos, a warm and genial white-haired man. It was a very rich mix.

The three host couples produced a copious dinner of gefilte fish, chicken soup with matzo balls, made by Ruth, turkey roasted by Amos, two noodle kugels, a sweet and an herb, a salad, a compote of apricots, prunes, and raisins, and chocolate matzo cake and macaroons.

The service concluded, a variety of Passover songs were offered by the guests, songs remembered from their childhood. Malka Locker, though apparently frail and feeble, boomed out East European songs in a deep contralto, Bar-Josef sang some in Ladino and Yiddish, and the rest enthusiastically joined in with Hebrew songs. It was a most memorable "this year in Jerusalem" in the home of my "old" friend, Ruth Levin, whom I had only now come to really know.